The Lost Decade

The Lost Decade

*Altman, Coppola, Friedkin and the
Hollywood Renaissance Auteur in the 1980s*

Chris Horn

BLOOMSBURY ACADEMIC
NEW YORK · LONDON · OXFORD · NEW DELHI · SYDNEY

BLOOMSBURY ACADEMIC
Bloomsbury Publishing Inc
1385 Broadway, New York, NY 10018, USA
50 Bedford Square, London, WC1B 3DP, UK
29 Earlsfort Terrace, Dublin 2, Ireland

BLOOMSBURY, BLOOMSBURY ACADEMIC and the Diana logo
are trademarks of Bloomsbury Publishing Plc

First published in the United States of America 2024

Copyright © Chris Horn, 2024

For legal purposes the Acknowledgements on pp. ix–x constitute an
extension of this copyright page.

Cover design: Eleanor Rose
Cover image: Harry Dean Stanton in *Fool For Love*, 1985,
Dir. Robert Altman © United Archives GmbH / Alamy Stock Photo

All rights reserved. No part of this publication may be reproduced or transmitted
in any form or by any means, electronic or mechanical, including photocopying,
recording, or any information storage or retrieval system, without prior
permission in writing from the publishers.

Bloomsbury Publishing Inc does not have any control over, or responsibility for,
any third-party websites referred to or in this book. All internet addresses given
in this book were correct at the time of going to press. The author and publisher
regret any inconvenience caused if addresses have changed or sites have ceased
to exist, but can accept no responsibility for any such changes.

A catalog record for this book is available from the Library of Congress.

ISBN:	HB:	978-1-5013-9445-4
	ePDF:	978-1-5013-9447-8
	eBook:	978-1-5013-9446-1

Typeset by Integra Software Services Pvt. Ltd.

To find out more about our authors and books visit www.bloomsbury.com
and sign up for our newsletters.

Contents

List of figures	vii
Acknowledgements	ix
Introduction	1
Defining the Hollywood Renaissance and the blockbuster era	2
1980s Hollywood: Ideology, industry and society	4
The 1980s and the difficulties of periodization	7
Defining the Hollywood Renaissance auteur	10
Film history, auteurs and authorship	12
1 Hollywood in the 1980s: Industrial change and the marginalization of auteurist filmmaking	19
Locating finance and distribution	20
The studio system	23
Independent cinema	28
2 Hollywood Renaissance auteurs in the 1980s	33
Enhanced reputations: Martin Scorsese and Brian De Palma	34
Hits and misses: Peter Bogdanovich and John Milius	44
Down and out: Arthur Penn and Hal Ashby	49
Hardly working: Bob Rafelson and Dennis Hopper	53
3 Robert Altman: Escape from LA	61
Filming theatre	63
1980–1982	65
1983–1984	69
Streamers	70
Secret Honor	76
1985–1986	83
Fool for Love	85
1987–1989	92

vi   *Contents*

4   Francis Coppola: Post-apocalyptic adventures   95
     1980–1981   97
          One from the Heart   100
     1982–1983   108
          The Outsiders   109
     1984–1986   117
     1987–1989   119
          Tucker: The Man and His Dream   121

5   William Friedkin: Ambiguity and anti-heroes   129
     1980–1982   131
          Cruising   132
     1983–1985   142
          To Live and Die in L.A.   144
     1986–1989   152
          Rampage   153

Conclusion   163

Appendices   169
     Appendix 1: Directors and their 1980s feature films: Production
     and distribution by industry sector   169
     Appendix 2: Top grossing 1980s films directed by Hollywood
     Renaissance auteurs   170

Notes   171
Bibliography   202
Filmography   215
Index   219

Figures

2.1	Jesus meets John the Baptist in Scorsese's controversial 'art movie'	39
2.2	Cebe murders her abusive father before killing herself and her mother in *Out of the Blue*'s devastatingly bleak finale	57
3.1	The drunken sergeants provide the humour but also serve as a tragi-comic reminder of the effects of war	72
3.2	Altman uses a 'Rear Window' effect to show a more carefree existence in the world outside	74
3.3	Philip Baker Hall's intense, physical performance as Richard Nixon	79
3.4	The images on the CCTV monitors are like watching old film of 'the windbag' in action	81
3.5	The increased budget allowed Altman to expand the setting to include a downbeat motel complex	86
3.6	May's contemplative mood reflected in the motel's windows and neon signs	91
4.1	Hank's backlot of retired neon signs and assorted detritus symbolizes Las Vegas' absurdity	105
4.2	A Michael Powell-like visual exuberance as Hank dreams about Leila before their date	106
4.3	Some of *The Outsiders*' cast of future superstars (from left to right: Estevez, Dillon, Cruise, Lowe, Howell, Macchio)	111
4.4	Sunsets in *The Outsiders* evoke both the perfection and the fleeting nature of youth	114
4.5	Coppola used nineteen of the surviving Tucker cars which are driven to the courthouse at the end of the film	124
4.6	Coppola uses his 'live cinema' techniques to film the Tuckers on either end of a telephone call	125
5.1	Friedkin's depiction of sado-masochistic practices in the leather clubs was deliberately provocative	134
5.2	The final ambiguous shot of Pacino looking in the mirror has invited a range of interpretations	140

viii *Figures*

5.3 The filming concentrated on rundown, industrial parts of Los Angeles rather than the usual fashionable views of downtown and Beverly Hills 150

5.4 No one in the film can be trusted including Friedkin who 'cheats' with a male stand-in 151

5.5 When Reece is re-captured, he is covered in blood from some unseen act of depravity 157

5.6 The killer stalks an ordinary neighbourhood seemingly drained of colour and light 160

Acknowledgements

This book represents a culmination of my fifty-year-long obsession with the cinema and, in particular, a fixation with American film directors whom I hero-worshipped in my late teens in the same way as the rock stars with whom I was equally infatuated. In the 1980s, with only one other like-minded soul occasionally for company (hello to Stuart Batsford), I followed Coppola, Altman et al.'s every move while bemoaning the critical indifference to their films (why did *everyone* hate *One from the Heart*?). At the same time, this book also seems like a logical conclusion to my middle-aged diversion into academic study – completing a BA, MA, then a PhD. So there are a lot of people I could acknowledge – and over a long period of time – so apologies to anyone that I have forgotten to include.

Firstly, sincere thanks to Guy Barefoot for his guidance, encouragement and patience. I want to record my heartfelt gratitude to Simon and Jude Clegg for their enduring friendship and for helping me believe in myself over many years. The influence of my older brother, Peter Horn, should also be acknowledged, not least because it was when he bought me my first serious book about a director (Hitchcock, of course) that set me on this journey. A special mention for Scott Freer, who has been a constant source of inspiration and support – and for flattering me enough to make me realize that I *may* be knowledgeable/clever enough to produce a book such as this. Rebecca Styler also provided thoughtful and encouraging advice and thanks also to Ian Hunter for his help. In addition, there are a lot of highly knowledgeable scholars who enriched my knowledge of, and love for, films during my several years of study at the University of Leicester who deserve a mention, including Jenny Stewart, James Chapman, Claire Jenkins and Marina Spunta. Thank you as well to Yannis Tzioumakis for his encouragement and advice about the best way to get this research into book form.

Then there are those who provided valuable assistance during my archival research: the staff at the University of Michigan Special Collections Department in Ann Arbor, at the Margaret Herrick Library in Los Angeles and at both the BFI Reuben Library and Film Finances Limited in London. I also appreciate the help of Charles Drazin for kindly arranging access to Film Finances' files that are not usually available to researchers.

I also want to gratefully acknowledge the funding I received from the Arts and Humanities Research Council via the Midland3Cities (now Midland4Cities) Doctoral Training Partnership. Most importantly, this financial support enabled me to carry out the vital American research trip.

Last (but not least), I am especially grateful to Katie Gallof – and everyone else at Bloomsbury Academic involved in the production of this book – for giving me this opportunity to disseminate my research and opinions in print.

And finally, this book is dedicated to the memory of my mother, a teacher whom I disappointed more than I like to remember when I chose not to go to university when I was eighteen years old – I hope she would be proud.

Introduction

The dominant view of late 1960s and early 1970s American film history is that of a 'Hollywood Renaissance', a relatively brief window of artistry and critique based around a select group of directors.[1] By contrast, the period that followed is usually seen as the era of the blockbuster and of 'Reaganite entertainment', as the 'Renaissance' seemingly evaporated in the aftermath of the unprecedented success of *Jaws* (Steven Spielberg, 1975) and then *Star Wars*[2] (George Lucas, 1977), compounded by the spectacular failure of several big-budget auteurist projects.[3] When Peter Bogdanovich melodramatically told Peter Biskind that 'I'd blown it, Friedkin had blown it, Altman went into eclipse, one flop after another. Francis went crazy, even *Raging Bull* didn't do any business. Everybody kind of blew it in varying shapes and sizes',[4] he epitomizes the perception that emerges from this 'standard' version of 1980s Hollywood: that the careers of almost all of New Hollywood's auteur-stars rapidly went into a steep decline. Yet many of these directors actually remained active throughout the decade, and this book begins with the premise that their work has been obscured by a narrow, singular model of American film history, which has placed undue emphasis on White House occupancy and box-office hits. This then is an analysis of 1980s Hollywood from a fresh perspective, through the prism of a group of filmmakers lavished with praise for the creativity of their 1970s films but whose subsequent careers have frequently been dismissed in perfunctory terms. It will demonstrate that the 1980s careers of directors like Robert Altman, Francis Ford Coppola and William Friedkin, far from conforming to a monolithic pattern of decline, show diverse and complex responses to societal and industrial changes. The notion that, as Justin Wyatt puts it, 'by the end of the [1970s], the period of auteurism and formal experimentation had ended'[5] is therefore interrogated through a specific focus on the 1980s work of the three above-mentioned directors and through broader examinations of market conditions and filmmakers' experiences.

While this study is concerned with the wider industrial context and extra-textual circumstances that influenced the ability of directors to get their work made, it is also very much about individual films, bringing to light a range of unheralded cinema that seems to invite an auteurist interpretation. These films are appraised in terms of their directors' artistic sensibilities and in the manner in which their direction was distinctive. The decade-long narratives of the auteurs under consideration were disparate and the film analysis is attuned to the particularities of each one's experience. Thus, Robert Altman's decade is examined in terms of the relationship between film and theatre, analysing how the director made a virtue of limited resources in making cinematic a series of inexpensive theatrical adaptations while with Coppola, there is a focus particularly on his attributes as a visual stylist and on the ways that his background and personal influences manifest themselves in the texts. William Friedkin is a different example again. At first glance, he seemed to cling to more conventional routes for the realization of his creative impulses and, as with Coppola, the manner in which he mostly operated within popular genres is scrutinized. Yet he also showed in this work that he was unable to resist undermining his own conventionality through narrative structures that veer towards the incoherent, and by his layering in levels of ambiguity, thereby undermining his films' chances of box-office success. Although all these films directed by the three case-study directors divided critical opinion (at best) at the time of their release, what makes them particularly fascinating is how they challenged prevalent mainstream tastes at a time when populist cinema dominated at the box office.

Defining the Hollywood Renaissance and the blockbuster era

Before proceeding further, it is worth clarifying more precisely how I will be using the terms 'Hollywood Renaissance' and 'Hollywood Renaissance auteur', and why the 1980s have been singled out as a specific frame of reference. The term 'Hollywood Renaissance' is but one of a number of terms that have been used to describe certain changes in 1960s and 1970s American filmmaking. In journalism and in popular culture, a far more common term for this historical phase is 'New Hollywood' but in academia this has been complicated by the term having been used to indicate different time frames and developments.[6] In an influential article, 'The New Hollywood', Thomas Schatz uses the phrase to

Introduction 3

indicate the period and circumstances that followed on from the record-breaking blockbusters of the mid-1970s – and others, such as Kristin Thompson, have followed Schatz's lead.[7] Some writers simply use New Hollywood as a catch-all for all the developments in the post-classical era while there are those who have further confused the term's use in other ways, such as Geoff King who breaks it down into two periods, 'New Hollywood Version 1: The Hollywood Renaissance' and 'New Hollywood Version II: Blockbusters and Corporate Hollywood'.[8] This does, at least, have the advantage of indicating the symbiotic relationship between the two time frames, both being underpinned by the involvement of Hollywood's power structures. 'American New Wave' is another alternative term but, in contrast to the French variety, the American movement was not so radical as to represent a complete break from the practices of classical Hollywood, more a modification of a common mode of practice.[9] A more discrete, precise term then is 'Hollywood Renaissance' (which I will usually abbreviate to 'Renaissance') because it indicates renewal but also implies a revision of existing norms rather than definitive change.

Although these auteurs were singular creative artists with distinctive qualities, to understand the extent to which Renaissance-style filmmaking carried over into their eighties work, we should still take some account of its typical attributes to appreciate the relationship between films across the decades. One particularly succinct and precise explanation of what constitutes Renaissance-style cinema comes from a recent book by Nicholas Godfrey (while assessing why Friedkin's *The French Connection* [1971] is a 'New Hollywood' film): 'contemporary resonance; genre frustration and revisionism; an emphasis on performance over stardom; a downbeat, fatalistic ending; and a self-conscious foregrounding of film style'.[10] As a summary of traits, this works well as a broad marker, but in this book the examination of individuality expressed in the work of particular directors will be seen to be more revealing when considering a disparate mass of films that encompass any number of styles and approaches in numerous genres, and with many different thematic interests. I do concentrate almost exclusively on directors as individual creative agents, an approach broadly in line with Robert Kolker's convincing argument, in the preface to the third edition of his seminal work, *A Cinema of Loneliness*, for why he chose to focus on specific filmmakers:

> I find [auteurism] still the most convenient tool to work through the complex, sometimes overwhelming, output of Hollywood … If coherence and influence can be pinned on one figure, then it seems reasonable to let that figure and the work be set as the object of study.[11]

There is a difference here, however, because I am more interested in reinstating the authorial coherence and influence that others have questioned, whereas Kolker's career-long examinations tend to foreground his subjects' most accomplished work.

Most accounts identify the Renaissance's dawning with the unexpected box-office successes of *The Graduate* (Mike Nichols) and *Bonnie and Clyde* (Arthur Penn) in 1967.[12] Subsequently, this much-praised period – recent edited collections have variously described it as *America's Most Celebrated Era*[13] and *When the Movies Mattered*[14] – enabled the emergence of a new breed of film directors, many of whom were young and inexperienced, with backgrounds in film school and television (as opposed to having worked their way up through the system, as had been habitually the case in the classical era). This relatively brief moment, when innovation was encouraged, was terminated, as the usual story goes, by the emergence of a 'blockbuster era' that, arguably, is still with us some forty-plus years later. Indeed, the directors of *Jaws* and *Star Wars* have frequently and forcefully been blamed for the Hollywood studios' rejection of auteur filmmaking, despite their early careers having been associated with the Renaissance. Robin Wood pejoratively described what emerged in the aftermath of these huge hits as the 'Spielberg-Lucas Syndrome'[15] while David Thomson is absolutely clear whom he considered at fault when grandly declaring in 1996 that 'I fear the medium has sunk beyond anything we dreamed of, leaving us stranded, a race of dreamers. This is more and worse than a bad cycle. This is something like the loss of feeling, and I blame Spielberg and Lucas.'[16]

1980s Hollywood: Ideology, industry and society

This book addresses a gap in the study of American film history, and it should be no surprise, therefore, that very little of the scholarly literature dealing with 1980s filmmaking is concerned with the careers of Renaissance auteurs, with the caveat of the relatively limited work devoted to specific directors. Initially, academic study about 1980s Hollywood tended to focus on ideological tendencies. In 1986, Andrew Britton wrote a polemic, 'Blissing Out: The Politics of Reaganite Entertainment', for the journal *Movie* that would have a significant influence on critical perceptions – indeed, the terms 'Reaganite entertainment' and 'Reaganite cinema' have now passed into popular usage. Britton reveals, and castigates, the conservative ideology of contemporary Hollywood and argues that blockbuster films, which dominated the domestic box office at that time, were representative of 'a general movement of reaction and conservative reassurance in the contemporary Hollywood cinema'.[17] There is, perhaps, an inherent contradiction in Britton's argument because, on one hand, he asserts that this form of entertainment is devoid of meaning and 'never asks us to feel anything', yet also insists that it also invites its viewers to 'take pleasure' from the conservative 'Reaganite' values that the films promote.[18] If these films promote a firm ideology, however unconsciously received, can they be empty? Britton's answer to this conundrum seems to be that the paucity of meaning inherent in these films is merely a mask behind which lies an ideological agenda. In order to fully understand Reaganite entertainment in its appropriate cultural context, later writers like Stephen Prince would argue that it is necessary to take some account of the industrial and commercial factors that fuelled the type of product Hollywood made at the time.[19] Yet Britton set the tone for much of the critical work about the 1980s that immediately followed it with his trenchant pessimism about the overwhelming box-office dominance of the type of films he disparages.

Many of Britton's attitudes about the perilous state of the industry in the mid-1980s were echoed shortly afterwards by his mentor, Robin Wood, in his equally influential book, *Hollywood from Vietnam to Reagan,* and both writers are regularly cited in the common conception of the decade's cinema as a reflection of the sitting president's political ideology. For Wood, the commercial failure of intelligent films like *Blade Runner* (Ridley Scott, 1982) – he also cites *Heaven's Gate* (Michael Cimino, 1980) and *The King of Comedy* (Martin Scorsese, 1983) – only encouraged the idea that 'today, it is becoming difficult for films that are not *Star Wars* (at least in the general sense of dispensing reassurance, but increasingly in more specific and literal ways) to get made, and when they do the public and often the critics reject them'.[20]

In academia, this emphasis on right-wing ideology as characteristic of the decade's cinema was soon challenged, yet writers still remained mostly fixated on the most popular films of the decade. In the early 1990s, two important books, by Timothy Corrigan and Justin Wyatt, examined aspects of filmic culture that arose out of contemporaneous industrial changes. Corrigan's 1991 contribution, *A Cinema without Walls: Movies and Culture after Vietnam,* examines films made between 1967 and 1990 and specifically focuses on the changes in viewing habits that developed during this period. In terms of this book, the most relevant section is when Corrigan discusses 'the commerce of auteurism'. Conceiving of directors in such a context, he argues that Coppola is a 'useless' auteur, not because he makes films of inferior quality but because 'the spectacle of self-destruction becomes a way back to self-expression'.[21] Corrigan's use of Coppola as an example of commercial auteurism was influential on perceptions about the director in the 1980s, most pointedly in Jon Lewis's later book about the travails of Coppola's difficult decade.[22] Corrigan does acknowledge that the importance of the filmic text has been relegated in contemporary notions of auteurism yet follows the same path himself, making little reference to Coppola's films.

Corrigan is interested in a number of aspects of cinematic culture, but Justin Wyatt's 1994 book, *High Concept: Movies and Marketing in Hollywood*, is concerned with a singular issue, one that he persuasively argues 'can be considered as one central – and perhaps *the* central development – within post-classical cinema, a style of film molded by economic and institutional forces'.[23] Wyatt defines 'high concept' filmmaking and examines how it became the dominant force in Hollywood in the 1980s, with the success of *Jaws* and *Star Wars* (once again) identified as the crucial turning point. Wyatt provides a list of about eighty films (made between 1975 and 1992) that conform to at least one of three identifiers of high concept, 'the look, the hook, the book' (spectacular imagery, marketing opportunities and reduced narratives).[24] By yoking high concept directly to commercial success, Wyatt's singular interpretation of contemporary cinema is aligned to the conception of 1980s American filmmaking as being dominated by blockbusters, formulaic cycles and repetitive sequels. By 2000, with the benefit of ten years' reflection, Stephen Prince's entry in the estimable 'History of American Cinema' series, *A New Pot of Gold: Hollywood under the Electronic Rainbow, 1980–1989*, takes a broader view of the decade, opposing monolithic opinion conceived in ideological or box-office terms, when he challenges what he calls the 'critical misapprehension' that supposes 'orderly and tidy' historical models of 'Reagan or blockbusters'.[25]

Although Prince does broaden perceptions of the decade, he still largely follows the usual path of suggesting that the careers of almost all of the other directors who emerged in the Renaissance went into decline at the beginning of the blockbuster era, a view that has led to the conventional perception of the 1980s as a 'lost decade' for this group. Peter Biskind, in his oft-cited if sensationalistic book, *Easy Riders, Raging Bulls*, contributed significantly to this perspective, observing hyperbolically that 'the New Hollywood directors were like free-range chickens; they were let out of the coop to run around the barnyard and imagined they were free. But when they ceased laying the eggs, they were slaughtered'.[26] Although this is certainly an amusing analogy (and

Introduction 7

fits neatly with Biskind's overarching rise-and-fall narrative), its depiction of a 'slaughter' is misleadingly unnuanced in describing the fate of a wide group of disparate filmmakers.

Much of the scholarly literature about the 1980s then has habitually focused on ideology, industry and society.[27] In the decade and beyond, the place in American cinema of formally inventive and thematically challenging films is more usually viewed from the perspective of the films made by younger directors who emerged in the eighties in the burgeoning independent sector, such as Spike Lee, Jim Jarmusch and the Coen brothers.[28] In fact, if film historians had been more inclined to make connections between the trajectory of the Renaissance auteurs' careers and these developments in independent cinema, and to link them to the afore-mentioned cadre of emerging filmmakers, then they might not have been quite as eager to assert that the careers of most Renaissance auteurs were in decline. At the same time, academic research about the 1980s has tended to move away from authorship and more towards issues of gender, race and sexuality.[29]

The 1980s and the difficulties of periodization

It is undoubtably true that, by the late 1970s, audiences were tiring of the more complex, frequently downbeat Renaissance cinema and the box-office successes of the 1980s had a decidedly broader, family-friendly appeal than films like *The Godfather* or *The Exorcist*. It is also important to remember that even in the Renaissance era, many of the biggest hits were still films, as with *Love Story* (Arthur Hiller, 1970) and *Fiddler on the Roof* (Norman Jewison, 1971), that attracted a more traditional viewership. After *Star Wars*, however, the focus of studio filmmaking became focused far more on trying to replicate its appeal to children and adults alike, epitomized in 1982 by Spielberg's *E.T. the Extra-Terrestrial* which even exceeded *Star Wars'* all-time box-office records. It is also true that most of the 1980s films directed by Renaissance auteurs were commercial failures, although there were occasional exceptions.[30] But, whereas in literature about the 1970s, these directors' successes or failures in commercial terms are habitually kept separate from aesthetic assessments of the work (so that the most acclaimed and studied films are not necessarily the most successful), their 1980s work has suffered, by comparison, from a tendency to conflate these different ways of describing a film as 'successful'.

8   *The Lost Decade*

The supposed end of the Renaissance can be attributed to a number of reasons, but what sometimes gets lost in trying to be definitive about this issue is the extent to which these factors are interlinked and interdependent on each other. I will return to this in more detail in Chapter 1, but the attitudes of the conglomerated Hollywood studios and the rise of the independent sector can be related directly to the way audience tastes were changing, that led in turn to an increasingly focused production of expensive blockbusters. Another frequently cited reason for the demise of the Renaissance is the notion of auteurs out of control, as a number of high-profile financial disasters were attributed to directorial profligacy. William Friedkin's *Sorcerer* (1977) and Francis Coppola's *Apocalypse Now* (1979) were but two of a number of such films but the culmination of this tendency was *Heaven's Gate* which effectively bankrupted United Artists.[31]

So when did the Renaissance end? Or is even trying to put a date on it a schematic and over-simplistic way to characterize the period? Indeed, why use the 1980s at all to frame the present discussion? Peter Krämer and Yannis Tzioumakis recently assessed the first of these questions, concluding that 'there does appear to be a general agreement that, as a group, the directors associated with the Hollywood Renaissance did most of their best work between 1967 and 1974, with overall decline setting in thereafter'.[32] Others have found different reasons to deem almost every subsequent year in the seventies as the 'end'. Examples include the unprecedented success of *Jaws* and the last year that Renaissance cinema featured at the top of box-office lists (1975); Carter's accession to the presidency and *Star Wars* (1977); or the end of the decade as a superficially natural and convenient marker of the end of an era, as well as being the year of the *Heaven's Gate* debacle (1980). This last timeline allows for a conception of the Renaissance that includes a number of important films made after 1974 by directors associated with the period that *have* been discussed in terms of individual creativity, such as Altman's *Nashville* (1975), Scorsese's *Taxi Driver* (1976), and Cimino's *The Deer Hunter* (1978) and *Apocalypse Now*.

This sort of periodization, of designating eras or using decades as limiting markers, always presents such difficulties in terms of definition. It also provides some inevitable contradictions here because I am questioning whether prescribing a specific end point to the Renaissance has led to a failure to make meaningful connections with more acclaimed earlier work and by extension with the characteristics of the Renaissance. However, in order to make this project both manageable and clearly comprehensible, some form of delineation

Introduction 9

is necessary and there are good reasons to begin in 1980 and to consider the decade in its entirety. One is that, as I have already indicated, *Heaven's Gate* was the culmination of one strand of what is deemed to represent the complete demise of the Renaissance because the effect of its catastrophic costs led directly to a focusing of minds in the boardrooms of the Hollywood studios. Beginning with 1980 also works on a more specific level because all three of the directors used as key case studies, by the turn of the decade, were perceived to be in trouble following what were thought of as costly and extravagant failures: Friedkin and *Sorcerer*, Altman and *Popeye* (1980), Coppola and *Apocalypse Now* (although, in fact, the latter two both eventually made good profits despite their reputation).

While there are strong reasons to begin this examination of post-Renaissance developments in 1980, the justification to end it in 1989 is not as immediately apparent. There is, however, one important development in American film history that does particularly encourage the treatment of the 1980s discretely. In 1989, *sex, lies, and videotape* (Steven Soderbergh) was a break-out low-budget success which, according to Yannis Tzioumakis, 'precipitated the subsequent growth in independent cinema, paving the way for the establishment of a powerful institutional apparatus that supported a particular brand of independent filmmaking'.[33] Tzioumakis is pointing here towards the beginnings of what is sometimes called 'Indiewood' cinema, a name given to the collaborative practices and takeovers that emerged in the 1990s between Hollywood studios and independent production companies.[34] He also asserts that 'critics have repeatedly referred to *sex, lies, and videotape* as the film that changed the face of American independent cinema and have labelled 1989 … a "watershed year"'.[35] The film's success, and the attention conferred on it, was a catalyst for the discourse surrounding auteurist filmmaking shifting towards a newer, younger breed, rather than on those under consideration here, and encourages the validity of ending this study in 1989. On a more specific level, the 1980s can also be understood as being particularly discrete for Coppola and Altman. For the former, the decade straddles *Apocalypse Now* and his reluctant return to that which made his name, *The Godfather: Part III* (1990); Altman, meanwhile, left Los Angeles in 1980, changed his mode of filmmaking and returned ten years later. There are also a number of others' careers that can be easily understood in terms of pre- and post-1980, such as Hal Ashby whose last critical and commercial success was *Being There* in 1979 and who died in 1988. Even Martin Scorsese could be considered in these terms because the eighties span two of

10 *The Lost Decade*

his most lauded films, *Raging Bull* (1980) and *Goodfellas* (1990) – although, as I make clear later, the suggestion of a steep career decline for Scorsese in the decade, often propagated by the director himself, is largely a misconception.[36]

Defining the Hollywood Renaissance auteur

Who then can feasibly be described as a Hollywood Renaissance auteur, which of them will be discussed, and why? There are quite a number for whom one might apply the term because many different directors made films considered to be key texts of the period, and whose work seemed to fit in with its broad characteristics. Of course, no one should be surprised that this group was almost exclusively white and male, although a recent book by Maya Montañez Smukler has provided a counter-narrative with her detailed account of those few women who did manage to direct films at this time.[37] Unfortunately, in the 1980s, none of the filmmakers featured in Smukler's book managed to forge a career in mainstream cinema. Elaine May, the female director most obviously aligned with New Hollywood filmmaking in the 1970s, only made one film in the eighties, the Warren Beatty and Dustin Hoffman vehicle, *Ishtar* (1987), a late, post-*Heaven's Gate*, entry in the infamous series of auteur-led box-office disasters.[38] The greatest focus, particularly in popular culture, has always been on a group that David Cook calls "'Film Generation" Auteurs, or the "Hollywood Brats"', young cine-literate filmmakers who were influenced by the arthouse cinema about which they learned at film school.[39] Cook's designation is derived from an influential 1979 book, *Movie Brats: How the Film School Generation Took over Hollywood,* by Michael Pye and Lynda Myles which features Coppola, Brian De Palma, Lucas, John Milius, Martin Scorsese and Spielberg.[40] Another important group of new filmmakers emerged via the independent production company, Raybert Productions (later BBS Productions) owned by Bert Schneider and Bob Rafelson (and later Steve Blauner) which included Rafelson himself, Dennis Hopper and Peter Bogdanovich. A number of older directors who made significant breakthroughs at this time had begun their careers working in television including Altman, Friedkin and Arthur Penn. At the same time, a number of the key texts associated with the Renaissance were directed by those who already had established careers, either in Europe or in the United States; by 1980, many of these had left the United States or moved determinedly with the times into the mainstream. Examples in this category

Introduction 11

include John Schlesinger, Sam Peckinpah, Roman Polanski, Michelangelo Antonioni, Milos Forman and Sidney Lumet.

These names are but a few of those associated at various times with the Renaissance and, given the amount of literature devoted to the period and its filmmakers, it is not surprising that different writers have paid attention to a range of diverse auteurs. This book, though, confines itself to a relatively narrow group whose careers can be said to have been largely defined by the films they directed between 1967 and 1980.[41] So I have excluded those who had already established their careers before making films associated with the Renaissance (for example, Stanley Kubrick and John Cassavetes). I make an exception and include Penn (who had achieved some success as early as 1958 with his feature debut, *The Left Handed Gun*) because of his influence on, and centrality to, virtually every writer's understanding of the Renaissance.[42] I have also not included those directors who, by the eighties, had moved firmly into the mainstream and whose names are usually excluded from canonical lists of Renaissance-era auteurs (Sydney Pollack, Mike Nichols, Paul Mazursky and, of course, Spielberg). I also omit those who did not begin their directorial careers until the Renaissance either was on the way out or, according to some, had already ended (for example, Cimino, Alan Rudolph and Paul Schrader).[43] This leaves a core group of eleven (three of whom are singled out for close attention), comprising 'Movie Brats' (Scorsese, Coppola, De Palma, Milius), those who started in television (Altman, Friedkin, Penn) and the key Raybert directors (Bogdanovich, Rafelson and Hopper), plus one slight outlier because he became a director after making a name as an editor (Hal Ashby).

The choice of the three directors to examine as case studies in individual chapters is made principally because their cases are particularly strong examples of the tendency to marginalize or dismiss all of their 1980s films relative to other parts of their careers. This body of work has either been largely forgotten or been saddled with reputations based more on extra-textual factors that have distorted appreciation of the actual films themselves. Furthermore, these three directors were responsible for some of the most successful and acclaimed films of the entire Renaissance period, including Altman's *M*A*S*H* (1970), Coppola's *The Godfather* (1972) and Friedkin's *The Exorcist* (1973). It is not that these directors' 1980s narratives have been entirely ignored – emphatically not so in the case of Coppola – but it is more that the films themselves, in terms of content, style and substance, have tended to be sidelined or summarily dismissed. Two directors, Scorsese and De Palma, who were the most successful both in commercial terms

12   *The Lost Decade*

and for remaining true to their own personal styles and artistic choices, are *not* chosen for closer evaluation because, unlike almost all of the other Renaissance auteurs (again with the obvious exceptions of Spielberg and Kubrick), their 1980s work has not been so obviously ignored (their decades are dealt with in Chapter 2).

Film history, auteurs and authorship

This book combines two interlocking approaches which might be broadly thought of as context and text. In simple terms, the context comprises the use of film-historical critical frameworks while the text is the study of authorship in specific films from specific directors. In analysing the context that influenced, determined and problematized the authorship of Renaissance auteurs and then showing how that authorship manifested itself in specific texts, the result is a symbiotic discussion where industrial and other extra-textual determinants inform an understanding of the films, while the analysis of specific films offers an understanding of what was the result of the interplay of all these factors.

This book is concerned with auteurs and I use the term repeatedly (and fairly loosely) to identify a particular type of director. I use it in a way that is broadly equivalent to Peter Lehman's definition: 'a filmmaker of substance who shapes and forms films with careful thought and attention to style, not just as window-dressing but as integral to storytelling'.[44] In contemporaneous eighties scholarship, where the validity of auteurism had begun to be more frequently challenged, discussions tended to move away from textual analysis, and towards a focus on industrial strategy, so that by 1991, according to Corrigan, directors now tended to be situated 'along an extratextual path in which their commercial status as auteurs is their chief function as auteurs'.[45] Yet, while it is important to acknowledge this aspect of auteurism, it is surely fundamental in revealing how reputational capital is constructed for film directors, to also identify how authorship (which can still be construed in collaborative terms) manifests itself within primary texts. Only some form of textual analysis can complete an understanding of where creative agency lies, sitting alongside the broader factors that condition a director's ability to generate employment opportunities and retain artistic control. In this regard, in the chapters that examine specific auteurs' films, I seek to identify authorial agency in such a way that, for example, in a film like *Fool for Love* (Altman, 1985), what is thought of as a faithful

Introduction 13

adaptation of Sam Shepard's play is revealed to be far more of an 'Altmanesque' film than has been previously recognized. By addressing such aspects of the films, I am able to examine the 1980s in ways that contrast with those who have been inclined to use specified directors' films only as a backdrop to their studies of reputational standing and related industrial contexts.

In one sense, this study of authorship also looks back towards the original conception of 'auteur theory' because I am interested in discerning what Sarris called 'the distinguishable personality of the director as a criterion of value'.[46] Heralded as auteurs in the 1970s, this book is concerned with what happened in the 1980s to a group of directors who were heralded as auteurs in the previous decade, and what this tells us about the model of Renaissance auteur beyond the Renaissance. Unlike Sarris and the *Cahiers* critics though, my concern with the extent of, or limitations on, directors' creative control means explaining the processes by which films are made as well as through textual analysis. This is an approach that can be related to more recent thinking about the study of cinematic authorship, which has moved on from the post-structuralists' complete disavowal of auteurism to what Pam Cook has called 'post-auteurism' where consideration is given to 'the social and industrial contexts of particular film-makers, or to the cultural context in which scholars, critics and historians choose to employ one or more of many auteurist models'.[47] In this book, this is seen through the exploration of institutional tensions and the production histories of individual films, linked to how authorship is manifested in the specific titles under discussion. V. F. Perkins, in his assessment of 'Direction and Authorship' in *Film as Film*, assessed the problems and impact on a director's creativity from external pressures, stating that 'probably the director's bitterest subjection is not to the taste of the public nor to the occasional ineptitudes of his employers, but to the industrial system, the mechanism of movie finance, production and distribution'.[48] If the decade is examined from the perspective of how directors dealt with the impact of such pressures, then care is still needed to avoid making assumptions that meaning is only derived from a singular vision, essentially a romantic but largely unsustainable conception. What is particularly relevant for directors in the 1980s is Perkins's assertion that 'creative freedom does not guarantee, nor does industrial production rule out, a good result'.[49] I will examine, therefore, the case-study auteurs' contributions to the films they directed by taking account of the impact of institutional power while still teasing out influences and characteristics shared with their peers, as well as thematic and stylistic similarities across the breadth of their own careers. In considering the historical background, and in paying attention to its effect on the construction of the films under consideration, my approach is broadly in line with principles proposed by advocates of New Film History, as when James Chapman, Mark Glancy and Sue Harper argue that the film historian can 'add a material dimension to the analysis by showing how struggles for creative control can be glimpsed in the visual texture of the film itself'.[50]

The dissection of the progression of the Renaissance auteurs' careers in the 1980s will underpin, and expand, the uncovering of authorship within the filmic texts, and the use of material from archives, critical literature and biographical work informs an understanding of the films. The archival research is a particularly valuable resource, one that is highly informative for both the contextual and textual dimensions of this project. The Altman archives, lodged at the University of Michigan, are employed as a means to fill in the intricate details of his project's production histories (including, in brief, some that were unmade). The range of information available from the director's papers is wide, from the financial details of projects, which expand and deepen our understanding of low-cost contemporaneous filmmaking, to correspondence that questions the accepted authorship and production histories of films. In addition to Altman's papers, two other archival sources inform the complicated ways that these directors managed to get their projects financed and distributed. The more limited of the two is the archives of the British completion guarantee company, Film Finances Limited. This is a valuable resource that is usually only open for projects made before 1980, but an exception was made that enabled me to examine the production files for the two Coppola films, *The Outsiders* and *Rumble Fish* (both 1983), that the company underwrote. This access allows me to reveal how the manner of authorial control on these two films has been previously somewhat misread in terms of the impact on creativity from institutional pressures. The third archival source, Friedkin's papers at the Margaret Herrick Library in Los Angeles, informs the discussion of production contexts in his 1980s work but their use is more focused on screenwriting material. Draft screenplays, notebooks and correspondence are used to illuminate his processes from the initial adaptation of the source novel, through numerous draft scripts, and on to the final version of the film as shot.

In recent work on the Renaissance, the centrality of the director in the academic study of the period has been challenged, with Aaron Hunter, for example, insisting that 'the canon that has been constructed around New Hollywood is heavily auteurist in nature, much to the detriment of a better

Introduction 15

understanding of the era'.[51] While Hunter and others have argued persuasively for new ways to move the discussion of the Renaissance away from directors, there are still methods that do not negate the use of auteurism and that can offer alternative and original perspectives on the period and its aftermath: in this regard, I prefer to take a diametrically opposite approach to those who would lessen the focus on the director-as-author. If Altman, Coppola and Friedkin can be considered as auteurs in the same way claimed for the likes of Hitchcock or Hawks (two directors who also operated within the Hollywood system), this should mean that an appreciation of their craft should be wide ranging and not necessarily determined by when specific films were made (although this does present an existential problem due to this project's calendar-based focus, as I have already noted). In this regard, it is therefore important to appreciate directors' auteurist qualities across artificially created historical boundaries. All the familiar reasons expressed – directorial excess, the runaway successes of high-concept blockbusters, changes in audience preferences (often linked directly with Reaganite politics) and the conglomeration of studio ownership – are valid as part of an explanation for the changes that occurred from one era to the next but what tends to be missed from these familiar explanations for the demise of the Renaissance is much nuance in terms of individual filmmakers' responses to these changes.

This book progresses from the general to the specific, so Chapter 1 is a broad analysis of the circumstances and production contexts that determined the place of the Renaissance auteur in the decade, examining the cinematic marketplace as it existed in the 1980s. The difficulties of locating finance and distribution, and the prevailing background in both the studio and independent sectors are shown in relation to the individual auteurs' struggle for creativity. As I have indicated, this book is partly about challenging the inclination to homogenize the group's fortunes, and for this reason, Chapter 2 illustrates the diversity of their experiences through a relatively brief discussion of the individual decades of eight directors, in pairs and ordered according to levels of career success and productivity in the 1980s (rather than according to any past connections).

When the book arrives at the three director-specific chapters, the emphasis does shift towards authorship and creativity in the individual films. A consistent structure in each chapter allows for an easy appreciation of the differences in each individual's career progression. A chronological review of each auteur's decade-long work practice is accompanied by the exploration of authorship in three films each. Chapter 3 deals with Robert Altman's unique decade when

16   *The Lost Decade*

he directed a series of low-budget, independently financed, adapted plays that appear to stand apart from the director's typical methodologies, not least because of their seeming fidelity to their sources. Altman directed more films (for cinema and television) in the 1980s than any other Renaissance auteur, and how he managed to attain such a level of productivity is also discussed. I do not include for close analysis Altman's most well-known and critically acclaimed 1980s film, *Come Back to the 5 and Dime, Jimmy Dean, Jimmy Dean* (1982) because it has attracted the most scholarly attention elsewhere.[52] The three films that are assessed – *Streamers* (1983), *Secret Honor* (1984) and *Fool for Love* – represent particularly interesting examples of how Altman expressed his artistic sensibilities.

Chapter 4 looks at Coppola's troubled, event-packed decade, one that has received extensive, if often superficial and disdainful, coverage elsewhere. Coppola is the most famous of the three and there have been at least six biographies or general interest books in English about him with such proliferation meaning that there is no issue with understanding the biographical details of Coppola's 1980s career.[53] Yet in much of this literature, and in the relatively scarce academic work about Coppola at this time, the films themselves are routinely treated perfunctorily, invoked merely as symptoms of his financial troubles and supposed 'Napoleon complex'.[54] My approach, while still discussing the significant events, is to emphasize the ways that these external factors impacted on Coppola's authorship within the filmic text and I consider three 1980s films in which he was able to retain a high degree of authorial control: *One from the Heart* (1981), *The Outsiders* and *Tucker: The Man and His Dream* (1988). *Rumble Fish*, the most admired of his eighties work, is not examined in close detail because, relative to the other eighties work, it seems in far less need of academic and critical recuperation.

The third case study, in Chapter 5, is perhaps the most representative of the overall struggles suffered by Renaissance auteurs, in that William Friedkin encountered enough difficulties to be restricted to directing only four feature films. Even then, only two of the four fall unambiguously in the decade because *Cruising*, released in early 1980, was made in 1979 and *Rampage*'s 1987 release was confined to only two showings in the United States, eventually only being released more widely in 1992. His decade is particularly interesting as an example of a director striving, frequently unsuccessfully, to remain within the embrace of the system. With the choice of three films to examine closely, I omit 1983's *Deal of the Century*, a feeble comedy vehicle for Chevy Chase, because it was

Introduction 17

developed by others and is the project in which Friedkin was the least engaged. By contrast, his other three films in the decade – *Cruising, To Live and Die in L.A.* (1985) and *Rampage* – all represent fascinating instances of his personal authorship. Not only was he involved in these projects from the start but, for the only time in his career (at least in terms of screenwriting credits), he single-handedly wrote all three of the films.[55] His overarching career has rarely been understood in auteurist terms, yet his 1980s films, despite having been inevitably assessed in terms of a steep career decline, can still be persuasively compared with each other in terms of both theme and filmmaking practice.

The examination of the films and fortunes of these three directors is not simply about shining a light on undervalued work but also as a way to provide insight into the transition between the 1970s and the 1980s. There were fundamental changes that made finding work more difficult for these filmmakers but what is interesting is the extent and the manner in which this was achieved. The detailed examination of the directors' 1980s career arcs allows the discussion to be about both artistry and industry and also to be about the difficulties of negotiating the tensions that are intrinsic to the relationship between the two.

1

Hollywood in the 1980s: Industrial change and the marginalization of auteurist filmmaking

In the 1980s, the industrial conditions in the Hollywood marketplace in which the Renaissance auteur strived to find meaningful work were entirely different from those prevalent during the earlier period in which they made their names. According to Philip Drake, 'filmmaking is a collaborative enterprise, with filmmakers able to exercise more creative control at some times than others, while some films are perceived to have more "indie" qualities than others. These factors shift over time and depend on cultural and historical contexts'.[1] What Drake's observation suggests is that historical determinants have a considerable effect on any film director's creative independence. In the 1980s, restrictions that arose through the industry's structural changes affected both the ability of filmmakers to generate finance for personal, often seemingly uncommercial, projects as well as the circumstances in which they might be employed to handle properties developed by others. This chapter will provide an overview of the pressures and wider implications that characterized the working environment in American filmmaking at this time and the ways this specifically affected this book's subjects.

During the brief heyday of the Hollywood Renaissance, the major studios were falling over themselves to get involved with the emergent auteurs of the time. However, by the beginning of the 1980s, in a post-*Star Wars* marketplace, these directors now found themselves in a difficult position if they wanted to retain some degree of creative agency. As Geoff King puts it, 'the price of success for auteurist control at the industrial level remains ... either modesty or a large measure of multi-market, mainstream conformity'.[2] However, it was not entirely true in the eighties that those directors who were able to remain in the studio system were *always* obliged to compromise in order to attract a mass audience. Similarly, it is too simplistic to think that those who looked to the independent sector may have had to work cheaply but could do so without much interference. Renaissance filmmakers did not work solely in one or the other sector in the 1980s, rather tending to move between the two in pursuit of adequate finance. Each individual director's arc displays varying degrees of compromise and rebellion as well as diverse reasons for choosing, or being chosen for, projects. Furthermore, even in this period that is closely associated with the studios' singular focus on high-concept and populist filmmaking, it was not always the case that working for the majors necessarily equated with more commercial cinema; conversely, an independently funded film did not automatically mean the opposite. Executives responsible for green-lighting projects in both sectors made decisions based on a range of factors that might include the state of the director's reputational capital or their ability to remain within budget but also for any number of reasons not directly associated with the director. One significant factor, which gained greater traction in the 1980s and played a role in determining a director's ability to land finance, was the increasing power of agents who brought to projects ready-made package deals that might include stars, directors, or even writers. Mark Crispin Miller points out that while the studios re-established, post-Renaissance, a high degree of control over both distribution and exhibition, 'they no longer plan the films themselves. This crucial process is now dominated by the giant talent agencies ... that in effect, run Hollywood'.[3] The perceived value of an auteur's star image was crucial for agents to include them in such preordained arrangements. A case in point is Martin Scorsese who signed up to the all-powerful Michael Ovitz's Creative Artists Agency (CAA) in 1987, directly leading him finally to make *The Last Temptation of Christ* (1988), which he had been struggling for years to get made.[4]

Locating finance and distribution

Before considering the different ways that Renaissance auteurs' films were brought to market, it is important to understand how the term 'independent' can mean a number of different things in order to appreciate the relationship between studios and other sources of finance. According to Tzioumakis, '"independent cinema" may be best conceived as a *discourse* that changes over time and is continually redefined'.[5] He has interrogated this problem of definition in some detail, as have a number of other writers.[6] For the purposes of this discussion, however, it suffices to use Emanuel Levy's simple explanation: 'two

Hollywood in the 1980s

different conceptions of independent film can be found. One is based on the way indies are financed, the other focuses on their spirit or vision.[7] The first categorization, which places films in their institutional context, relates to funding and distribution that derives from outside Hollywood's major studios, whereas the second is more about what Richard Maltby describes as 'something between European arthouse cinema and the mainstream star vehicle and delivering an attention to theme, character relationships, and social relevance'.[8] Although I will occasionally refer to the 'spirit' aspect of the term, my focus here is primarily concerned with the industrial definition, while bearing in mind, as Tzioumakis points out, how its meaning continues to mutate over time.

In Appendix 1, I have provided a detailed breakdown of the 1980s output of the book's featured auteurs (as detailed in Introduction) in terms of their production and distribution according to major studio, mini-major or independent designations.[9] The director-specific detail will become more relevant when the career arcs of individual filmmakers are discussed in the following chapters, but what is interesting and particularly relevant, in terms of the industry's overall direction at this time, is how the proportion in favour of independent over studio finance is reversed when distribution is considered. Studios funded only 34 per cent of the forty-nine feature films made by the group, but they distributed 67 per cent of them with a further 20 per cent handled by the mini-majors. It was only those films with the smallest budgets and limited profiles that were distributed independently. There are only six such titles: three directed by Altman (for very particular reasons, examined at length in Chapter 3) while the other three – *They All Laughed* (Bogdanovich, 1981), *Out of the Blue* (Hopper, 1980) and *Rampage* – barely managed any theatrical release at all (as will be seen in Chapters 2 and 5).

In the context of this study, it is important that the way distribution worked in the eighties is understood because it illustrates one crucial way that the Hollywood major studios were still able to retain a large degree of control over the wider marketplace which, in turn, can be related to why, and how, directors struggled to maintain creative autonomy. It is the effect on authorial agency relating to the circumstances of production and distribution that is particularly relevant to identifying the place of the Renaissance auteur in the 1980s. In this respect, it is not enough to know whether the production company was independent, but also who was responsible for distribution. The major Hollywood studios – by the 1980s, the significant players were Universal, Warners, Paramount, Fox, Columbia and Disney while MGM/UA struggled to retain a significant presence – still maintained an iron grip on the distribution of the most popular films. Not only that, but what can be missed when talking about a studio's influence over a filmmaker's creative independence is how important it is to understand at what stage the distributor made their deal. Thus, if a studio's financial interest formed part of the initial fiscal structure, where distribution rights were wholly or partly responsible for the raising of the funds needed, the studio will likely have some authority over the making of the film, thereby potentially diminishing a director's authorial control. In the 1980s, however, a common arrangement, which, according to Maltby, was responsible for something like one-third of all box-office revenues, was for films produced independently to have their distribution rights sold on a 'pick-up' basis once production was complete.[10] In this circumstance, the distributor clearly has no input into content or production budget while the (small) independent company's ability to turn a profit becomes precariously entirely dependent on selling the rights at a fair price.

Another problem in understanding the relationship between independent finance and creative control is that independent film companies do not necessarily only make 'independent-style' films. Furthermore, even when they profess to offer a director complete freedom, they can still be just as interfering as a Hollywood studio. Independent films may usually mean lower budgets, but a small film company will likely be even more desperate than a studio *not* to lose money. Drake illustrates this when discussing Hal Ashby's disastrous relationship with Lorimar making *Second-Hand Hearts* (1981) and *Lookin' To Get Out* (1982), arguing that 'independence is sometimes more readily available within rather than outside of mainstream Hollywood cinema'.[11] When someone like Ashby, with a well-documented reputation for profligacy and unreliability, was involved, independent companies, who tended to exist on a financial 'knife-edge', could be even more restrictive and interfering than the major studios.

In the early part of the decade, the number of films made by independent companies, but distributed by the majors, remained fairly constant but as the decade progressed, there was a need for extra product to satisfy the burgeoning video market. In the United States, ownership of video recorders in the decade rose from 2 million to 62 million (two-thirds of all households) while sales of pre-recorded videotapes grew even more quickly, from 3 million in 1980 to 220 million in 1990. At the same time, the number of cable subscribers was also growing rapidly.[12] The number of films distributed independently started rising to accommodate the increased demand, from 125 in 1983 to 242 in 1986.[13]

Generally, these were cheap genre films and it is not surprising, therefore, that established filmmakers were typically unwilling to lower their expectations as far as the 'straight-to-video' market. As the decade progressed, while independent production rose at a rapid pace (193 in 1986, 277 in 1987 and 393 in 1988), 40 per cent of all independent films received no theatrical release and of those that did, most were commercial failures.[14] According to Peter Biskind, for a film to make more than $10 million in the 1980s, it would have 'to play the suburban multiplexes', a facility simply not available for most independently distributed films.[15] Budgets were rising in all sectors in the 1980s, and this fed into lower end productions as well so that escalating costs 'also raised the earnings threshold requirements for an independent movie to be considered a success'.[16]

The studio system

The changes in ownership of the studios, shaking off the remnants of the classical mogul-driven era, resulted in more hard-headed decision-making by executives who frequently had no experience of the industry, and no interest in films other than as vehicles for generating profits. As Miller puts it, 'the lawyers and MBAs now managing the movie business are ... obsessed with blockbusters, they prize a movie only as a multiply [sic] exploitable resource, like a vulnerable company with lots of assets'.[17] Increasingly, the conglomerates identified what Maltby calls the 'ultra-high-budget film' as their most efficient vehicle for generating massive returns. The average cost of a studio film rose from $9.4 million in 1980 to $26.8 million in 1990 (and $39 million by 1995). It was the expanding 'stable secondary markets' of television and video, as well as market globalization, which provided 'a financial cushion for movies that fail at the theatrical box-office'.[18]

The expenditure required to finance blockbuster crowd-pleasers now tended to be balanced by a more cautious and parsimonious approach to other projects. However, the studios did not entirely reject medium-budget productions and the tendency to decry Hollywood's singular approach, as with Britton and Wood, needs to be contextualized and understood in a more nuanced way when discussing the Renaissance auteur. Stephen Prince argues that, in fact, the majors in the eighties still 'funded and distributed many pictures with limited commercial prospects and whose style and sensibility were outside the commercial mainstream'.[19] However, it is important to understand that this support was often highly conditional and not stable. Majors were perfectly capable of dropping out of projects at the last minute, as Martin Scorsese found with his first attempt to make *The Last Temptation of Christ* in 1983 (five years before it was eventually made). After eleven months of pre-production and $5 million spent, Paramount dropped out only four days before principal photography was due to start.[20] In fact, natural expectations could sometimes be confounded with studios, for all their wealth, being particularly risk-averse in comparison with the independent sector, as when Warners pulled out of backing Friedkin's *Cruising* once Al Pacino became attached because they were not willing to pay his going rate of $2 million.[21] In such a cautious environment, the problem for many of the Renaissance directors was that a maverick reputation made studios much more wary, particularly with regard to keeping to a film's budget. It was no longer as attractive, in the eyes of bottom-line-obsessed executives, to take the opportunity to market films in terms of a director's public persona and status as a commercial auteur. The debacle of *Heaven's Gate* and the other notorious auteurist box-office failures cast long shadows in the 1980s and most directors found that trust had now to be hard-earned. As Manohla Dargis has observed, *Heaven's Gate* was regarded as 'a $44 million object lesson in directorial ego and executive incompetence.'[22] The latter is particularly important because no one in authority at the majors wanted to repeat the catastrophic mistakes made at United Artists in failing to control the production's spiralling costs. A cautious approach now meant that star-led projects were more likely to be given to filmmakers who were considered to be fiscally reliable. In the case of directors who had made films that are seen as emblematic of the New Wave, it tended to be those who gravitated towards the mainstream who were considered trustworthy, such as Sidney Lumet or Mike Nichols.[23] This is not to say, as we shall see, that the major studios did not sometimes place faith in maverick filmmakers, if only occasionally, and in particular circumstances.

The unprecedented success of *Jaws* and *Star Wars* might have initially been the stimulus that led the Hollywood majors to alter their policies about funding and distributing feature films, but there were other factors at play than simply chasing similarly extravagant box-office numbers. Profitability was no longer as firmly yoked to domestic theatrical attendance with ancillary revenue streams, including home video, cable television and music soundtracks, as well as a growth in international sales, becoming more important in terms of measuring success. Douglas Gomery explains the modern Hollywood studio's aims: 'vertical integration, the bedrock of the classical era, is still part of the basic strategies, but

Hollywood in the 1980s

the emphasis is on horizontal integration to capture synergies with other media businesses'.[24] This becomes absolutely clear when one considers how, in 1980, US theatrical attendance was responsible for about 30 per cent of film revenues whereas by 1990, this had dropped to only 16 per cent. At the same time, home video's share moved from 7 per cent in 1980 to 39 per cent in 1990.[25] These factors had a negative effect on any property not obviously suited to exploitation beyond a first-run theatrical release. If a project was not likely to be a good prospect in terms of a broad appeal that lent itself to repeat viewings on television and on video, did not have a marketable soundtrack or was not deemed to be a likely hit overseas, it would increasingly hold little interest for a studio. For example, even an enormous success such as *Tootsie* (Sydney Pollack, 1983), which earned $94 million domestically, had *considerably* less overall potential than *Back to the Future* (Robert Zemeckis, 1985) despite their theatrical receipts being almost identical.[26] The latter film would prove to be more exploitable, its broad demographic appeal leading to great success in video sales and rentals, as well in merchandising and its soundtrack; like so many of the decade's most successful films, it also spawned successful sequels in 1989 and 1990. *Back to the Future*'s multimedia qualities have also played a key role in its continuing appeal across the generations.

In the 1980s, the major studios who fared best were those who consistently produced the very biggest hits with Universal, Warners and Paramount accounting for about 45 per cent of the domestic market in the decade.[27] The first two had positioned themselves best to fully exploit the growth in ancillary markets; the amount of conglomeration, mergers and acquisitions (as well as some de-conglomeration by the end of the decade) was fuelled by other studios' attempts to catch up with Universal and Warners. Lew Wasserman's Music Corporation of America (MCA), originally a talent agency, had bought Universal in 1958 and quickly became a significant player in television production and music publishing as well. Wasserman was a pioneer who, according to Gomery, 'created the modern Hollywood system – just as Adolph Zukor invented the classic studio system'. He was the first to recognize the opportunities for exploiting cinematic properties in different media sectors by accumulating a library of titles, then selling – and reselling – them to broadcast and pay television.[28]

Warners consistently performed well in the 1980s through similar structural advantages over the competition, in their case through their established record label and music publishing company. Steve Ross, who had bought Warners in 1969 for his Kinney Corporation, was the first studio head 'to understand the viability of the home video market'.[29] Paramount too were very successful at the box office in the decade but were owned by a conglomerate, Gulf and Western, who held holdings, unlike Universal and Warners, in a diverse range of industries entirely unconnected to the film business. When owner, Charlie Bluhdorn, died suddenly in 1983, his successor, Martin Davis, followed Wasserman's example by divesting the company of nearly all its interests, including financial services, sugar cane and auto parts, leaving only their still substantial assets in entertainment and publishing. In 1989, the parent company was renamed Paramount Communications.[30]

A similar lesson was eventually learnt by Coca-Cola. They purchased Columbia in 1982 for $823 million and conducted an unsuccessful seven-year experiment in whether a film studio could be run by MBAs. The pursuit of synergy proved elusive and Coca-Cola sold out to Sony, a company seemingly more obviously aligned with the film business, for $3.4 billion in October 1989.[31] Columbia had always carried a reputation for following rather than innovating but the Coca-Cola era did see them involved in the formation of Tri-Star Pictures in 1983, an enterprise seemingly ideally placed to take the fullest advantage of prevalent marketplace opportunities. According to Prince, despite only being a short-lived experiment, the new company carried 'a special, emblematic importance in the developing Hollywood of the 1980s'.[32] Columbia, HBO (the television subscription channel) and CBS Records formed Tri-Star with the intention of becoming the eighth major studio, its structure designed to immediately take advantage of the interaction between the three media sectors involved. The company immediately announced that they had the finance in place to produce an annual slate of thirty-five films, a comparable amount with the other majors. What seemed potentially so significant about Tri-Star was its inherent synergistic characteristics. HBO, owned by Time-Life, was completely dominant at that time in pay-television with more than 60 per cent of the nation's subscribers.[33] All the studios were obliged to make deals with HBO if they wanted to profit from this growing revenue stream. Yet, despite their considerable inbuilt benefit, Tri-Star went the way of many of the other mergers and acquisitions in the decade when CBS sold out in 1985 with Time-Life following suit in the next year, leaving Tri-Star to continue as a low-key, subdivision of Columbia. It had not been able to find the sure-fire hit or franchise that was necessary to sustain such an ambitious enterprise. The company's only interaction with the Renaissance filmmakers was via two Coppola films: one of their more profitable titles, *Peggy Sue Got Married* (1986) followed by a box-office failure, *Gardens of Stone* (1987).

Other changes in studio ownership during this period included Rupert Murdoch's takeover of 20th Century Fox in 1985, which led to the corporation becoming more singularly focused on the bottom line and to a rapid and ambitious expansion into television.[34] Universal also finally changed hands when MCA was bought for $6.3 billion in November 1990 by Matsushita Electric of Japan, a direct competitor to Sony, the recent purchaser of Columbia. Universal's relatively superior status is indicated by MCA's sale realizing approximately double the amount that Columbia had managed just over a year previously.[35]

In the 1980s, the studios relied more and more on a small number of individual titles and franchises to sustain the sort of returns on their investment they expected. This seems unsurprising from a purely commercial perspective because the company which enjoyed the greatest share in each year in the 1980s was also always responsible for one of the top two best-performing films in that twelve-month period. This was most apparent in 1982 when Universal's 30 per cent share of the market (easily the highest share of any year in the decade) was largely attributable to the record-breaking $228 million domestic returns of *E.T.*, more than three times those of the number-two performer that year, *Rocky III* (Sylvester Stallone).[36] The consequence for auteurist directors of this singular focus on blockbuster success was that production finance became increasingly difficult to source from the majors. Although independent money often became a necessity if a director wanted to keep working and retain some degree of creative autonomy, the issues from the past that dogged Renaissance auteurs' relationships with Hollywood executives could still sometimes be a problem because borrowing funds was often conditional upon first securing a distribution deal with a studio. The majors' share of the overall domestic market, approximately 80 per cent across the decade (with another 9 per cent for mini-majors, Orion and TriStar), is a fair indicator of why studios felt disinclined to bother with anything other than blockbusters and franchises.[37] Although ancillary markets and alternative revenue streams were now more valuable than box-office returns, success at the latter still provided the best indicator of a film's potential in the former. For the right sort of blockbuster property, under prevalent market conditions, revenues could grow at an exponential rate. Sequels, soundtracks, transmission on cable and the opportunity for repeat viewings on home video all contributed to their profit potential. Almost every major studio had at least one successful franchise in the 1980s, including *Indiana Jones* and Paramount, *Back to the Future* and Universal, as well as *Star Wars* and Fox. Thus, the cross-media opportunities derived from a small, select number

28   *The Lost Decade*

of 'tent-pole' films meant studio executives were not overly concerned with the less-commercial properties usually favoured by auteurist filmmakers.

However, as I have already noted, the major studios did not only produce populist franchise films and they could still be persuaded to finance non-blockbuster cinema. There was a variety of factors that might affect a decision whether to 'green light' projects, including the attraction of a currently popular star being attached, or a pre-sold bestselling source novel; all-powerful agents often would provide a package deal that combined the two. Studio heads even still occasionally courted directors but only those with the highest reputation for hit-making, as when Spielberg was 'successfully wooed away' from Wasserman at Universal by Warners' Steve Ross.[38] Where majors were involved in the decade with Renaissance auteurs, it was often when a particular director became involved in something more obviously commercial than their usual fare. Appendix 2 shows the most successful films at the domestic box office (over $20 million) directed by the select group of eleven auteurs. The top four titles on this list were funded by studios and were the most mainstream films made by these filmmakers in the decade. Excepting perhaps Altman's *Popeye*, they are among their most untypical work as well, and for Scorsese and De Palma, it was a deliberate move towards commercial success through conformity. The dominance of the studios in terms of distribution is indicated by all thirteen of these films being distributed by majors or mini-majors, illustrating how independent distribution, at this time, did not yet possess the tools or the financial backing required to reach a substantial audience.

Independent cinema

American cinema's independent sector underwent a significant but faltering upturn in the 1980s. Tzioumakis identifies a period from the late 1970s to the end of the 1980s as the first of three phases ('Independent', 'Indie' and 'Indiewood') that he uses in order to provide a periodization of contemporary American independent cinema. During this first phase, a market was established away from Hollywood which achieved some limited commercial distribution and a small measure of box-office success, leading some critics to declare a new era in independent filmmaking.[39] Ever since the traditional studio model had begun to break down in the 1950s, the financial packaging of deals from sources other than the major studios had become increasingly prevalent. In the eighties, the demand for a greater amount of product was stimulated by the expansion in subscription television and from the sudden growth in home video, yet it appears that the sector was not yet sufficiently mature to flourish and to sustain itself. It was not until *sex, lies and videotape* (Steven Soderbergh) was screened at Sundance in January 1989 that, as described by industry insider, John Pierson, 'the corpse stirred'.[40] The difficulties of operating in Hollywood on an independent basis in the 1980s are amply illustrated by the fact that *all* of the decade's most successful independent production companies either had gone out of business by the early 1990s or, in a few select cases, were acquired by a major studio. It was the latter examples who were best positioned to take advantage of the 1990s upsurge in popularity for independent-style films. By acquiring companies like Miramax (Disney in 1993) and New Line (bought by Turner Broadcasting in 1994, who in turn were bought by Warners in 1996), or by setting up their own specialist divisions (Sony Picture Classics in 1992, Fox Searchlight in 1994),[41] the studios played a major role in the accelerated success of so-called independent cinema through their increased interest in financing *and* distributing 'indie-style' cinema. Miramax, 'the undisputed leader of the speciality film market in the 1990s and early 2000s', along with New Line, have consistently been the focus in much of the literature that has examined the impact of independent cinema, which also has tended to concentrate principally on the 1990s onwards.[42]

In the 1980s, those independent film companies who made the most significant impact in financial terms were those who participated in the populist 'franchise' sector of Hollywood filmmaking, rather than those who supported unconventional, 'indie-style' filmmaking. Such companies achieved a short-lived success by developing the type of films that fit quite easily into the 'Reaganite entertainment' template described by Britton and Wood. Carolco Pictures has been described as 'the most significant' of the 1980s independent companies but despite a number of massive hits including the Rambo films and *Terminator 2* (James Cameron, 1991), it eventually overextended and went bankrupt in 1995.[43] A major factor for its downfall is indicative of the way the independent market worked at the time. The expected revenues from such huge hits did not materialize because the company was pre-selling the rights to various territories in advance of production. This was a necessity to be able to generate the substantial budgets needed to sustain the spectacle that their style of cinema demanded. The result of this policy was that most of the vast revenues generated were immediately passed onto the various distributors worldwide.

30   *The Lost Decade*

Carolco did not engage much with the type of cinema more commonly deemed to be 'independent' in terms of content or vision, but other overtly commercial independent companies, who did *occasionally* finance more creatively ambitious films, also expanded too rapidly. The most visible of these was the Cannon Group, bought by Menahan Golan and Yoram Globus in 1979, which, in many ways, operated along similar lines to Carolco, specializing in 'B-movie' action cinema, often starring Chuck Norris or Charles Bronson. However, Cannon's eccentric owners also occasionally tried to boost their credibility by investing in films made by recognized arthouse auteurs including Altman (*Fool for Love*, 1985), Jean-Luc Godard (*King Lear*, 1987) and John Cassavetes (*Love Streams*, 1984). Of these, the only commercial success was Andrei Konchalovsky's *Runaway Train* in 1985. Not helped presumably by these 'arthouse' indulgences, Cannon followed what was a familiar pattern. When they attempted to take on the studios by distributing their own films, they overreached and, in 1986, Golan and Globus were obliged to sell out to Pathé.[44]

Of course, there were plenty of non-blockbuster films being made by smaller companies, stimulated by the need to accommodate the expanding video market, and a number of independent organizations and individuals were more closely engaged with this sort of cinema and with Renaissance auteurs. One example was Dino De Laurentiis, a flamboyant, long-established independent producer in Italy and Hollywood, who produced John Milius's successful, highly influential *Conan the Barbarian* in 1982, although this fantasy crowd-pleaser was hardly typical of the type of cinema most Renaissance auteurs were trying to make. A preference for muscular cinema was also apparent when in 1985, De Laurentiis surprised many by getting involved with New Hollywood's own *enfant terrible*, Michael Cimino, producing *Year of the Dragon*, his first film since the *Heaven's Gate* debacle. Arthur Penn observed that 'it was brave and Cimino came through for [De Laurentiis] in the sense that he did a very responsible job for him fiscally'.[45] In the same year, much like Cannon, De Laurentiis decided to try to compete on a more equal footing with the majors when he formed the Dino de Laurentiis Group (DEG), purchasing Embassy Pictures to handle distribution, as well as his own 32 acre studio lot.[46] DEG never produced a significant hit and critical credibility from films like *Blue Velvet* (David Lynch, 1986) did not translate into the sort of profits necessary to keep solvent a fully fledged studio operation: by August 1988, it was DEG's turn to file for bankruptcy. Its last gasp productions included two collaborations with Renaissance auteurs: Bogdanovich on the disastrous *Illegally Yours* (1988) and Friedkin's *Rampage*, the release of which was caught up in the company's bankruptcy resulting in it being left on the shelf until 1992.[47] Another indie whose demise was similarly associated with Renaissance directors was Filmways, which initially made its name in television but, by the late 1970s, had become heavily involved in film production and was in financial trouble. In 1981, Filmways put its future on the line with two films directed by established Renaissance filmmakers, Penn's *Four Friends* and De Palma's *Blow Out*. Both performed poorly, with *Blow Out*'s chances seriously undermined by John Travolta's huge salary.[48] The company was sold to Orion in 1982, another company with ambitions to compete on an equal footing with the majors, who itself barely survived the 1980s, also declaring bankruptcy in 1991.

It is apparent that those independent production companies who flourished in the decade were unable to cope with rapid expansion because they did not possess the substantial reserves of capital required to bolster themselves against the inherently precarious nature of the business. John Pierson's explanation for so many independents coming undone seems harsh but fair: 'The companies that had competed and failed in the 1980s were essentially the same companies that either overspent on production and overhead, or simply didn't have a clue how to pick films.'[49] Of course, in the film industry, virtually every project is a massive gamble from the moment it is green-lit. Yet, as Pierson implies, the causes of the demise of these companies seem to have come at least as much from a reckless and over-ambitious approach to running their businesses as from the broader structural and fiscal advantages that inherently favoured the conglomerates. Pierson also accuses these companies of being unable to spot a good film when they saw it and, as the man who secured lucrative deals, at the start of their careers, for Spike Lee, Michael Moore and Richard Linklater among others (to which the title of his memoir refers), he had a grandstand view of the 1980s independent scene.

What distinguishes the independent market in the 1980s from its 1990s upsurge is partly attributable to the difficulties of surviving outside of the Hollywood studio behemoth, but another reason was that the video market did not prove to be the expected bonanza for low-medium-budget films generally, and specifically for the type of films favoured by Renaissance directors. The most successful titles in the video market were still almost always the same blockbusters and family-oriented fare that dominated at the cinema. Although there was a growth in independently financed titles released in the decade to service the home video market, adventurous or challenging new cinema tended to fall in the gap between bestsellers and the more forgettable, disposable fare intended solely as 'straight-to-video'. For individual directors and their films, as we will see shortly, it was an adherence to mainstream norms, a willingness to compromise and the support of significant budgets from the major studios that was still the most likely route to commercial success. Where filmmakers engaged with the independent sector, this sometimes afforded them a measure of creative freedom but the unstable finances and inherent inability to get films into cinemas made commercial success unlikely.

2

Hollywood Renaissance auteurs in the 1980s

The mavericks and auteurs of the Hollywood Renaissance found the eighties especially testing ... The careers of Friedkin, Bogdanovich, Rafelson, Coppola and others went into terminal decline.

– Barry Langford[1]

The tendency to treat the post-1980 careers of the Hollywood Renaissance auteur as one of collective failure provides one of the reasons for this fresh look at their experiences and is aptly illustrated by Barry Langford's fairly sweeping assessment above; indeed, his citing of two of this book's three key case-study directors aptly illustrates the necessity for a more nuanced approach in order to show how these filmmakers experienced varying degrees of 'decline' and even a little success. This chapter will certainly show that it is indeed accurate to say that the decline of *some* of the filmmakers associated with the Renaissance was 'terminal', although those whose downfall was most precipitous are not necessarily the auteurs that he highlights. On the other hand, there is Stephen Prince's observation:

> One of the most remarkable facets of the industry's cultural history during the period [is that] Hollywood itself was attacked by a range of critics and special interest groups that deemed the industry's products to be unacceptably lewd, bigoted, or sacrilegious.[2]

What makes this particularly interesting in the present context is how this indicates that there were Renaissance directors who did not disappear without trace in the 1980s. Of the five films that Prince uses to illustrate the 'unacceptably lewd, bigoted, or sacrilegious' in eighties cinema, four were directed by filmmakers featured in this book: Friedkin's *Cruising*, De Palma's *Dressed to Kill* (1980) and *Body Double* (1984), as well as Scorsese's *The Last Temptation of Christ* (the other example is *Caligula* (Tinto Brass, 1980)).[3] It is clear, therefore, that, for all their oft-mentioned lack of commercial success, a number of the directors who emerged in the 1970s still maintained a significant public profile, even if often only perceived negatively due to their association with controversy. As the previous chapter showed, the structural changes and evolving commercial environment of the industry in the 1980s point us towards why these directors experienced difficulties, but the diversity and characteristics of their individual narratives need to be understood to be able to fully identify a more complete picture of their place within the decade's cinematic history. What follows is a description of specific auteur filmmakers and their films from the 1980s that shows how they made use of, for better or worse, the opportunities that either they were given or they managed to generate themselves.

Established directors used to auteurist levels of control did not all respond in the same way to the changing marketplace. Some managed the difficult feat of remaining productive by moving between highly commercial and more challenging, innovative work, while others moved more firmly into the mainstream. Then there were those who persisted, frequently in vain, in trying to get Renaissance-style films made at the studios, and there were others who just contented themselves with smaller budgets. While few of these films were commercially successful, there were exceptions for certain films and directors and if the decade taken in its entirety can be said to represent a continuing diminution of many of the Renaissance auteurs' careers, a small number saw their reputation and marketability actually enhanced.[4] Outside of the narrowly defined group covered here, there were directors like Nichols, Lumet, Sydney Pollack and Paul Mazursky, whose 1970s films have been sometimes associated with the Renaissance, who forged a reputation for reliability.[5] Philip Drake observes that 'when filmmakers are able to exercise almost absolute creative autonomy it is usually because they either have considerable industry reputation and clout, or are positioned industrially in such a way as to be able to make the films they want'.[6] In the 1980s, however, while this can generally be seen to be true, such power was not easily earned and, unless your name was Spielberg – or maybe Kubrick – few were able to achieve anything close to 'absolute creative autonomy'.

Enhanced reputations: Martin Scorsese and Brian De Palma

Martin Scorsese and Brian De Palma, two 'Movie Brats' of Italian heritage, have been studied in tandem with each other by a number of writers and for a variety of reasons: as postmodern auteurs; in terms of their shared interest in

Hollywood Renaissance Auteurs in the 1980s 35

examining male sexuality; and in their approach to genre.[7] The development and progression of their careers in the 1980s also invite a close comparison because, of the directors considered in this volume, De Palma and Scorsese are the only ones who can be said to have finished the decade with their reputation and marketability markedly enhanced. Yet neither Scorsese nor De Palma enjoyed a trouble-free eighties and each felt cause to question their position in Hollywood at one time or another in the decade. Indeed, they both experienced a high degree of opprobrium for controversial films that were deemed either blasphemous (Scorsese) or exploitatively sexual and violent (De Palma). Yet, by the end of the decade, they had both proved that they could handle a star-laden film and bring home a profitable studio assignment without too much trouble. Not only were *The Color of Money* (1986) and *The Untouchables* (1987) each director's most successful to date, in the following decade both enjoyed even bigger hits that moved them further towards the mainstream.[8] Unlike many of their peers, Scorsese and De Palma also consistently managed to retain, to varying degrees, their signature styles: these are filmmakers whose coherent and personal approach to filmmaking encourages an auteurist discourse.

Scorsese

Martin Scorsese often talks about his experiences in the 1980s in a negative light, but in doing so, he is really only referencing the period between *The King of Comedy* in 1982 and *The Color of Money* in 1986. This is the context when he aligned himself with Robert Altman by declaring that 'in a way he was sent to the diaspora for ten years, and so was I'.[9] This is a wilful exaggeration because his relatively short-lived issues bear little comparison with Altman's ten-year-long exile from Hollywood. When Scorsese was discussing why he decided to make *The Color of Money*, he said he no longer wanted to be 'a director who'd have five years between films'.[10] Again, he protests too much because, in fact, the *three* years between *King of Comedy* and *After Hours* (1985) is actually the longest time he has *ever* gone between films in the entire course of his career, a statistic indicative of the extent to which he has managed to consistently retain the industry's confidence. Unlike so many of the Renaissance auteurs, including Altman, Coppola and Friedkin, Scorsese's behaviour never resulted in a long-term breakdown in his relationships with the majors, for all his talk of falling out of favour.

At the end of the 1970s, however, Scorsese's position in the industry was not as secure as one might expect: while established as a critical favourite, unlike many of his peers, he had never had a genuine hit – although, according to Todd Berliner, *Taxi Driver*'s modest success actually earned almost ten times its negative cost due to its surprisingly small budget.[11] *New York, New York*'s costly failure in 1977 had been his contribution to the cycle of auteur-led commercial disasters yet it seems his reputational capital was still sufficiently high for him to be able to remain at this point within the embrace of the studio system. In 1980, Scorsese was persuaded by Robert de Niro, apparently against his better judgement, to take on *Raging Bull*, about the boxer, Jake La Motta, leading to the powerful producers, Robert Chartoff and Irwin Winkler, taking the project to United Artists, their usual partner. After reading Paul Schrader's screenplay, Steven Bach, the studio's head of production, said that they could not 'afford' a film that was 'written as an X'. De Niro and Scorsese quickly rewrote (uncredited) a more acceptable version and the studio now gave the go-ahead.[12] Thus, even an apparently personal and artistically innovative film like *Raging Bull* was subject to institutional influence amid the necessity to find a sensible place in the marketplace. It was, however, United Artists' habit of not interfering once they approved a script (a policy not unrelated to the *Heaven's Gate* debacle) that led to *Raging Bull* being unsparing and formally challenging in its portrait of an unsympathetic protagonist. The studio's light touch was surely a contributory factor in the film's enduring vaunted reputation, yet at the time of its release in November 1980, while it garnered positive reviews, *Raging Bull* was not a success: costing $17 million, it took only $10 million at the domestic box office.[13]

Scorsese's next project was yet another collaboration with De Niro and their continuing ability to get films funded by major studios must have had something to do with the prestige that the pair carried as a package. Backed by Fox, *The King of Comedy* was not an easy film to market; its use of comedy in the title and the presence of Jerry Lewis raised expectations of humour that the film was uninterested in meeting. At the time, the film divided critics but at the box office it was 'an unmitigated disaster', taking a mere $1.5 million before Fox withdrew it after only four weeks.[14] The film's reputation has grown in subsequent years, its influence identified by critics in a range of cinema, as with the recent example of *Joker* (Todd Phillips, 2019) in which reviewers detected obvious allusions to the Scorsese film.[15] The film's dismal performance and the subsequent cancelling of what Scorsese intended to be his next project, *The Last Temptation of Christ*, left the director dejected: it was specifically the critical and commercial failure

Hollywood Renaissance Auteurs in the 1980s 37

of *The King of Comedy* that seems to have prompted Scorsese's later downbeat depiction of the decade as a whole.

It is not really true, however, as Scorsese has been known to claim, that at this point Hollywood turned their back on him: the director himself has said that Paramount offered him both *Beverly Hills Cop* and *Witness*, made successfully by other directors in 1984 and 1985, respectively.[16] When Scorsese made the choice to move into the independent sector with his next film *After Hours*, although less starry auteurs had already made such a move, it was the more visible Scorsese, and the fact that he made the film *so* cheaply, that attracted so much comment. The film was funded by The Geffen Company for only $4.5 million, with distribution on a pick-up basis that left Scorsese without any external interference.[17] Scorsese showed himself, and others, that he could work quickly and cheaply: principal photography took forty days and the director only received a quarter of his normal salary. Its returns were healthy, considering its budget, making $10.6 million.[18] However, Scorsese reported that 'when I went to Hollywood to promote my next film I found, to my surprise, some people resented that we had made it for so little', the implication being that it would now be expected that everyone could work that way.[19] In the context of Scorsese's overall career, *After Hours*, although it has moments of characteristic invention (like all his films), has less of the more flamboyant touches that are characteristic of his most-acclaimed work. As a relatively discrete entry in Scorsese's *oeuvre*, it was also unusually for a director who tends to plough a singular furrow, very much of its time, forming part of a brief, concentrated cycle of 'yuppie nightmare' films, a sub-genre that now seems especially reflective of the Reaganite era in which these films were made.[20]

In September 1984, Scorsese was approached by Paul Newman with an offer to direct *The Color of Money*, an adaptation of Walter Tevis's sequel to his novel, *The Hustler*. The film of *The Hustler* had been a notable and much-admired success for Newman in 1961 and he had secured the sequel's rights and sourced the finance from Touchstone, Disney's adult division. According to Scorsese, his previous relationship with Michael Eisner and Jeffrey Katzenberg, who had just left Paramount for Disney, also contributed to the decision to finance the film.[21] In fact, following *After Hours'* moderate success, Scorsese was again in demand, including an offer to direct *Dick Tracy* for Warren Beatty (which Beatty eventually directed himself in 1990).[22] In explaining why he took on such a conventional project, Scorsese has said that, at this stage in his career, he was interested in seeing if he could be the sort of director who can handle a mainstream film starring a Hollywood legend like Newman. The director proudly described how he finished in forty-nine days, instead of the scheduled fifty, and brought it in for $13 million, $1.5 million below budget.[23] This boast about an achievement, which was only slightly better than the mere fulfilment of a contractual duty, gives us some sense of how maverick directors like Scorsese had become habitually accustomed to exceeding allocated financial limits and timescale. This is reflected in Scorsese and Newman, despite their combined status, having to agree to put up a third of their salaries as surety against the film going over budget.[24] Yet perhaps it should not come as that much of a surprise that Scorsese could work efficiently with limited funding: his early schooling with Roger Corman had, according to Berliner, taught him 'how to give a professional a look to a low-budget film'.[25] *The Color of Money* earned Newman his long overdue Best Actor Oscar although, from the perspective of Scorsese's authorial discourse, it is unsurprisingly not especially interesting. It was his highest performing film to that point, taking $52.3 million at the domestic box office: an indication of Hollywood's habitual 'short-termism' was his immediate receipt of a two-year 'first-look' deal with Disney.[26]

Scorsese was now finally able to make his long-cherished project, *The Last Temptation of Christ*. Scorsese observed wryly that when he moved agents on 1 January 1987, 'the film has been the laughing stock of cocktail parties in Hollywood until the minute I signed with CAA – then it was made'. Universal, the one studio who had never courted the director, agreed to take on the project, but in a partnership with Cineplex Odeon.[27] This collaboration between a studio and a theatrical chain arose out of a law change that encouraged yet more conglomeration within Hollywood's power structures, but its significance has rarely been noted. In 1986, the 1948 'Paramount Decree' that had dismantled Hollywood's vertical integration, was annulled and MCA, Universal's owner, immediately acquired 50 per cent of Cineplex.[28] Effectively, then, the financing came from a single source, but the fiscal arrangement ensured that *Last Temptation* would receive an adequate release, an insurance against the possibility that some theatre owners might refuse to screen it. Such trepidation was justified when, as Michael Morris described it, 'a public outcry of a magnitude unprecedented in the history of religious films' came to pass.[29] Support for the film *within* the industry was, nevertheless, extensive and both the Directors' and Writers' Guilds berated those theatres that refused to show the film. Its box-office performance of $8.4 million domestically and $4 million overseas was seen as reasonable, considering that, as its director put it, 'it's an "art movie" ... not a commercial mainstream movie. It runs 2 hours and 43 minutes and it was not made for exploitative reasons'.[30] After the relative conventionality of *After Hours* and *The Color of Money*, *Last Temptation* was a bold return to a more ambitious and personal style of filmmaking which, in hindsight, appears all the more remarkable considering how much populist filmmaking dominated at the time (Figure 2.1). For Carl Freedman, '*Last Temptation* is even more radically Scorsesian than *Taxi Driver* in its fascination with human unconnectedness.'[31] It is perhaps a little surprising that the intellectually complex and visually splendid *Last Temptation* is rarely included when Scorsese's best work is discussed, but its artistry seems to have been somewhat overshadowed by its headline-grabbing controversies. In academia, the complex religious questions that the film, and its source novel, raises have tended to overshadow the consideration of its aesthetics: there have been three books alone devoted to the subject since the turn of the century.[32] Reflecting changing attitudes to risk as the decade progressed, Scorsese was obliged in 1988 to make the film for about half of its 1983 budget ($7 million compared with $12–16 million), indicating again that he could manage on small budgets, this time in pursuit of something more formally adventurous and intellectually challenging. Scorsese worked for no salary and was equally parsimonious on set, shooting the film in sixty-two days and restricting himself to three takes for any shot.[33]

Figure 2.1 Jesus meets John the Baptist in Scorsese's controversial 'art movie'.

40   *The Lost Decade*

Scorsese finished the decade with his contribution, 'Life Lessons', easily the best of three short films in the anthology, *New York Stories* (1989), with the others directed by Coppola and Woody Allen. As Disney aggressively pushed for a greater share of the adult market, Touchstone financed the film, according to Grist, to 'enhance the company's institutional and critical prestige'.[34] In 1990, Scorsese returned to a familiar subject – Italian-American gangsters – with *Goodfellas* which achieved the rare combination at that time of both commercial appeal and critical acclaim. His next film, *Cape Fear*, was his most successful to that point, earning $79 million domestically alone.[35] Scorsese subsequently enjoyed an uninterrupted run of well-funded films, with some more personal, and less commercial, than others.[36] By the end of the 1980s, Scorsese had established a reputation for reliability and respectability that he still retains today.

De Palma

Brian De Palma's 1980s career is unlike all the other Renaissance filmmakers because the films he made in the decade became fundamental in defining both his controversial reputation and divisive authorial image. By the 1980s, according to Paul Raemaker, his approach to filmmaking comprised a 'prevalent aesthetic imperative, manifest in virtuosic displays of authorially-motivated visual stylization'.[37] Although *Carrie*'s success in 1976 was an important breakthrough for the director, four of the seven films he directed in the eighties – *Dressed to Kill, Scarface* (1983), *Body Double* and *The Untouchables* – are, for different reasons, significant texts with which to consider both De Palma and contemporaneous developments in Hollywood cinema. Somehow De Palma steered his career towards respectability despite vituperative attacks aimed at the first three of these films. The result is that his work has polarized opinion more than any of the other Renaissance auteurs. In more recent times, there has been a belated torrent of scholarly interest in De Palma, much of which offers carefully argued defences of the most frequent criticisms of his filmmaking: his slavish devotion to Hitchcock, his predilection for extreme depictions of violence and the objectification and exploitation of his female characters (and actresses).[38] As well as recent defenders, there were a few earlier staunch supporters like Robin Wood and Kenneth MacKinnon, but more common attitudes about the director were similar to Robert Kolker, who dismisses De Palma outright because of his 'career of the most superficial imitations of the most superficial aspects of

Hitchcock's style, worked through a misogyny and violence that manifest a contempt for the audience exploited by his films'.[39] The visibility of De Palma and his films has markedly increased outside the academy as well, spearheaded by the omniscience of *Scarface* as a cultural artefact (according to Chris Dumas, 'the single-most widely influential film of the last thirty years'),[40] as well as at least four retrospectives in 2016. These were inspired by the well-publicized release of the 2015 documentary, *De Palma*, a fascinating, if extremely solipsistic, overview of his career comprised solely of the titular subject talking to camera with clips.[41] De Palma's visual style is undoubtedly grandiose, and his debt to the 'master of suspense' is all too apparent in much of his work. While much of the scholarship that identifies the director as a consummate filmmaker is persuasive, many of his films seem hidebound by the assault on the senses that derive from his overdetermined homages to Hitchcock and from his hyperbolic style. In the 1980s, *Blow Out*, arguably, stands apart because it wears its influences more lightly, and its style is delivered in a lower register than in the overblown excess of *Scarface* or in the other more lurid 1980s Hitchcockian thrillers, *Dressed to Kill* and *Body Double*.

De Palma began the decade with the independently funded *Dressed to Kill*, from an original screenplay he wrote himself. Filmways offered De Palma the opportunity to make the film on a budget of only $7.5 million but its performance, realizing $31 million, was good enough for Filmways to readily agree to fund De Palma's next film, *Blow Out*.[42] *Dressed to Kill*, as already noted, attracted angry accusations of female exploitation and objectification and was also embroiled in a ratings row when striving to obtain an 'R' rating. There are interesting parallels here with Friedkin's *Cruising*, released in the same year, with both enduring disputes with protestors and censors. Both directors were contractually obliged to deliver an R-rated film, their rows with the ratings board played out through the press. Curiously, De Palma was also briefly attached to a version of *Cruising* before Friedkin, with elements of his script 'repurposed' for *Dressed to Kill*.[43] As David Greven identified in his 2013 book, De Palma and Friedkin also share an interest in the exploration of male psycho-sexual behaviour and ambiguous notions of heroism (see Chapter 5 for more on this aspect of Friedkin's work).[44]

Blow Out was an attempt to make, according to De Palma, something 'more serious and reputable'[45] and distance himself from the horror genre, although the film remains a continuation of his Hitchcock project, by way of both Antonioni's *Blow-Up* (1967) – as foregrounded in the film's title – and Coppola's *The Conversation* (1974) – itself inspired by Antonioni's film. Filmways effectively gambled their future on the film when the budget ballooned from $5–6 million to $20 million after John Travolta came on board. Independent producers banking on a star presence was not unusual in the 1980s but the strategy failed badly for *Blow Out*, which returned only $8 million. It has a devastatingly downbeat conclusion and De Palma said, '[N]o-one saw it until it was finished. When they saw the ending, they nearly died.'[46] Indeed, *Blow Out*'s final moments are as bleak as anything from the 1970s and the final shot of a broken Travolta recalls Gene Hackman's despair at the end of *The Conversation*. These final scenes are astonishingly rendered, described by Robin Wood as 'among the most remarkable achievements of modern Hollywood cinema.'[47]

Despite *Dressed to Kill*'s controversy and *Blow Out*'s failure, De Palma still found work within the studio system for the remainder of the decade (and beyond), making five films for four different studios. With *Scarface*, De Palma once again displayed an apparently thin skin regarding criticism of his trademark style when he now claimed that he wanted 'to move into a different world' because he had grown 'tired of making these Brian De Palma movies'.[48] The remake of Howard Hawks's 1932 film of the same name originated with Al Pacino who initially recruited De Palma along with playwright and aspiring screenwriter, David Rabe, who was rapidly replaced by Oliver Stone.[49] Stone, in turn, also departed after falling out with De Palma because, at least according to the former, he had the effrontery to confer directly with Pacino.[50] It is hard to understate *Scarface*'s abiding presence in popular culture today but at the time of its release, after the film's projected cost of $15 million spiralled to $25 million, its box-office performance only just about managed to match its budget.[51] Critics disliked it for its excess of graphic, cynical violence but the film was later picked up by the hip-hop generation, drawn to its portrayal of a supposedly glamorous 'drugs-and-guns' culture. The initial lukewarm performance of the film may also be traced to yet another ratings issue. After returning unsuccessfully to the censors three times in order to get an 'R' rating, De Palma decided not to change it anymore, even putting everything back in he had removed.[52] It is no wonder, then, that critics and audiences were so shocked by the film's violence.

De Palma's next move shows he was not yet entirely reconciled to working within the system – and indicates that he took a perverse pleasure in his own notoriety. In 1984, he was given a three-picture deal with Columbia, including an office on the studio lot, quite an achievement given the prevalent industrial circumstances.[53] His first project, *Body Double*, was a return to his familiar Hitchcockian horror-thriller mode that can only be seen as a deliberate act

Hollywood Renaissance Auteurs in the 1980s   43

of provocation, not least because De Palma made no secret of his intentions. Anticipating and relishing the power from the expected success of *Scarface*, he even sounds a little unhinged when, speaking from the set, he told Lynn Hirshberg:

> I'm going to go out and make an X-rated suspense porn picture ... I'm sick of being censored. *Dressed to Kill* was going to get an X rating and I had to cut a lot. So, if they want an X, they'll get a *real* X. They wanna see suspense, they wanna see terror, they wanna see SEX – I'm the person for the job. It's going to be unbelievable. I've been thinking about this for years: BRIAN DE PALMA'S *BODY DOUBLE*! I can't wait.[54]

Body Double delivered on De Palma's promises, making what Linda Badley calls his retaliatory 'self-parodic dirty joke'[55] and including a notorious, unpalatable 'driller-killer' murder scene that Prince opines is 'the decade's ghastliest sequence of sexual slaughter in a mainstream film'.[56] Without any big stars, the film cost a reasonable $9 million yet still barely covered its costs. No one was surprised when Columbia cancelled his contract and De Palma once again was expressing a need to 're-invent myself' and do something where 'no-one could accuse me ripping off Hitchcock'.[57] *Wise Guys* (1986), a lukewarm gangster comedy, was another commercial failure, a mixed genre film that may have confused audiences expecting another *Scarface*. However, according to Keesey, because De Palma brought the film in on budget, and on time, he proved to Hollywood that he was a team player.[58] This may have influenced Paramount's decision to hire him for *The Untouchables* which would become, by far, his most successful film to that point.

A major project with stars (Kevin Costner, Sean Connery and De Niro) and a budget in the region of $20 million, *The Untouchables* was critically and commercially well received and made $76 million at the domestic box office and $186 million worldwide.[59] De Palma had now moved onto another level within Hollywood, leading to him being entrusted, disastrously, with *The Bonfire of the Vanities* in 1990. Before that film, De Palma first used his new-found power to make a heartfelt film on a serious topic, somewhat sacrificing his usual hyperbolic tone to suit the subject matter. Based on a real incident, *Casualties of War* (1989) was his contribution to the late eighties cycle of Vietnam films, a harrowing tale that may have suffered from its similarities to *Platoon*, Oliver Stone's award-winning 1986 film. It returned a reasonable $18.5 million but not enough to cover its prohibitive $22.5 million cost.[60]

44   *The Lost Decade*

For all the furore surrounding some of his films in the eighties, De Palma had gone from one film to another without too much difficulty. Seemingly against the odds at times, he managed to negotiate the system sufficiently well in the decade, despite setbacks, to remain firmly located within it. Like Scorsese, his body of work encourages an auteurist perspective because he so consistently adopts a signature visual style. Any De Palma film will inevitably feature the use of split screens, spilt dioptres (and split personalities), 360-degree shots and overblown, theatrical staging, a schema that he frequently used as complementary to his thematic concerns exploring sexuality and psychology. Even in those films he made in the decade that he did not develop from scratch, De Palma's visual sensibility is still obviously present, very much so in the case of *Scarface*'s operatic style and excess of violence. Despite the high-profile, expensive failure of *Bonfire*, De Palma was now a big-name Hollywood director and when he made *Mission Impossible* in 1996, he moved into genuine blockbuster territory.

Hits and misses: Peter Bogdanovich and John Milius

Peter Bogdanovich and John Milius are very different filmmakers, although their work does share an allusive quality that invokes both classical Hollywood – particularly John Ford – and more arthouse influences. Renaissance auteurs regularly railed against the interference of executives in creative matters with Milius and Bogdanovich sharing with the likes of Penn and Ashby an inability to adapt themselves to the system's confines in the 1980s. Despite this, they both briefly belied their decline with box-office successes: Bogdanovich with *Mask* (1985) and Milius with *Conan the Barbarian* and *Red Dawn* (1984). This section considers the circumstances that allowed these two to manage this small degree of success in the 1980s even if they still appeared to be en route to 'terminal decline'.

Bogdanovich

Bogdanovich is, in many ways, the epitome of the Hollywood Renaissance auteur who, in his own words (borrowing from *Easy Rider*), 'had blown it' as the new decade beckoned.[61] However, his particular experiences tell us how important it is to take account of a director's individual circumstances, even when considering them as representative of a wider group because the trajectory of Bogdanovich's troubled downhill career is particularly unique. By 1980, Bogdanovich had already managed to severely damage the reputation he rapidly established with three consecutive critical and commercial successes: *The Last Picture Show* (1971), *What's Up Doc?* (1972) and *Paper Moon* (1973), films that defined his career. What followed subsequently in the 1970s was a series of expensive failures that fostered a reputation for rampant egotism that caused Irwin Winkler to describe him as 'easily the most arrogant person' he had ever met in the film business.[62] By the turn of the decade, any remaining vestiges of his good reputation were destroyed by the effect on Bogdanovich of the tragic events of 14 August 1980. In a luridly notorious incident, his girlfriend, the Playboy model Dorothy Stratten, was murdered by her estranged husband,[63] and the professional consequences for Bogdanovich led to an absence from directing for four years following his reckless, unfathomable actions regarding the completion and release of *They All Laughed* in 1981 (featuring an unconvincing Stratten in a leading role). The box-office failure of the film placed him in financial straits that eventually led to his bankruptcy in 1985.[64]

They All Laughed, one of Bogdanovich's frequent attempts to capture the spirit of classic screwball comedies, was funded by Time-Life Films who were trying to establish themselves in Hollywood. They put up $7.5 million but Bogdanovich fell out with the producers during shooting. Then came the tragedy and he felt obliged, according to Andrew Yule, 'to complete the movie for the sake of Stratten and all she had meant to him'.[65] When Fox, the film's distributor, became reluctant to put more money in, Bogdanovich's somewhat crazy solution was to buy the film himself from Time-Life, also paying Fox half a million dollars to get the rights reverted to him. He made a deal with Mark Damon's Producers Sales Organisation, who managed to sell the film in forty overseas territories but, as in the United States, returns were paltry.[66] It earned less than $1 million at the domestic box office and ended up costing Bogdanovich at least $5 million of his own money.[67]

Bogdanovich's disagreements with an independent might appear to support the notion that it was often as difficult to achieve creative autonomy in that sector, but what happened on his next project, *Mask*, a return to a Hollywood major, indicates that, in his particular case, it was more about his failure to recognize how much the power dynamic had shifted in contemporary Hollywood. Late in 1983, Universal offered Bogdanovich the opportunity to direct *Mask*, a melodrama about a disfigured boy and his mother, based on a real story and budgeted at $12 million. After handing over the film, the studio ignored the director's right of 'final cut' and re-edited the film, dispensing with eight minutes running time. Bogdanovich sued the studio for $11 million but it was Universal's version that appeared on 8 March 1985. For all the director's protests, the film was a success, earning $48 million domestically, prompting him to see sense and drop the lawsuit.[68] Placing Bogdanovich in this section *is* based on *Mask*'s success and it is telling that again it was a firm move into the mainstream financed by a studio that was his solitary eighties hit. Considering his behaviour, it is not a surprise that the film's success did not provide any form of rehabilitation: on the contrary, Bogdanovich asserted that 'suing the studio was the single worst thing I ever did in this business. The whole town really got scared of me'.[69]

Mirroring what happened to Francis Coppola (as Chapter 4 will show), the result of filing for bankruptcy was that Bogdanovich was obliged to find work. Dino De Laurentiis, with his penchant for working with New Hollywood auteurs, offered him *Illegally Yours*, another screwball comedy, starring Rob Lowe, supposedly in the vein of *What's Up Doc?* The unfunny film that resulted was a disastrous shoot, with DEG closing in on bankruptcy and myriad other problems arising on set. According to its director, '*Illegally Yours* was without question the worst experience of my career from beginning to end'.[70]

After *Illegally Yours*, Bogdanovich was looking to return to the scene of his greatest triumph with *Texasville* (1990), a sequel to *The Last Picture Show*, which proved to be yet another financial disappointment. Stylistically and tonally unlike the original, it is a rather undervalued gem, certainly when compared with anything Bogdanovich made in the 1980s. How the film came about recalls Scorsese and the making of *Last Temptation*: like Scorsese, Bogdanovich signed with CAA in the late eighties and they managed swiftly to get independent backing to make *Texasville*.[71] Bogdanovich's personal experiences coloured his professional ones in the 1980s and his difficulties indicate how important it was for directors to find some accommodation with the demands of an industry that perpetually threatened to undermine their creative impulses.

Milius

John Milius was part of the 'film school generation', attending the University of Southern California (USC) where he became firm friends with George Lucas. He stands apart from all the other 'brats' because of his publicly expressed right-wing views, embodied in a persona deliberately constructed to provoke.

His promotion of himself as a hyper-patriotic warmonger, a baiter of both liberals, and of liberal ideas, led Milius to claim that 'I've been blacklisted for a large part of my career because of my politics – as surely as any writer was blacklisted back in the 1950s'.[72] This seems to be supported by the fact that, between 1970 and 1991, he only directed eight feature films. Yet many of his public pronouncements often seem made more out of a sense of mischief than any serious intent, as when he asserted in a 2013 high-profile documentary (that has partially rehabilitated his reputation), 'I am not a fascist. I am much closer to a Maoist. However, I *am* a Zen-anarchist'.[73] Such playfulness notwithstanding, his films can certainly be read as reflective of his political concerns, and it is a body of work that displays a tightly knotted group of themes and obsessions. While not easily aligned with that of his contemporaries, in this sense, his films do exhibit the coherence of an auteur. Yet they are far more ideologically nuanced than is usually perceived with his public persona working against a balanced understanding of his films' thematic subtleties. This illustrates how an authorial star image was not always seen as an asset in the carefully controlled environment of 1980s Hollywood. In fact, because Milius, as Alfio Leotta notes, 'mobilized extreme political discourses to develop a distinguishable and marketable persona', it is hardly unreasonable that there has been a tendency to understand Milius's films as unabashed expressions of his right-wing views.[74] Kolker finds his work as distasteful as he does De Palma's, commenting that 'his work is overblown with portent and violence, full of the racism, misogyny, meanness, and vulgarity that go with his ideology'.[75] This is not an uncommon view (although his 1970s work such as *Dillinger* (1973) and *Big Wednesday* (1978) has its admirers) but where Milius has been most appreciated creatively, especially among his peers, is as a writer: as well as originating and co-writing *Apocalypse Now*, he is renowned for heroic work as an uncredited script-doctor – as Spielberg put it, 'none of us could tell a story like John'.[76]

Conan the Barbarian (1982) prefigured and inspired a whole range of fantasy cinema and television, the influence of which is still felt today, not least in the wildly successful television series, *Game of Thrones* (2011–2019). Not only did *Conan* have an impact on the fantasy genre but the presence of the muscular Arnold Schwarzenegger, playing the eponymous hero, also heralded, alongside Stallone in the same year's *First Blood*, the 1980s obsession with what Susan Jeffords calls 'hard bodies'.[77] *Conan*'s original script was written by Oliver Stone who collaborated with four different Renaissance directors in the 1980s and fell out with all of them, after which the directors all rewrote his screenplays (or obtained rewrites).[78] Stone's version would have been expensive, costed at an unfeasible $40 million.[79] The version that ended up being made, complained Stone, 'was silly and so far from what was once conceived'.[80] *Conan* was produced by De Laurentiis who co-financed the film with Universal. With a budget of $19.5 million, it was a successful film and Leotta claims its cult following and home video sales led to it eventually grossing $300 million.[81] Its success led to Milius's next film, *Red Dawn*, being backed by United Artists and distributed by parent company, MGM.

Red Dawn, another right-wing fantasy, depicts an invasion on American soil by Russian and Cuban forces and shows a ragbag of youthful rebels fighting back, guerrilla style. Milius, promoting it at the time, said that 'I see it as an anti-war movie, in the sense that if both sides could see this, maybe it wouldn't have to happen'.[82] The film did well with a domestic return of $38 million against a budget of $17 million.[83] *Red Dawn* may offer a fantasy of American derring-do, but it is a downbeat film and it can be argued that Milius's real target in *Red Dawn* was not communism but the federal government. Milius's films all emphasize the importance of an individual's ability to make their own decisions. No matter that the film displays a certain ideological nuance, this has not stopped *Red Dawn* being adopted as a totemic emblem of American right-wing extremism.

The message in both *Conan* and *Red Dawn* of the value in self-determination would be even more central to Milius's final 1980s film, *Farewell to the King*. The film is the story of a rogue American soldier (Nick Nolte), who has established a mini-empire in the jungles of Borneo during the Second World War; the character carries obvious similarities to Kurtz in *Apocalypse Now*. Amidst a flurry of Vietnam films around the same time, with its similar jungle setting, it may have struggled to distinguish itself sufficiently to arouse much interest: it was not successful, only earning just under $2.5 million, a fraction of its $20 million budget.[84] Milius blamed the film's failure on cuts imposed by Orion but it was the beginning of the end, with his career petering out in the 1990s – he directed only one more feature film, *Flight of the Intruder*, in 1991.[85] Milius's problems seem to have stemmed from his confrontational personality and by not being willing to compromise sufficiently to find remunerative work. Yet it was probably his public espousal of problematic political views that most scared executives: the studios may have simply thought that he was not worth the bother.

Down and out: Arthur Penn and Hal Ashby

Arthur Penn and Hal Ashby directed some of the most revered films of the Renaissance period and both enjoyed, for a while, an unbroken run of critically acclaimed work. By the 1980s, however, although they strived to remain in gainful employment, there followed a dramatic and permanent downturn in both their fortunes. Ashby died in 1988 and Penn never made another film for the cinema after 1989's *Penn and Teller Get Killed*. Not one of the eight films they directed between them in the decade could be said to have even achieved a modest degree of success or critical praise. Penn, the acclaimed auteur behind *Bonnie and Clyde*, has attracted scholarly interest in the past, not least from Wood and Kolker, but his name recognition, if not his most well-known films, has diminished in recent years.[86] Ashby's status as an auteur star of the Renaissance has progressed in the opposite direction. In the past, he was frequently excluded in canonical lists of the period's auteurs, although his lack of profile *has* been exaggerated by those seeking to correct it. From about 2009 onwards, however, a sudden surge of interest resulted in a number of books and articles, as well as a recent documentary.[87] Yet even Ashby's staunchest defenders struggle to find much good to say about his 1980s films and Penn is much the same. The circumstances that led to this pair's artistic and commercial decline were different, of course, but, in both cases, can be most obviously related to the prevailing market conditions. Neither seemed to be able, or were insufficiently inspired, to get the sort of projects made that they had managed in the previous decade. They were obliged to compromise with what seemed like atypical subject matter and styles simply in order to remain in gainful employment.

Penn

Much like Bogdanovich or Altman, Penn struggled during the latter part of the 1970s to get even close to the outstanding commercial performance of *Bonnie and Clyde* (1967), the film that cemented his reputation, yet his critical standing remained largely intact. However, the relative box-office failure of *Night Moves* (1975) and *The Missouri Breaks* (1976) made it difficult for Penn to get projects off the ground in the latter part of the decade. This was the context that led to Penn accepting the opportunity to direct *Four Friends* in 1980, a coming-of-age drama set in the 1960s, written by Steve Tesich, a follow-up to his surprise 1979 hit, *Breaking Away* (Peter Yates). Filmways who, as noted earlier, were

50   *The Lost Decade*

struggling to survive, gambled their future on *Blow Out* and on Penn's film. It is a coming-of-age drama that depicts the 1960s in a fairly original way and, while it is not obviously relatable to Penn's earlier work, it is the most interesting of his eighties work. However, as Kolker points out, it 'is harmed by an inability to deal with the contradictions of nostalgia and bitterness'.[88] It is largely unregarded, or even known or seen, although Penn did claim in 1986 that 'there were certainly different opinions of the film. It has very strong supporters in Europe'.[89] It did feature as a fairly recent entry in *Sight and Sound*'s 'Lost and Found' column (that re-examines unavailable and obscure films) where Geoff Andrew makes a somewhat debatable case for the film's rehabilitation: 'far from negligible … it interrogates the migrant's dream of America as a land of plenty and freedom'.[90]

It was another four years until Penn's next film, *Target*, a further retreat into conventional genre filmmaking, and his least characteristic to date. The circumstances that led him to accept the film are illustrative of the diverse ways that Renaissance directors found work at this time. In 1984, Penn had been approached about directing *Falling in Love*, a contemporary melodrama in the vein of *Brief Encounter* (David Lean, 1945), which was to reunite Streep and De Niro after *The Deer Hunter*. Meanwhile Ulu Grosbard was attached to *Target* but left it to replace Penn on *Falling in Love*, supposedly because of a friendship with De Niro. The directors shared an agent, Sam Cohen, so *Target* was offered to Penn, by now desperate to make almost anything. Penn explained to Lippe and Wood some of his thinking when he accepted *Target*:

> I took it fully with my eyes wide open knowing the limitations of it, knowing the kind of film it was. But I thought also there was another part of it, and this is a question of vanity. I thought, dammit, I'd like to show that I can do this kind of high-kinetic action movie.[91]

What is left unsaid in this account is why the film company, CBS Films, thought Penn a suitable choice for a generic action thriller. Once again, it can be seen how an interrelated web of circumstances can come into play in order to understand how Renaissance auteurs found work at this time. When cineastes and scholars try too hard to justify why auteurs make work of which they seem unworthy, they can be too preoccupied with romantic notions of a thwarted creativity, whereas, in fact, the reasons can actually often be quite prosaic. *Target* is an acceptable example of a routine spy thriller but is of little interest because of its steadfast generic conformity. For Robert Kolker, *Target* 'signifies nothing less than an exhausted liberal filmmaker surrendering to the reigning neoconservatism of the 1980s' and *Dead of Winter* (1987), Penn's penultimate film, was also conventional, a pedestrian and predictable gothic horror. His final feature film, *Penn and Teller Get Killed* (1989), was a vehicle written by, and starring, the eponymous magicians which Kolker calls 'a cute trick' and which seems to have disappeared almost without trace in the intervening years.[92]

Even in 1986, Penn seemed resigned to the decline of his career. When he was asked if he might consider following Altman's example with low-budget theatrical adaptations, Penn responded enthusiastically, commenting, 'certainly Altman is a very good model to use, someone who has always found a way around orthodoxy. I've got to do more of what he does'.[93] He never did move into this type of lower budget filmmaking which he may not have really seen as a realistic option: very few filmmakers have Altman's flexibility and work ethic. It is perhaps no surprise that Robin Wood's Marxist sympathies led him to read Penn and other left-leaning directors' difficulties finding meaningful work at this time as being linked to their politically motivated unwillingness to compromise their artistic integrity. Not that Wood believed that studios' objection to any form of radicalism was ideologically determined, rather that any move towards the left, and away from the prevalent Reaganism, was considered likely to be unprofitable.[94] In the final analysis, perhaps Penn's age – he was the oldest of all the Renaissance auteurs and in his sixties – might suggest that the fading of his career was simply attributable to the fading of his creative light.

Ashby

Between 1970 and 1979, from *The Landlord* to *Being There*, Hal Ashby directed seven films that were all critically and (in varying degrees) commercially successful. In sharp contrast, the four films he made in the 1980s were all financial and critical catastrophes, described by Christopher Beach as 'one of the saddest and most surprising reversals in the history of Hollywood directors'.[95] No other Renaissance auteur's 1980s arc so starkly illustrates the differences between the decades. The reasons for this dramatic turnaround, according to Aaron Hunter, 'are complex … but one cause is clear … three were taken away from him before and during the editing process and cut or re-cut by a different editor'.[96] The cruel irony was that Ashby made his name as an editor, including winning an Oscar for *In the Heat of the Night* (Norman Jewison, 1967). Hunter is not alone in downplaying the extent that Ashby's behaviour was a significant, maybe *the most* significant, reason for the downturn in quality of his films, and the comment about Ashby's removal from the editing of his films as a 'cause' seems incomplete because it elides *why* he was removed. It was his behaviour that caused him to be removed and the effect was poorly edited films. Philip Drake's observation that Ashby's 'films made in the eighties ... are rarely examined, and when they are, the approach tends to be in terms of artistic compromise and decline' does not seem to allow for the fact that such a stance may be justified.[97] *Second-Hand Hearts* is unavailable in any commercial format, but the other three films are generic exercises that are difficult to reconcile with the director of *Harold and Maude* (1970) or *Shampoo* (1975).

In 1978, after the success of *Coming Home*, Ashby was offered a multi-picture deal with Lorimar Productions, a successful independent television production company, who were in the process of establishing a cinematic presence. By attaching themselves to a critically admired auteur, Lorimar, as with other independents, believed they could bolster their credibility and create a public profile. The deal was particularly attractive for Ashby, coming with both creative control and profit participation.[98] He decided to shoot the first two films of the deal back to back and, surprisingly, the much-admired *Being There*, released in 1979, was actually shot after *Second-Hand Hearts* which did not come out until May 1981, despite principal photography being completed in September 1978.[99] Ashby had already fallen out with Lorimar over what he felt was inadequate marketing for *Being There* when the film company took exception to the excessive time Ashby was taking editing *Second-Hand Hearts*. When it did finally come out, the film was greeted by vicious put-downs and Beach concludes that 'the film suffers from the performances of the lead actors, from a weak plot, and from a lack of tonal consistency'.[100]

Ashby's relationship with Lorimar deteriorated even further on *Lookin' to Get Out*, to such an extent that they ended up in the law courts for several years. Haskell Wexler, the film's cinematographer, commented that '*Lookin' to Get Out* was a lousy script ... There was one weakness Hal had. Hal was confident that he could weave gold out of flax'.[101] Ashby was not in full control as he was trying to re-edit *Second-Hand Hearts* while shooting *Lookin'* at the same time. By October 1981, Lorimar had enough and, with the film already over $5 million over its $10 million budget, Ashby was forced to accept that another editor would now recut the film that was, at that stage, prohibitively long at 2 hours 45 minutes. By October 1982, after protracted arguments in the courts, Ashby allowed Lorimar's cut to be released. The film finally cost a staggering $21 million but only registered gross receipts of $1.6 million, largely derived from video and cable sales.[102]

Hollywood Renaissance Auteurs in the 1980s   53

The wider consequences of Ashby's inability to forge a sustainable working relationship with Lorimar became apparent in June 1981 when Ashby signed a contract with Columbia to direct *Tootsie*. This was a clear indication that, at this stage, Ashby's reputation was still solid. Despite his contract with Lorimar being non-exclusive, they complained to Columbia that Ashby was still employed by them editing *Lookin' to Get Out*. By October, wary of a lawsuit from Lorimar, Columbia had replaced Ashby with Sydney Pollack.[103] To add insult to injury, the film was hugely successful, the second-best performing film of 1983. However much blame might be attributed to Lorimar, and it is inevitable that there must have been some, it is apparent that directors like Ashby, who were unable to adapt a more responsible approach to filmmaking, were now finding it difficult to survive.

Ashby's next film, his penultimate, *The Slugger's Wife* (1985), was a weak comedy written by Neil Simon on which the director was dismissed from the film by Columbia for 'unprofessional conduct and material breeches of conduct [*sic*]'.[104] When the studio released the film in a recut version, it earned just $1.3 million on a budget of $19 million.[105] Ashby's final film, *8 Million Ways to Die* (1986), is an all-action, generic thriller and unlike anything else he had previously made. Produced by Mark Damon, and his company PSO, it was a chaotic project from the outset with Ashby even more uncooperative than usual; two days after shooting ended, in December 1985, he was once again fired. After a legal battle, in an echo of what happened on *Lookin'*, Ashby had to concede and allow PSO's edit to be released. Ashby died in 1988 and *8 Million* provided a sad coda to his career, as he yet again lost control of a film. Hal Ashby's career decline may have been symptomatic of the times but, in his particular case, there seems little doubt that much of the blame was his own.

Hardly working: Bob Rafelson and Dennis Hopper

Dennis Hopper and Bob Rafelson worked together on one of the most important films of the Renaissance era when Hopper directed *Easy Rider* in 1969 for Raybert Productions, co-owned by Rafelson. Despite both achieving significant early breakthroughs (Rafelson with *Five Easy Pieces* in 1970), it is striking how their subsequent directorial careers are characterized by a paltry number of projects realized. Hopper directed seven feature films between 1969 and 1994 and Rafelson, ten between 1968 and 2002. In the 1980s, they managed

54 *The Lost Decade*

to direct just two features each, yet with their second films, *Colors* (1988) and *Black Widow* (1987), they actually managed to achieve some box-office success, albeit with no discernible long-term benefit to their overall careers.

Rafelson

Bob Rafelson has never attracted much considered attention, his relatively meagre output only resulting in a 1996 book by Jay Boyer and a smattering of articles and features.[106] The exception is *Five Easy Pieces* (1970) and, to a lesser extent, *The King of Marvin Gardens* (1972). Indeed, according to one reference book, 'had Bob Rafelson never made a film again after *Five Easy Pieces*, his name would still be remembered in American history'.[107] Much like Bogdanovich and Friedkin, Rafelson's subsequent career seems to be overshadowed by these early critical favourites. Rafelson had founded Raybert Productions with Bert Schneider (later BBS Productions with Steve Blauner joining them) who made their name originally in television with *The Monkees* (1966–1968), featuring the eponymous pop group. Armed early on with an enviable six-film deal with Columbia that only allowed budgets under $1 million, but crucially promised no creative interference, BBS went on to produce some of the most important films of the early Renaissance, notably *Easy Rider*, *The Last Picture Show* and *Five Easy Pieces*.[108] It is difficult to fully grasp why Rafelson struggled to get films made for the majority of his career, but his inability to keep within prescribed limits, or to countenance interference from those controlling the purse strings, certainly played its part. The environment at Raybert, 'the single best example of a workable break with studio orthodoxies' according to Andrew Schroeder, may have contributed to Rafelson (and potentially Hopper and Bogdanovich as well) being unable to accept outside influences that he saw as distorting his personal vision.[109]

Since *Stay Hungry* in 1976, Rafelson had been vainly trying to get projects off the ground or secure directing assignments. Among these putative opportunities was *Brubaker*, a Robert Redford film eventually directed by Stuart Rosenberg in 1980, for which Rafelson signed a contract with Fox but after ten days of production, behind schedule and over budget and after an argument with a studio executive on set, he was fired. He claimed he had spent a year in preparation alone. Jack Nicholson, who looms large in Rafelson's career, now offered him the opportunity to make a new version of James Cain's novel, *The Postman Always Rings Twice* (1981), which had been adapted twice before in

Hollywood Renaissance Auteurs in the 1980s 55

the 1940s.[110] Close friends for many years, Nicholson starred in five of the ten films Rafelson directed as well as being attached to a number of his unmade projects.[111] The offer was attractive, coming with the promise of the sort of autonomy he had enjoyed at BBS. Co-funded by Lorimar and MGM, with a script by David Mamet, the film aimed to stay closer to its source text than the earlier adaptations. With a scrupulous attention to period detail and deep-focus photography from Sven Nykvist that made use of 'several distinct visual planes but also allowed for a high contrast of colors between these planes – something [Rafelson] coined "Gregg Toland in color"', it is a stylish film that recalls the neo-noirs of the Renaissance period.[112] It is not just the presence of Nicholson that is evocative of *Chinatown* (Polanski, 1974). While the film's raunchy sex scenes attracted some publicity, Cain's protagonists, anti-heroic murderers, were not to audience tastes in 1981 and the film performed modestly, earning $12 million domestically. As usual, Rafelson struggled to get anything made in the aftermath and it was another six years before he directed *Black Widow*.

Meanwhile, Rafelson's greatest frustration around this time was *Heaven and Earth*, a film he was set to make for Warner Bros about Diane Fossey. Universal had a similar project in the works, *Gorillas in the Mist*, so the studios joined forces, and Michael Apted, the director attached to the Universal project, was given the job. Rafelson had invested considerable time and effort on the Fossey story only for him to see someone else effectively make the film.[113] His career seems to have been predicated on such misadventures although, on this occasion, there is nothing to suggest he was at fault. In 1986, proving he was not entirely forgotten in Hollywood, Fox (who fired him from *Brubaker*) offered Rafelson *Black Widow*, a large-scale studio project with nearly hundred locations in five states, a challenge for a director with no experience of working on such a scale. Although more conventional than his earlier work, it is a slick and sure-footed production showing that even a supposed maverick like Rafelson could adapt himself to market conditions. The film also has feminist credentials, with one reviewer praising 'its unique creation of a plot in which its two women protagonists interact directly with each other in their own right, rather than as mediated through a male psyche'.[114] Released in February 1987, *Black Widow* was fairly successful, earning about $25 million against a budget of $11 million, enabling Rafelson to realize his dream project, *Mountains of the Moon* (1990), an expensive failure about Burton and Speke's search for the source of the Nile.[115] His career limped on much as before after that, aided by his friendship with Nicholson who appeared in two more of his films.[116] Rafelson can be compared to many of the Renaissance directors because he found it difficult to interact successfully with studio executives or to compromise his artistic choices to pursue commercial success. This is hardly surprising as Rafelson had begun his career running his own independent film company, whose creative freedom had been 'the envy of every small film company on both coasts'.[117] Eventually, he seemed to recognize his problem: in 1990, he was self-aware enough to observe, 'you learn after a while that the guys from the studio have a job to do and you have a job to do, and it's never going to be the same job. But they're not the enemy'.[118] Such a belated understanding may have come rather too late for any return to the embrace of mainstream Hollywood.

Hopper

Dennis Hopper's travails were starker and more clearly defined than Rafelson's. Having broken through with *Easy Rider*, his follow-up, 1971's *The Last Movie*, infamously preceded all of the other directors' high-profile expensive failures. Its extravagant and chaotic production in Peru was dogged by negative publicity, the first incarnation of the New Hollywood auteur out of control. The freedom given to Hopper to make *The Last Movie* was a reflection of the early rush to cash in on the explosion of a 'New Wave' sweeping through Hollywood. Like many such follies, it has gradually undergone a critical rehabilitation. Hopper, infamous for his embrace of a hedonistic lifestyle, was subsequently effectively blacklisted by Hollywood. In 1983, Hopper was still finding it difficult: 'I've been working very hard to survive and trying to keep in the motion picture business … trying to establish the fact that I'm not a difficult person to work with'.[119] By 1988, just before *Colors*, he was still talking about his struggles to earn trust, observing that, with his reputation, it was much easier to get work as an actor, while as a director, 'I've been close before, but the deals never happened'.[120]

The next time Hopper was able to direct a feature film after *The Last Movie* in 1971 was not until 1980, and he arrived at the opportunity by chance. Hopper had signed on to act in a small Canadian film, *Out of the Blue*, to be directed by one of its writers. Hopper had recently begun to rehabilitate his acting career, starring in Wim Wenders's *The American Friend* in 1978 as well as his memorable cameo in *Apocalypse Now*. When the production hit trouble, both the backers and the director asked Hopper to take over. Once in charge, he recast the main roles, rewrote the script and did not use any of the footage already shot.[121] The resultant film is remarkable, an uncomfortable story of youthful alienation.

Its protagonist, Cebe (Linda Manz), is a punk- and Elvis-obsessed teen whose rebellious nature is starkly depicted as motivated by the extreme fecklessness of her parents (Hopper and Sharon Farrell). The film's title comes from the magisterial Neil Young song, 'My, My, Hey Hey (Out of the Blue)' that plays over the titles and at key moments in the film.[122] The film is an original and affecting examination of teenage alienation which makes it all the more surprising that the film has languished in relative obscurity, although Barbara Scharres's 1983 article, 'From Out of the Blue: The Return of Dennis Hopper', offers a perceptive and informative analysis of the film: '*Out of the Blue* involves a single-minded refining of [Hopper's] favourite themes to their most concentrated form, partly made possible by shaping the three central characters to embody different extreme aspects of the character type played by Hopper in his two previous films.'[123] The film was also featured in a recent season at the BFI in London, 'The Other Side of 1980s America', a selection of low-budget, relatively obscure films that offer an opposing view of the decade's dominant Reaganite perspective. In an article accompanying the season, Nick Pinkerton describes *Out of the Blue* as 'Hopper's finest film … the star of the counter-culture engages with emergent hardcore punk'.[124] It is the film's invocation of existential angst that is so powerful and, with the possible exception of *Blow Out*, its devastating ending is as bleak as any other American film of the period (Figure 2.2).

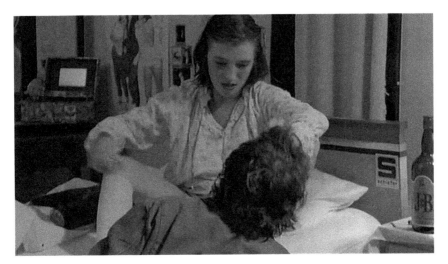

Figure 2.2 Cebe murders her abusive father before killing herself and her mother in *Out of the Blue*'s devastatingly bleak finale.

58   *The Lost Decade*

Out of the Blue disappeared without trace and it was another seven years before Hopper was given an opportunity to direct again. Orion only assigned *Colors* to Hopper, as he tells it, because 'Sean Penn wanted me to do it'.[125] Hopper demanded changes to the original concept with a white and a Black cop in Chicago replaced by a more traditional and familiar Los Angeles-set, all-white partnership of a tough old veteran (Robert Duvall) and a hot-headed rookie (Penn). When asked if *Colors* represented a move back onto the mainstream, Hopper's response was that it was the first film he has done as a member of the Director's Guild of America (DGA) (as if this explained everything about its conventionality).[126] Its box-office performance certainly suggests it was mainstream, earning $46 million domestically on a reported budget of only about $9 million, its success leading to Hopper enjoying a brief moment when he could get films made.[127] Two films he directed were released in 1990, *The Hot Spot* and *Catchfire*, but in the case of the latter, Hopper fell out so badly with the producers that he took his name off it, instead using the customary Alan Smithee moniker. As we have seen, Hopper is another of the Renaissance auteurs whose personal behavioural issues leaked into his professional life to the extent that notoriety as an unstable and intoxicated troublemaker was established early on in his directing career. Unlike others with similar reputations like Ashby or Rafelson, he never really established any sort of track record and, thus, financiers were even less willing in his case to take any sort of risk. This was already true in the 1970s but by the 1980s, such views were hardened by changes in audience tastes, leading studios to be even more reluctant to employ someone with such a troublesome reputation.

****

There are a number of factors that have been shown as frequent determinants in the relative success or failure of Renaissance auteurs in the 1980s. Behavioural issues and varying degrees of willingness to adjust to less-forgiving managerial environments were certainly key factors. Philip Drake's discussion of reputation, by way of the early 1980s experiences of Hal Ashby, also offers a useful perspective but only takes us so far in terms of an understanding of the Renaissance directors' place in 1980s American film history. Drake's suggestion about the analysis of reputation being more valuable than the study of authorship fails to take account of how a reputation is dependent on the quality and viability of films which are, of course, authored in some form or other, if with varying degrees of collaborative practice. Drake goes on to say:

> The analysis of ... archival materials enables nuanced accounts of creative decision-making to be built, alongside detailed production histories, offering a useful corrective to auteur studies that emphasise individual rather than collaborative or negotiated film authorship. These allow us to consider how processes as well as people author films.[128]

I would suggest that it is more accurate to think of 'processes' as the means by which authorship can be understood even if derived from multiple sources, as when a director's contract allows substantive outside interference. These processes, rather than authoring films, can offer nuanced ways with which to understand authorship as more than just an expression of an individual's artistic vision. My somewhat broader employment of archival resources than Drake, particularly using script materials, will enhance a more complete perspective in the following chapters when closer discussions of Altman, Coppola and Friedkin's decades places them more precisely within, or outside of, the Hollywood system with individual films closely examined as expressions of authorship within that context. Their very different arcs will highlight the shortcomings of a homogenous approach to the 'downfall' of the Hollywood Renaissance.

3

Robert Altman: Escape from LA

Altman needed to make films like he needed to breathe.

– Robert Kolker[1]

Robert Altman's career in the 1980s has a very specific narrative. In the first year of the new decade, his relationship with the Hollywood studios broke down completely following a scabrous war of words with Paramount and Disney while making *Popeye* and when his previous film, *HealtH*, was deemed unreleasable by 20th Century Fox.[2] With one unfortunate exception (*OC and Stiggs,* made in 1983 and released in 1987) that further hardened the director's alienation from the majors, Altman worked throughout the decade away from Hollywood. But the most remarkable aspect of his eighties films, including his television work, is that until *Tanner '88* (1988), all are straight adaptations of plays with the screenwriter, in every case, listed as the playwright (*Beyond Therapy* (1987) is also credited to Altman). This suggests, mostly if not entirely accurately (as I will illustrate shortly), that the dialogue in these films faithfully follows their original sources. As Pauline Kael observed about Altman at this time, 'it was as if he had just discovered theater, and he approached a playwright's text with a respect at the opposite pole from his treatment of a screenwriter's work'.[3] For the assistant director on several of Altman's 1980s films, Allan F. Nicholls, his adherence to the plays' texts was the filmmaker wagging his finger at his former institutional collaborators with a 'fuck you Hollywood … You haven't liked me when I improv[ise] and you give me shit … So then he took these scripted plays and filmed them'.[4] This fidelity was but one way that the decade represents a significant change in direction for a filmmaker more used to unpicking his screenwriting collaborators' work with cavalier abandon.

It was noted earlier that Martin Scorsese aligned himself with Altman in noting that 'in a way [Altman] was sent to the diaspora for ten years'.[5] Yet Altman's dismissal of such a notion that the 1980s represented a career regression at all is amply illustrated in his response in 1993 to a journalist who had the effrontery to call *The Player* a comeback: 'making *Secret Honor* and *Streamers* and those pictures meant just as much to me as making *Nashville* or *MASH*. I've been here all the time. So you're the comeback'.[6] This should hardly seem surprising given that this alleged decade-long 'banishment' actually resulted in him directing eight films for the cinema, five for television at feature length, one short in an anthology and an eleven-part television series. As if this workload was not enough, all this was topped up with various digressions into theatre and opera direction, as well as a significant number of unmade projects. In 1994, an assertion by one British critic about the director's so-called comeback with *The Player* offers what is a fairly typical summation (and, entirely coincidentally, uses this book's title as well): 'Altman emerged from the eighties – his lost decade – with a trail of flops and his maverick reputation in disrepair'.[7] Yet it is surely hard to square any notions of a 'lost decade' or a 'reputation in disrepair' with such a volume of work. This level of productivity also begs the question as to how this level of output was achieved and what were the circumstances that led Altman to such different material and circumstances of production, especially in the context of his decision to flee Hollywood's all-embracing institutional power.

This chapter examines these issues through an analysis of Altman's 1980s filmmaking journey to provide a picture of a period that represents an outlier in the director's career and that has tended to be habitually undervalued, under-examined and misunderstood. Often working with miniscule budgets, Altman retreated to small, emerging markets away from studio interference, exploring opportunities provided by the need for content from the burgeoning videotape and cable markets. As Altman himself observed about these new areas, 'there are now more ways to get the money back. It means you've got a better chance of raising the money in the private sector'.[8] However, as Chapter 1 showed, commercial viability in the independent sector was limited at this time and Altman's engagement with alternative financial sources may have secured the funds to make his films but rarely allowed for adequate levels of distribution to achieve any discernible box-office success.

Running concurrently with the chronological description of Altman's 1980s travails will be the closer analysis of three films in order to understand how he brought his authorship to bear on the filming of scripts largely left as they were performed in the theatre and how these transcriptions can be understood in terms of the relationship between theatre and cinema. Unlike many commentators who have tended to see these adapted plays as simply inferior to Altman's earlier work, Armond White shrewdly appreciates their differences when he argues that 'by breaking through the artifice of theatre, Altman, the great atmospheric filmmaker of the 1970s, becomes our great expressionist'.[9] Altman's approach to these plays, the process by which he made them cinematic, is a re-adjustment, or even a refinement, of the methodology that defined his more renowned films of the previous decade. In some respects, it will be seen that the work can be more easily compared to his more characteristic films than is usually supposed, a viewpoint that seems to have resulted from the lack of much substantive analysis of these films. Certainly Altman's new choice of material was unsuited to his trademark overlapping dialogue and populous visual tableaux and, as Yannis Tzioumakis suggests, 'the limited settings force Alman to eschew his "free floating" camera'.[10] Yet, while this is largely true, it may be more accurate to say that, while it may not float as freely in the more confined spaces, the camera in the 1980s work often still retains Altman's characteristic fluidity. As always, he uses the zoom liberally, and unconventionally, and where opportunity allows, he still retains his penchant for filming characters through windows or mirrors, using reflected and refracted images to symbolize underlying themes, a trait that runs through his entire *oeuvre*.

Filming theatre

Before examining Altman's filmed plays more specifically, a brief look at the relationship between theatre and the cinema provides a framework for understanding what these films might be seeking to achieve. André Bazin observed that 'the relations between theater and cinema [are] certainly not limited to what is generally and deprecatingly called "filmed theater"'.[11] Misleadingly, and inaccurately, some writers, such as Gayle Sherwood Magee, have also damned Altman's 1980s work with this pejorative phrase.[12] While seeking a more balanced understanding of the relationship between the two media, Bazin does suggest that films derived from plays have a tendency 'to overcompensate by the "superiority" of [their] technique' because of 'an urge to "make cinema"'.[13] This seems particularly relevant to the way that Altman resisted overt cinematic flourishes and largely avoided 'opening up' his filmed plays. He subjugated many of his familiar techniques to the needs of the material he was adapting (undoubtedly, a lack of funds was also a contributory factor) and he seems to have recognized that, as Bazin observed about Cocteau, 'the role of the cinema was to not to multiply but to intensify'.[14] Susan Sontag also argues that adapting theatre well does not mean necessarily expanding the diegetic space. She observes that 'it is no more part of the putative "essence" of movies that the camera must rove over a large physical area, than it is that movies ought to be silent'.[15] In the cinema, the camera operator is able to roam about and reorientate the space seen within the frame, but a director can still resist an entirely natural urge to be expansive in doing so. Films can, theoretically if not always practically, depict any number of dramatic settings but, in the theatre, as Martin Esslin observes, a single frame (or proscenium arch) 'has to serve for a multiplicity of possible spaces'.[16] Thus, when a director chooses not to revise or 'open up' a play, especially if on a restricted budget, he or she is more likely to adapt those that depend on single locations. Indeed, nearly all of Altman's 1980s work is mostly confined to just one space.

In the theatre, each audience member uniquely chooses where to look, but from a fixed point (their seat). In the cinema, everyone shares the same view but their perspective of the action taking place is 'directed' by the choices made about what images are presented and in what way. Differing shots can deliberately encourage the viewer to question whose point of view is being privileged and, as Sontag tells us, 'this ambiguity of point-of-view ... has no equivalent in the theatre'.[17] A film director can place emphasis by purely cinematic means (most obviously with the close-up) and a camera is a flexible tool that can be used to interpret the same written material as performed on the stage but in different ways. Altman's judicious employment use of a zoom lens (frequently discussed in the context of his more usual style) is an example of how the tools of filmmaking allowed him to direct attention on moments, characters or objects.[18]

When adapting a play for the screen, it is vital to select a suitable vehicle: plays that do not seem to be obviously cinematic will need expansion and revision and to be rewritten accordingly. Yet the adaptation of a revered play is more likely to offend those familiar with the original if it veers too far from its source or is unnecessarily expanded (as they see it). Andrew Sarris, for example, complained about *Fool for Love* that 'a very effective play has been stretched out into a very ineffective movie'.[19] On the other hand, reviewers frequently criticize films for failing to overcome the static nature of plays when they are not opened up sufficiently, as when Nigel Andrews called *Streamers* a 'four-wall screaming match'.[20] When a play is inherently claustrophobic, it is not absolute that any opening up will necessarily make it more cinematic, one notable example being the much-admired *Twelve Angry Men* (Lumet, 1957), a one-room play that retained to great effect its single setting in its transfer from stage to screen. Whereas Altman used the camera as a tool to overcome the static nature of such constricted material, Sontag argues that 'filmed theatre' does not even have to necessarily do this to be effective cinema. She is especially complimentary ('a minor masterpiece') about how Carl Dreyer's *Gertrud* (1964) makes a virtue of its theatrical qualities, with long and formal dialogue filmed almost entirely in static medium shots.[21] Conversely, Altman's stated strategy 'was to put the audience among the characters. In a close-up, you can tell so much about a person'.[22] Technological advances aided Altman in achieving this intimacy. Charles Champlin, reporting from the set of *Streamers*, described the details of the equipment that facilitated Altman's style: 'a camera mounted on a counterweighted boom, a miniature version of the high-rising studio crane, and the whole unit is on a dolly, allowing for a fluidity of movement vertically and laterally'.[23]

1980–1982

The seventies were productive for Altman, establishing a work rate that he was able to continue right up to the end of his life. After the success of *M*A*S*H* in 1970, he was amply backed by the Hollywood studios and directed thirteen features in ten years. Films like *Nashville* and *McCabe and Mrs Miller* (1971) were championed by critics, their relatively poor returns mitigated by the majors' desire to bask in the reflection of Altman's auteurist prestige, and their fervent hope that another *M*A*S*H* was just around the corner. However, in Altman's later 1970s films, such as *A Perfect Couple* and *Quintet* (both 1979), the critical reception began to match their poor box-office returns. Hollywood and audience tastes were changing and the events of 1980 completed the breakdown of Altman's relationship with the majors. Firstly, *HealtH* was completed, an ensemble-led comedy in the anarchic, satirical style of *Nashville* and *A Wedding* (1978), which was the last film in a less than successful multi-picture deal with 20th Century Fox. Altman's support at the studio was dependent on production chief, Alan Ladd Jr., and his departure in 1979 led to *HealtH* being left on the shelf for a year by the studio's new regime before it was shown in just two theatres, one each in Los Angeles and New York.[24] At the same time, Altman was making *Popeye*, ostensibly his most mainstream project and armed with his largest ever budget. It began at $13 million but ballooned to an estimated $20–30 million.[25] Following a long, troubled shoot in Malta, the press was reporting that the film was a disaster in the making. The Hollywood Renaissance auteurs were now acquiring a reputation for profligacy and unreliability, and *Popeye* was seen as being the latest in a line of extravagant director-led flops.[26] Tim Anderson argues that at this time, 'the model for a high-concept blockbuster was still being established' and while the film's backers may have held out hopes in this regard, Anderson explains that 'what is often less understood are the many failures that are key to any long-term structural change. Such a failure was the case of *Popeye* as it tried to become a high-concept blockbuster'.[27] A simpler explanation for the film not meeting its franchise expectations might be that the hiring of Robert Altman for anything that might be called 'high concept' – or indeed a 'blockbuster' – could only ever have led to institutional frustration. In fact, *Popeye* eventually registered a reasonable profit with a domestic gross alone of just under $50 million, but the damage was already done in terms of Altman's reputation: he needed to work but no one was returning his calls. Altman had planned that his next film would be *Lone Star*, based on a play by James McClure about a returning Vietnam soldier, and MGM had expressed sufficient interest for a script to be written and for production plans to have been made. However, Norbert Auerbach, the new studio head, did not like what he was reading about *Popeye* and dropped the project while Altman was working on pre-production.[28]

This was the background to Altman's decision, in the summer of 1981, to leave California. After selling his studio and post-production facility, Lion's Gate, to a consortium headed by producer, Jonathan Taplin, for $2.3 million, and leasing his Malibu home to Diana Ross, Altman moved his family and offices to New York.[29] In 1985, he moved again, basing himself in Paris for the remainder of the decade. He had physically and mentally detached himself from the Hollywood machine. Yet there are different ways that Altman's self-imposed exile can be understood. As he had stated over the years, Altman never considered himself to be in the same business as the system's hit-making machine: 'The movies I want to make are movies the studios don't want. What they want to make, I don't'.[30] Patrick McGilligan, however, is insistent that his exile was a move born of desperation: 'Altman was seeking survival, and retreating to the small format as a last contingency in the downward spiral of his relations with major studios. He was entering a period of heightened isolation and paranoia, writer's block and writer despondency.'[31] McGilligan presents a picture of a man bereft of ideas and willing to do almost anything so long as it paid, but he fails to offer any tangible evidence to this effect. As will be seen shortly, the archives show that McGilligan was wrong on one count because Altman never stopped writing, even if he struggled to get anything made. Others have offered different perspectives on his decisions at this time. Stephen Farber, when he interviewed the director in 1985, concluded that 'far from discouraged, Altman feels creatively invigorated by the new direction his career has taken.'[32] The actor and director, Mark Rydell, also praised the director's indefatigability and independence: 'Bob never let the industry beat him. He created his own initiative. He went out and got the money to make his pictures. He rejected the status quo and would not be deterred.'[33]

Altman now found himself in a situation where this determination found him having to explore small-scale, low-key opportunities. This was very much of his own making but was also influenced by the changes in the film industry at the turn of the decade. As Justin Wyatt put it, 'Altman's projects, usually lacking stars, an exploitable premise, and an obvious marketing approach, deviated significantly from [the] overall change in the industry'.[34] It has already been discussed how 'auteurs' were struggling to find a place in a marketplace that was irrevocably altered by the effects of the 'Spielberg-Lucas Syndrome' but Altman's breakdown in his relationship with the studios was also because he was not willing to concede *any* control over his work (he always insisted on final cut). Altman was fighting against the prevailing tide, and this unwillingness to compromise his filmmaking principles meant, in Wyatt's opinion, that 'Altman falls into the category of auteurs who failed to adapt to high concept'.[35] Perhaps it is more accurate to say that he never even tried to adapt in the first place.

In June 1981, Altman was invited to direct *Rattlesnake in the Cooler* and *Precious Blood*, two one-act plays by up-and-coming playwright, Frank South, at the Los Angeles Actors Theatre. After enabling its transfer to St Clements Theatre, off-Broadway, Altman filmed the pair there, under the title *Two by South*, for transmission on ABC's Cable Arts Network in early 1982. The result was that Altman, who invested $114,500 of his own money, registered a net profit of $22,501 on the project.[36] These types of opportunity from new revenue streams would provide Altman with a way to keep working on several later occasions in the decade.

Later in 1982, Altman agreed to direct Ed Graczyk's 1976 play, *Come Back to the 5 and Dime, Jimmy Dean, Jimmy Dean* at the Martin Beck theatre on Broadway. Assembling a formidable cast (all of whom went on appear in the film) that included Cher in her first acting role, as well as Altman regulars Karen Black and Sandy Dennis, the play was a moderate success but was particularly hampered by a scathing review by influential critic, Frank Rich, in the *New York Times*. Not only was the play 'a dreary amateur night' but Rich blamed Altman for staging it 'at the pace of a dripping faucet'.[37] At some point, an aspiring producer, Peter Newman, approached the director about adapting the play for cable television channel Showtime. He had obtained finance, about $850,000, from Mark Goodson, a successful game show producer.[38] Altman had already thought about filming *Jimmy Dean* after he had noticed, one night, 'that there were things on these actresses' faces which the audience couldn't see'.[39] Only one week after the play closed in spring 1982, shooting was underway. Altman wanted a theatrical release and Showtime reluctantly agreed to let him take the film around the festival circuit. Newman and Altman subsequently took it on a whistle-stop European tour and in just two weeks, the pair attended four festivals and five screenings (as well as three screenings of *HealtH* that the ever-enterprising director was also trying to sell at the same time).[40] For all this work, and reasonable deals for video distribution from at least six territories around the world, a financial statement from March 1985 shows that the film had still, to that point, only recouped $737,045 against final costs of just over $1.8 million.[41]

Jimmy Dean is the Altman film from the period that has attracted the greatest amount of focused academic attention, not least because, thematically, it can easily be aligned with other Altman films, such as *Images* (1972) or *3 Women* (1977), which place female consciousness at their centre. According to Robert Kolker, *Jimmy Dean* can be compared to these films because it 'deals with the crisis of women confronting the oppressions of patriarchy by dissolving them into neuroses'.[42] Altman himself acknowledged the similarities but said that he did not notice the connections with his other female-led films until after he had filmed it.[43] It tells the story of a group of women reuniting in the small Texas town where they grew up together (and where two of them still live). A mysterious outsider, Jo (Karen Black), is the catalyst for the revelation of the truth about what happened twenty years ago. On the stage, these past events were played downstage, with different lighting and by different actresses; in the film, Altman pulls off what appears to be a technically complex effect in showing the historical scenes play out through the mirror at the back of the eponymous 5 and Dime store. The camera alights on a character thinking about events twenty years ago and then pans across to the mirror where what actually happened is shown (with the same actresses only nominally altered in appearance). The effect is achieved relatively simply by using a 'Mylar mirror', which reflects as a normal mirror until light is put behind it when you can see through it (like a window).[44] As he would do in almost all the eighties work, Altman cleaves fairly faithfully to the original text of the play.[45] *Jimmy Dean* was Altman's most acclaimed film for some years although McGilligan claims that he was, nevertheless, no happier: 'the critics ceased to have any real meaning. The director was still scrambling, wretched, vindictive'.[46] Whatever his state of mind, it seems that the experience of directing the play on stage, then filming it inexpensively, set the template for the way Altman would manage to keep working for the reminder of the decade.

1983–1984

In June 1982, Altman had accepted an offer from the University of Michigan to become their Marsh Visiting Professor of Communications and the next year, he directed opera for the first time in a university production of Stravinsky's *A Rake's Progress*. He put his own money up so that he could lay on a spectacular production with a cast of 140 characters and lavish art direction.[47] Diverting into a new medium that employed aspects of both music and theatre allowed Altman, according to Magee, 'a unique opportunity to synthesize these seemingly disparate elements'.[48] Meanwhile, *Streamers*, the third play in a 'Vietnam trilogy' by David Rabe, had been circulating as a film property since its 1976 production.[49] A winner of 'Best American Play' at the New York Drama Critics Circle Awards under the direction of Mike Nichols, producers Robert Geisler and John Roberdeau obtained the rights to adapt the play for the cinema and invited Altman to direct. Shooting was under way at Las Colinas Studios near Dallas when Altman realized that the pair did not have the funds to make the film. Altman was obliged to pay them $280,000 plus 5 per cent of net profits to acquire ownership and managed to complete shooting in 'eighteen days with a twenty-man crew for something under $2 million'.[50] Altman was saved when his agent found a financier, Nick Mileti, willing to buy the rights for approximately $3 million.[51] As with *Jimmy Dean*, Altman travelled extensively to promote *Streamers*, visiting festivals in Chicago, Milan, Rome, London and Cleveland on the search for distribution deals.[52] At Venice, in September, it was in competition and carried away six Golden Lion awards for 'Best Actor' for its ensemble cast. Following this achievement, United Artists Classics, who had become the first studio to launch their own specialist division, agreed to distribute the film

70 *The Lost Decade*

with one executive consciously exploiting Altman's retreat from studio fare in describing *Streamers* as 'an American movie that breaks the Hollywood mold'.[53] Altman had been willing to dip into his own pocket to make *Streamers*, and would do again on *Secret Honor*, suggesting that Altman's personal financial situation was not as desperate as McGilligan implies and that his motivation at this time, in the face of ongoing difficulties in raising finance, was to keep busy at all times and to get his art seen, rather than the simple necessity of earning a living.

Streamers

When Altman was promoting *Streamers*, he frequently remarked that he was 'telling the same story as *M*A*S*H* but it just isn't funny anymore'.[54] This made a good sound bite, a way to try to sell *Streamers*, but it is a comparison that only works in the broadest possible terms. In relying on the early hit that made his name in this way, Altman illustrated the difficulty of marketing a film like *Streamers*. In the age of blockbusters and sequels, it was inevitable that a low-scale film, one that takes place in the confined setting of a barracks room and centres around the conversations between four young men awaiting orders to go to Vietnam, would struggle to find an audience on its own terms. Whereas the satire of *M*A*S*H* explored the futility and absurdities of war, its Korean setting could really have been any conflict. According to Philip Kolin, *Streamers* is also more concerned with an 'archetypical theme – the rite of passage into manhood – in the lives of four young soldiers'.[55] Yet the specificity of its setting and the distance of the film from both the events it portrays, and from when the play was first performed, offers a more objective hindsight about the events its viewers know will occur in Vietnam shortly after the play's events. The tragic and violent conclusion of the play prefigures the deaths that likely awaited soldiers waiting for orders in 1965 (when the play is set). According to Carol Rosen, the way the play uses the titular song, adapted from the popular song 'Beautiful Dreamer', turns it 'into a universalising song about all meaningless deaths ... a motif for *everyone* fallen in lost causes in absurd wars'.[56] Rabe explained the song and the title: 'Our lives are all like streamers, because ultimately, the chute doesn't open – we're all going to die.'[57] But in *Streamers*, Vietnam itself is not used universally, as Korea was in *M*A*S*H*, but as a specific and recognizable marker for most Americans of such meaningless deaths. It is, however, not only about war, and some analysts of the play, like Sabine Altwein, argue how it only uses its historical setting as a vehicle to explore its underlying themes of 'racial prejudices, political ignorance, religious hypocrisy, and the rejection of the "Other" in the broadest sense'.[58] In keeping with the wider concerns of this book, however, the following analysis of *Streamers* is far more about Altman's authorial contribution than its interweaving of such themes. As in nearly all the adapted plays, his creative agency rests mostly outside of the written text. My focus is more on how Altman made cinematic a static, constricted and dialogue-heavy piece of theatre.

Whereas writers on the theatre have shown interest in Rabe, and particularly in *Streamers*, scholarly considerations of Altman's career have largely ignored the film.[59] Helene Keyssar justifies this by rather unfairly aligning *Streamers* with *Beyond Therapy* and *OC and Stiggs* as 'the most predictable productions' of the eighties.[60] While it is true that *Streamers* does not hold such obvious attractions for academics as the female perspective of *Jimmy Dean* or the political resonances found in *Secret Honor*, it is an adaptation that offers up an accomplished, and in many ways typical, example of the way Altman approached making small-scale films from contemporary plays. The setting is a barracks room, one corner of which is occupied by three young soldiers, awaiting orders to be shipped out to Vietnam. Billy (Matthew Modine), a white college graduate, and Roger (David Alan Grier), a working-class African American, appear to be close friends, having bonded over their fitness regimes and their pride in keeping their 'house' neat and tidy. Richie (Mitchell Litchenstein), from a wealthy background, affects a camp demeanour and constantly refers to his professed homosexuality. Billy and Roger keep telling each other that Richie is only joking until an outsider, Carlyle (Michael Wright), arrives and disturbs the trio's equanimity. He is a Black man from 'the streets' (as he puts it), disoriented by being dragged from his natural milieu, whose volatility and inability to assimilate to an alien environment lead to the violent denouement. Hovering on the fringes of the action, two sergeants, Rooney (Guy Boyd) and Cokes (George Dzundza), old comrades who served together, provide a tragi-comic reminder of the effects of war. They are inebriated throughout, their sense of self shattered by their experiences (Figure 3.1). By the end, Carlyle has murdered Rooney and Billy for almost meaningless reasons, the actions of a man for whom the experience of violence is already an everyday reality and whose fragile identity is unhinged both by a latent homosexuality he does not want to acknowledge and by his perception of institutional racial discrimination. As Christopher Bigsby observed about the play, 'the threat is already on the inside' because these men's 'existence seems to have no purpose

Figure 3.1 The drunken sergeants provide the humour but also serve as a tragi-comic reminder of the effects of war.

beyond its self-justifying routines'.[61] In such an environment, death occurs almost outside of the control of those involved.

In *Jimmy Dean* and later in *Secret Honor*, Altman begins with his trademark mobile camera on the prowl, exploring what will be the film's setting, delving into the dusty corners of the 5 and Dime store or taking in the accoutrements of Richard Nixon's study. *Streamers*' opening (although not its camera style) is quite different but its title sequence, which is mirrored in the end credits, is nevertheless an early indicator of Altman's intervention. The credits play while a group of highly disciplined soldiers carry out their drill. There is no music, only the eerie sounds of their routine from boots and rifles, the mood matched by images cast in a blue-grey haze. The shots of a ghostly military precision provide a counterpoint to the disorganized, dishevelled portrayal of the army that will constitute *Streamers*. The film itself then begins with a near-silent scene not in the play: the two drunken sergeants are playing a childish game with fuses and firecrackers. As well as introducing this pair much earlier than in the play, Altman does the same with Carlyle, the interloper, in these opening moments. He is seen outside the hut, through the window, looking anxious, before he enters and is intercut with the sergeants' antics, as he looks around uncertainly. The film joins up with the play, mirroring the slow build-ups initiated by Altman in the other adaptations, only after about five minutes when Richie goes into the bathroom and talks with Martin (Albert Macklin), a suicidal soldier who disappears from the play after this incident (although in the film he makes a brief re-appearance towards the end). Rabe recounted that he did not write these introductory scenes:

> No, that was not in the play, strictly the movie. I don't know if it was ever written. I think it was more or less an improvisation; it may have been written after they did it. Or maybe Bob Altman wrote it … I understand the reasons for it and I approve of Bob's impulse to have something to start off with that would be better – in terms of filmmaking – to lead you into the place and story.[62]

His reaction to this indicates that he felt able to accommodate himself to Altman's needs. As would occur with *Secret Honor*, any disruption of the fidelity to the original play's text mostly transpired, according to Rabe, after the filming: 'basically we shot the play and we created the screenplay in the editing room'.[63] The written screenplays in the archives confirm Rabe's understanding with only the 'Script as Shot' incorporating changes made to the original source text.[64]

The film does excise some fairly large swathes of the play's text and there is clearly some new dialogue worked out on set. Altman said that 'the actors had the right to interpret the roles' which suggests his customary working practice, where he allows actors a certain amount of freedom to work out their roles for themselves, was applicable in the 1980s work more than is generally supposed because of a close adherence to original sources.[65] According to Matthew Modine, when he approached the director for advice on the meaning of one of his monologues, Altman's response was, 'I hired you to be an actor. There were things about this role that you could interpret, that you could bring to life. If I was interested in my interpretation I would have played the part.'[66] In any case, according to Mark Minett's recent close reading of Altman's 1970s improvisational tendencies, he exerted a great deal more control over his actors than is usually thought.[67] The removal of dialogue sometimes functions, presumably, to keep the film to a manageable length but also works more subtly, showing how cinema can draw attention to emotional response, wordlessly, more effectively than in the theatre. This is because a viewer in a cinema is more guided than a theatregoer through the use of techniques such as the close-up and shot-reverse-shot convention. This is particularly noticeable when Cokes and Rooney are telling the young recruits a story about a soldier's death by faulty parachute. The young soldiers' spoken responses are written on the page in lines like 'Ohhhhh, geezus', 'un-fuckin'-believable', 'Jesus!' and 'Hey!'[68] All these verbal responses are omitted in favour of silent shots with close-ups on the individual, differentiated reactions of the characters. These begin with bemusement and contemplation and then are replaced with aghast and unbelieving expressions as Cokes's story becomes horribly absurd. In this way, a camera can pick up minute reactions that a theatregoer, from their distanced viewpoint, will never see.

Altman does not entirely confine the film to the single barracks room with three bunks that is the setting of the play.[69] The film slightly alters this by largely setting the action in the small corner of a long room where the three soldiers live, but the camera often allows us views of the extended space with many rows of bunks stretching away towards Rooney's office at the far end, as well as shots of the washroom that adjoins the barracks. Altman also uses what he called (*à la* Hitchcock) a 'Rear Window' technique, showing activity outside the hut only from within, through filthy windows.[70] These fleeting, unscripted scenes are employed as a symbolic contrast to the traumatic effects of the soldier's confinement with glimpses of the more carefree life that exists outside in the real world, including Cokes and Rooney childishly playing hide-and-seek and the happy reunion of an engaged couple (Figure 3.2). This partial unbuckling of the constriction of the single set does not dissipate the dramatic tensions that derive from the action within. Instead, the claustrophobic effect is heightened by staying indoors but offering tantalizing glimpses of a world that is close yet seemingly unattainable. It is the camera style that Altman developed with his regular cinematographer at the time, Pierre Mignot, that allows him to

Figure 3.2 Altman uses a 'Rear Window' effect to show a more carefree existence in the world outside.

retain this sense of confinement, which is not simply derived from the original theatrical setting but from the piece's thematic concerns as well.[71] The soldiers are imprisoned by their circumstances and it was important that Altman retained the play's claustrophobic essence in re-imagining it cinematically.

It is the way the camera is employed in *Streamers* that energizes the play, transporting the viewer into the action. This strategy illustrates how cinema is different from the theatre because, as Bazin describes it, it can 'free the spectator from his seat and by varying the shots give an added quality to the acting'.[72] The drama and tension in the play come from long scenes of charged conversation that gradually reveal the protagonists' damaged sense of identity. Altman heightens this melodrama with his inquisitive camera that allows him to examine more closely the behaviours and reactions of the soldiers as the developing tragedy is visited upon them. Keyssar observes about the 1980s work more generally that 'Altman places the camera in the middle of the single, enclosed space ... and wanders about in that space in a manner consistent with, but more subtle than, the promiscuous camera work in his films of the seventies'.[73] Perhaps the subtle but promiscuous camera is *the* defining characteristic of the 'Altmanesque in exile'.

Streamers attracted a mixed reception from the critics, although tending mostly towards the negative, in a pattern that was not too dissimilar to the reviews of Altman's later 1970s films. As Altman would find throughout much of the decade, what these independent films lacked was the distribution and marketing muscle of Hollywood and even the most positive critical reception would not result in box-office success for a film like *Streamers* because it played more on the arthouse circuit than through the large theatre chains. Although its domestic gross was a paltry $378,000, not even as much as Altman had been willing to spend of his own money on the film, there were always possibilities, with video and overseas sales, for such small-scale projects to eventually make a profit. Indeed, an undated 'Final Accounting Statement' shows the film eventually registering a net profit of $383,103.[74] Altman's next step, however, suggested that he remained frustrated by the limited scope of these inexpensive films.

✱✱✱✱✱✱✱✱✱✱✱✱✱✱✱✱✱✱✱✱✱✱✱✱✱✱✱✱✱✱✱✱✱✱✱✱

In 1983, Peter Newman (*Jimmy Dean*'s producer) funded the writing of a script from a *National Lampoon* article, 'The Ugly, Monstrous, Mind-Roasting Summer of O.C. and Stiggs', by Tod Carroll and Ted Mann. The 'teen' comedy was in favour at the time and the project attracted interest from several studios and

76   *The Lost Decade*

directors. At this point, Altman suddenly claimed to be affronted to have not been asked to direct and Newman, who still had faith in his 'hero', readily agreed to do so. The pair met with executives at MGM whose 'green light' was only granted when Altman promised, with apparent sincerity, to 'shoot the script' and to not bad-mouth the studio in the press. Armed with a $7 million 'go', shooting began in Phoenix where Altman proceeded to immediately, wilfully, break both his promises, tearing up the script and cutting off all communication with the studio. After a preview, MGM begged Altman to re-edit (he had final cut), but he refused and the studio shelved the film until 1987, when it was released only to clear rights for video release.[75] The film was panned and its domestic returns barely reached a mere $30,000. Whereas MGM were looking for a teen romp in the manner of *Animal House* (John Landis, 1978) and *Porky's* (Bob Clark, 1981), Altman professed to hate the genre and told himself he could make it as a satire.[76] Unfortunately the satire is barely discernible and there are only fleeting glimpses of the Altman style among the puerile humour and uninspired plotting. Altman's involvement and behaviour indicate a tension between a desire to keep working and an unshakeable disdain for Hollywood that manifested itself in him deliberately making promises he knew he would not keep. The difference between 1983 and the 1970s is that his creative capital in Hollywood was now entirely spent. *OC and Stiggs* cemented his estrangement and, even when his exile was over, he gravitated to the burgeoning independent market to finance his films.

Later in 1983, Altman was reluctantly dragged along by his friend, Bill Bushnell, to his playhouse, the Los Angeles Actors Theater, to see *Secret Honor, The Last Testament of Richard M. Nixon: A Political Myth*, a one-man play starring Philip Baker Hall. Altman was captivated by what he saw, especially what he called Hall's 'performance at a Shakespearian level'.[77] He immediately offered to get the play produced off-Broadway and it ran for about forty performances at the Provincetown Playhouse in New York in October and November. A pattern was now emerging for Altman in the 1980s: this was the third time in recent years he had involved himself in a theatrical project (although not directing this time) and it seemed inevitable that he would now film *Secret Honor*.

Secret Honor

Secret Honor was written by Donald Freed, a writer and playwright who was no stranger to speculating about outlandish political conspiracies, and Arnold

M. Stone, a lawyer allegedly with connections to the murkier corners of American politics.[78] It was, in the words of its original subtitle, 'a political myth' expounded through an extended monologue by *a* version of the disgraced ex-president. He becomes progressively inebriated as he delivers an unrestrained rant against his perceived enemies and mounts a defence, really a series of excuses and justifications, against a list of imagined charges against him. The revelation he eventually explicates, his 'secret honor', is that he deliberately constructed the Watergate affair to enable him to resign. Nixon's honour means he must extricate himself from, and therefore thwart, a conspiracy in which he was the mere figurehead for all-powerful American business interests who expected Nixon to continue the war in Vietnam and stand for a third term.

Secret Honor was made on a 'shoestring', initially financed entirely by Altman. As he observed, a one-man play set in a single room, about a figure that most Americans wanted to banish from their memories, did not exactly have a 'want-to-see factor'.[79] Altman asserted that 'it cost about $350,000 … I will probably lose $300,000! I can't afford to do it again for a while, but I'm glad I spent the money'.[80] No doubt he was exaggerating for effect, not only because international and video sales inevitably would mitigate the film's losses but also because, in December 1984, Altman had secured a seven-year distribution deal with Cinecom (who distributed *Jimmy Dean*) for 'sole and exclusive rights' in all domestic markets.[81] According to Cinecom's owner, Ira Deutchman, 'because of the successes of *Jimmy Dean*, he just came to us with it. There was no money involved. We didn't pay anything for it. He just asked us if we would release it, and we agreed'.[82] It seems apparent that Altman was, in fact, willing to spend as much money as he could afford to lose rather than deliberately keeping the cost down because he judged the film would fail. Although he may have seemed to be more concerned with working meaningfully than profitably, he could not entirely separate the two if he wanted his work to be seen. It was entirely unfeasible for Altman to keep financing his own films, however microscopic a budget with which he was able to manage.

One of the more interesting aspects of *Secret Honor* is its unusual production environment. It was predicated on the budget that Altman could afford to spend but also represents an interesting experiment in film production as teaching exercise by enabling students to collaborate with, and observe at work, one of America's most-admired auteur-directors. As a visiting professor at the University of Michigan, he was able to film *Secret Honor* there, using a student residential hall as his location. He employed students to fulfil most of the functions required of a film crew, apart from a few key roles given to professionals (including Mignot, his regular cinematographer and his son, Stephen as production designer). Students who wanted to work on the film filled in questionnaires listing their experience and strengths, as well as if they had a car that they were willing to use – possibly the most important attribute as far as the production team were concerned. The form demanded 'a full time commitment' for the seven days of shooting.[83] As well as students enjoying hands-on experience of making a film, Altman lectured during the process (and also offered public access, as reported on local news[84]), placed a camera in the room where the filming took place and set up monitors outside enabling students to observe the shooting as it took place. In keeping with his usual practice of encouraging everyone to watch the dailies, Altman even allowed any students who were so inclined to watch the rough footage at the end of each day.[85] Altman's use of proto-filmmakers as an alternative way of making films recalls Nicholas Ray's later years where he similarly collaborated with aspiring students on experimental work, as depicted in the documentary, *Lightning over Water* (1980), that he made with Wim Wenders at the very end of his life. Brian de Palma also did something similar at his alma mater on *Home Movies* in 1979.[86]

Altman scholars, when writing about the 1980s, have largely concentrated on thematic connections that develop from the written text or from the actors' characterizations.[87] This approach to the analysis of Altman becomes problematic when attempting any auteurist interpretation of his 1980s work. On *Secret Honor*, particularly, it does appear initially difficult to ascribe to Altman any significant degree of authorial agency. There was no screenplay and they filmed the entire play, only abridging it in the editing room. A comparison between the film and the published text of the play reveals the film's elisions to be relatively superficial and infrequent.[88] Hall had spoken the same words on many previous occasions and the celluloid record of his performance might be seen as the culmination of his own contribution to its ongoing authorship. His intensity and physicality are such that he becomes a fundamental part of the film's creative essence (Figure 3.3). It is no surprise that, according to Altman, Hall 'lost three to five pounds in each performance'.[89] Alongside Hall, there is also the contribution of the play's stage director, Robert Harders, to whom Altman was keen to afford a large degree of credit for the 'direction' of his film: 'Philip and Bob [Harders] were responsible for the authorship a lot, they gave it a shape.'[90] However, all the above notwithstanding, the transition from stage to screen is not achieved in a conventional or unimaginative manner: this is not

Figure 3.3 Philip Baker Hall's intense, physical performance as Richard Nixon.

'filmed theatre'. We can acknowledge that authorship is shared more in *Secret Honor* than in almost anything Altman directed but what is interesting is the way he, nevertheless, fashions it into a distinctive Altmanesque film.

Altman asserts his authorial presence from the very beginning. The play starts with Nixon seated, a drink in hand, staring into the fireplace. The film begins quite differently, with a shot of a clock (not mentioned in the play) that will mark the passage of time before, as the credits roll, the camera pans slowly left across the room, taking in the accoutrements of Nixon's study. The camera pulls back and tilts right, as George Burt's orchestral music rises, circling the room before eventually revealing, beneath a portrait of Henry Kissinger, a bank of four CCTV monitors. These are the most significant difference from the original theatrical presentation; the monitors are used frequently throughout the film as cutaways from Hall to fuzzy black-and-white images. The camera advances, framing the right-hand monitor which shows a set of security gates; the next monitor then reveals a hazy image of a man walking towards the camera down a corridor and turning left, before stopping and looking nervously back. The third now shows his back as he approaches a door. The sound of a key turning accompanies the camera panning away from the monitor to the door of the study. Richard Nixon enters tentatively, nervously clutching a briefcase. The camera trails Hall as he pours himself a sherry, prowls the room and stares at the monitors, as if he has never seen them before. He changes his drink for a whisky, and he swaps jackets. It is only now, with a medium long shot of Nixon, that the film joins up with the play's opening: 'He lifts out a large box. He opens the box and checks the gun inside.'[91] It is six and a half minutes into the film, and everything seen to this point flows from Altman's imagination and Hall's interpretation of his direction. Altman has set the scene, allowing the audience to become accustomed to the ambience of the setting alongside the time to think about what they already know about Nixon. They must get used to the fact that this 'Richard Nixon' does not really resemble, and will not sound like, the real one. Altman establishes the rhythm for the play's cinematic incarnation by the expedient addition of a silent prologue that introduces its character and establishes the boundaries of the film's mise-en-scène. By barely opening up the play, Altman can be seen to be upholding the virtues of Bazin and Sontag's ideas for filming plays effectively; at the same time, he makes use of cinematic techniques not available to a stage director.

The pattern that Altman establishes in these opening moments he carries forward into the film, employing a highly mobile, inquisitive camera, accompanied by extended panning shots and judicious cutting, to energize the drama. Altman takes the viewer into the midst of the action by allowing his camera to wander languidly among the confined setting. Altman (and Mignot) provides relief from Hall's emotional rants with the more distanced, blurred imagery on the monitors and he observed that he 'liked the bad quality of the image, it almost gave the impression we were watching old film of Nixon's appearances'.[92] According to Thomas Monsell, 'through [the monitors] we see Nixon, the windbag, impressing himself'[93] and Richard Ness suggests that they function in a similar manner to the windows and mirrors that feature so often in Altman's more typical work (Figure 3.4).[94] Altman uses an array of close-ups, shots from every conceivable angle and numerous cutaway shots that are all keenly attuned to the pacing of Hall's monologue. As he becomes mournful and contemplative, the cutting slows down and the camera lingers on the crumpled figure, particularly when he is talking about his mother. When Nixon is ranting, the camera often becomes restless, mimicking his mood. Altman, frequently and characteristically, uses a zoom lens to place emphasis on what Nixon is saying or feeling or on objects that bear some meaning, such as the gun with

Figure 3.4 The images on the CCTV monitors are like watching old film of 'the windbag' in action.

which he may commit suicide or the clock that indicates a form of deadline for that act (will he kill himself at midnight?).

After the extended opening, the film follows its original source faithfully until Altman chooses to extend the ending, making further expressive use of the monitors. Both play and film give us Nixon's angry riposte to the American people: 'They wanted me to stay down. They wanted me to kill myself.' He picks up the pistol, puts it to his head and thinks about it before angrily putting it down. He says, 'If they want me dead, they'll have to do it.' He triumphally raises his fist to the air and shouts at the top of his voice, 'Fuck' em!'[95] This is how the play ends, but Altman does not quite finish there. Hall carries on exclaiming the final line over and over, *sixteen* times in total, as Altman pans and cuts from one monitor to the next and the next, and rapidly panning back and forward again. The shots' speed increases exponentially so that Nixon appears to be, in Pauline Kael's words, 'splintering right before our eyes'.[96] Behind the ranting, a chorus of a mob chanting repeatedly 'four more years' can be heard getting gradually louder. This chorus continues as the screen goes fuzzy like a CCTV system gone wrong while the credits start to roll. Altman has taken the blunt sign-off of the play and extended into a crazed final riposte from the disgraced ex-president to all those who have tried to put him down. Keyssar reads this conclusion as a 'visual metaphor' for 'the dissolution of Nixon's speech into inarticulate babble'[97] and the employment of the monitors allows Altman to accomplish a stunningly realized, final evocation of the man's self-delusion. The unhinged, almost fascistic nature of his saluting gesture, the images multiplied by the rapid cutting, satirizes the triumphalism of despotic dictators – and, indeed, of victorious American presidents.

When identifying the position that the film holds in its director's canon, and what it tells us about his career in the 1980s, the plausibility of the political story that the film purports to tell us is not especially relevant. Nevertheless, the content chimes with Altman's leftist view of American politics, and he and Freed both promoted the film in interviews by attesting that large parts of the text were based on proven facts. Altman's wholehearted endorsement of Freed and Stone's fairly extreme conspiracy theories recalls other directors, like Milius or Fellini, whose public pronouncements cannot necessarily be taken at face value because they seem to be in the service of the deliberate creation of a marketable persona appropriate to their latest artistic offerings. In *Secret Honor*, while it is Hall's mesmeric performance that holds the audience's attention, the writing is provocative and mischievous with its blend of speculative invention and known historical fact, as when Nixon recounts that he is the puppet of a secretive cabal who gather at Bohemian Grove, a real-life retreat located deep in the redwoods of California.[98] It is a fictional portrait, however, and within this fictive interpretation of Nixon, *Secret Honor* is far more interested in, and interesting about, the essence of its real-life model's character as a vehicle with which to expose the instability inherent in American politics.

Secret Honor was shown at an early iteration of the Sundance Festival in 1984 but, failing to acquire adequate distribution, Altman's production company was obliged to secure individual deals with theatres and cinema chains across the country.[99] Despite various deals for video and European distribution, as late as 1989 a report for the Screen Actors Guild (on behalf of Baker Hall) was still reporting a gross to date of only $146,543.[100] The film was warmly received by many critics on both sides of the Atlantic although, unsurprisingly, the controversial, far-fetched political content attracted some criticism in the United States.[101] A largely positive reception, however, did not have the effect it might have had earlier in Altman's career. By 1984, Altman was so far removed from the Hollywood machine, and his profile so reduced, that what the critics said was unlikely to have any effect at all. The lack of distribution arrangements meant that readers will have been mostly unable to act upon the positive reviews by actually going to see the film. Nevertheless, maintaining a certain critical cachet must have helped the director to stay in gainful employment: his next theatrical adaptation would allow him a much larger budget.

1985–1986

In the second half of the decade, although continuing to insist that he had as little interest in Hollywood as it did in him, Altman was nevertheless constantly trying to get more substantially budgeted films made, but through alternative financial arrangements. The project that came closest to production was *An Easter Egg Hunt*, based on a novel by Gillian Freeman (who had written the screenplay for Altman's *That Cold Day in the Park* in 1969). A dreamy mystery set in a British girls' boarding school during the First World War, budgeted at about $6 million, it was 'nearly' financed by a Canadian production company in 1981, then by an American independent producer in 1984, followed by Euston Films in Britain showing considerable interest in 1986. As late as 1994, Altman was writing a fifth draft and his son, Stephen, revised it yet again two years later with a view to directing it himself.[102] *Biarritz*, from an original screenplay by Altman, was a European thriller with a surreal, potentially 'Altmanesque' flavour, set in a hotel in the eponymous location that also attracted enough interest to be close to production in late 1984, in 1987 and again in 1995.[103] Other scripts written by Altman in the decade which were never made also included *The Feud* in 1983, from a Pulitzer Prize-winning novel by Thomas Berger, and *Across the River and Into the Trees* in 1985, based on a Hemingway novel.[104] Altman also signed on to direct *Heat* in 1986, a generic Burt Reynolds vehicle with a script by William Goldman for which he was clearly unsuited, and he extricated himself from the project before production began.[105]

There was even the chance of a Hollywood redemption from a proposed 1988 sequel to the much-loved *Nashville*, to be called *Nashville XIII* (thirteen years after the original) that sought to reunite most of the main cast, picking up on the characters' lives thirteen years later. Jerry Weintraub, the original's producer, obtained finance from Paramount for $10 million and five drafts were written by Robert Harders and Altman (individually and together).[106] Although Karen Black and Henry Gibson, from the original cast, were firmly secured, a letter from the producers to Altman's assistant, Scott Bushnell, gives detailed, and individual, advice about what Altman needed to do to get eleven of the key cast on board. These were mostly the original line-up and, essentially, what was requested of Altman was to massage egos and make them feel wanted. This letter is a reminder that it is wise to never underestimate the extent of film stars' inflated sense of their own importance.[107] The efforts to try to coral this all-star cast dragged on for over a year and later drafts were now calling it *Nashville, Nashville*. In 1991, the protracted saga was unhappily concluded with the bankruptcy of Weintraub's production company.

In 1985, after several of these putative projects stalled, Altman moved his home and operations to Paris. He edited his next feature, *Fool for Love*, there but only shot two films in Paris itself, one for the cinema and one for television, and neither set there: *Beyond Therapy* and *The Laundromat*. Despite the flight to Europe, Altman remained drawn to settings, subjects and themes about his native country. *The Laundromat* was another one-act play, by Marsha Norman, that Altman produced and directed for HBO in 1985.[108] The opportunities for independent production in emerging formats are exemplified in this small-scale television film which cost $272,259 and generated a net profit of $601,022.[109]

Although Sam Shepard later claimed that he was approached by Altman and agreed only reluctantly to allow *Fool for Love* to be filmed,[110] the playwright actually sent Altman a handwritten letter on 14 January 1983 in which he comments that 'after seeing your "Jimmy Dean" film, which I thought was amazing, I started thinking you might be interested in this new play of mine as a film of some kind'. He goes on to say he has been reluctant, previously, to allow any film or television adaptation of his work because 'I just never trusted anyone's judgement about it but I'd be willing to turn this piece over to you to go in any direction you wanted to try'.[111] At some point, Cannon Films became involved and provided what was, at that time for Altman, a significant budget of $6 million to adapt Shepard's play for the screen. Altman immediately wanted Shepard to take the lead role, to which the playwright reluctantly agreed but only after some persuasion.[112] The difference in scale between this and Altman's other recent work can be seen in how the combined remuneration for him and Shepard alone exceeded the budgets of any of the earlier adapted plays: Altman received $750,000, Shepard $500,000 as actor and $100,000 for literary acquisition.[113] During the shooting of *Fool for Love*, it seems that Shepard and Altman enjoyed a difficult and distant relationship. The resultant film, nevertheless, is arguably the most interesting, in terms of authorship, of the adapted plays, particularly because of the way Altman made alterations to the play's conception despite almost no disruption to his now habitual adherence to the original dialogue.

Fool for Love

Of all the eighties films, *Fool for Love* is the one that is most reminiscent of the more unconventional narrative structures, elusive meanings and unmotivated protagonists of Altman's earlier films. It is therefore a little surprising that Robert Self's book-length examination of Altman's work as symptomatic of the attributes of art cinema does not take much account of *Fool for Love* at all.[114] In earlier work on Altman, Self had already compared the director's films with art cinema narratives that 'proceed ... by a concern with psychological as opposed to sociological realism. They subjectively portray complex characters, enmeshed in frequently aimless plots constructed not on action but inaction and reflection'.[115] This seems a description that might as easily be applied to *Fool for Love*. There are other thematic similarities: Kolker aligns the film with Altman's more female-centric films because it 'is also concerned with the oppressions of patriarchy – quite literally, as it describes the effects of his children on a man who kept two wives'.[116] My interest here, though, is much more about the visual style Altman employs and in his manipulation of the source material's nature, factors that foreground his personal contribution to the film. Altman said during *Fool for Love*'s production: 'I'm not going to alter the content ... I've concerned myself with the arena, the environment that the play takes place in – in other words, in the stage, the stage that I'm making'.[117] In particular, this analysis examines how Altman created this stage; in doing so, his changes made the play's opaque text yet more ambiguous.

The set-up of *Fool for Love* is a simple one. May (Kim Basinger) is working and living in a run-down motel in the middle of nowhere. She is visited there by Eddie (Shepard), a cowboy type in denim, with the trademark hat and pulling a horsebox trailer. *Fool for Love*'s larger budget enabled Altman to open up the play more than in the other films, expanding its one-seedy-room setting into a downbeat motel complex with a bar, scattered chalets, neon signs and assorted detritus (Figure 3.5). Whereas many critics like Stanley Kauffmann objected to this expansion that disturbed the play's claustrophobic dynamic ('the play is chattered and movieized away ... with a lot of troweled-on artiness'[118]), Neil

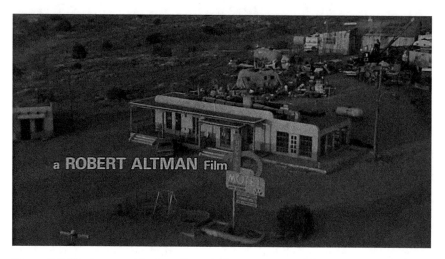

Figure 3.5 The increased budget allowed Altman to expand the setting to include a downbeat motel complex.

Norman's assertion that 'the extraordinary circular set of motel shacks lit by garish neon and Shepard's junkyard ambience remain faithful to his conceptual metaphor of America' is a perceptive one because it foregrounds the way Altman reimagined and reinterpreted Shepard's underlying dramatic concerns (by contrast with the closer adherence of the earlier films).[119]

From the very start, as he did in *Secret Honor*, Altman makes his authorial presence apparent. The play opens with Eddie already in the motel room with May, telling her 'I am not goin' anywhere. See? I am right here'.[120] In the film, there is a more elaborate set-up, a long sequence that introduces both the setting and the characters. Beginning with an overhead shot of the desert, the camera pans right to reveal the motel complex. May and the 'Old Man' (Harry Dean Stanton) seem nervous at the prospect of a visitor, shots intercut with those of Eddie in his truck, driving towards them, a photo of May tucked into his sunvisor.[121] The titles overlay these images and the silence is broken first by the Old Man's harmonica and by a country song heard on Eddie's car radio, then as May puts on her tinny transistor which plays the same tune. Eddie arrives, May hides and Eddie breaks in May's chalet door. They now confront each other and, twelve minutes into the film, they finally speak, with their early exchanges still not from the play. It is yet another couple of minutes before the dialogue begins to follow the original text (when Eddie offers to make May tea).[122] This extended opening establishes both the tone of the piece, and its location and protagonists, implying the nature of their relationships to each other in a near-silent prologue. It also seems to be Altman's authorial assertion that he is not producing a facsimile of the stage production; in contrast with the earlier adaptations, he does this by expanding (to a limited extent only) the play's constrictive one-room set. As the languid start makes clear, the film determinedly ignores Shepard's clear instruction at the beginning of the published text: 'this play is to be performed relentlessly without a break'.[123]

This immediate challenge to Shepard's original conception may have been a precursor to the difficult collaboration between director and writer/actor. According to Altman, 'I never talked to him about his own ideas for the play, as he wouldn't tell me, and I had my own ideas'.[124] Shepard later discussed the difficult collaboration:

> I don't think the movie works nearly as well as it did onstage … I think Bob did a commendable job. But in retrospect I don't think it works … There's never been any of my plays that was turned into a movie that was worth a shit. A lot of people have tried it and one after another they don't work … He had told me I was going to be involved in the editing process and this and that, and he … went to Paris and cut the whole thing there and that was it.[125]

The tension that clearly characterized their working relationship is explained convincingly by Kimball King when he says that 'Shepard is not haughty, but he is aloof and independent, hardly the sort to be molded by a director with an incompatible vision. It is difficult to separate the playwright from the filmmaker from the actor'.[126] Allan Nicholls explains it from Altman's perspective in similar terms: 'Bob was at loggerheads with Sam Shepard, because you can't really work with Bob if you think you are as big as him. Sam had a bit of an ego himself'.[127] Altman's determination to cast a reluctant Shepard in the film only seems to have confused the interaction between writer and director on one hand, and actor and director on the other. The various drafts of the screenplay (four plus the 'as shot' version) suggest that some of the alterations, and opening-up, were Shepard's but the substantial differences, particularly the Old Man's role and the ending, only appear in the 'as shot' script.[128] In trying to understand how Altman related to the writers of the filmed plays, it is worth noting that the playwrights with whom he fell out were those where the director altered their original concept in some significant way: Graczyk, over the decision to use the same actresses for young and old incarnations in *Jimmy Dean*; Shepard, when he altered the pacing of *Fool for Love*; and later Christopher Durang, after extensively rewriting *Beyond Therapy* in 1987 (a sole exception in terms of fidelity to the original plays).

88 *The Lost Decade*

To this point in his cycle of theatrical adaptations, Altman had maintained the constrictions that were inherent in their original settings and utilized his mobile camera as a means to insert the viewer into the action. In *Fool for Love*, the camera is still typically promiscuous, but here he provides a more expansive space in which it can operate. The film was shot by as usual by Mignot, but only after Altman had dispensed with the services of Robbie Müller: 'He's great but he was making a different film to the one I wanted. He was more interested in the composition of the frame ... Mignot ... understood better the fluid camera movements I like.'[129] It is interesting that Müller was the cinematographer on Wenders's masterpiece, *Paris, Texas*. While both are written by Shepard, the earlier film's wide-screen imagery of the vast deserts of the American South necessitated a different visual approach. As with the casting of Stanton, one might surmise the hiring of Müller was inspired by the earlier film. Altman's comments about the cinematography are revealing about his personal filmmaking style, showing that the camerawork in his 1980s films was still yoked to many of his characteristic methods. Altman's films were never slick productions, and the lack of concern with the aesthetics of the individual frame, retaining the rough edges that accompany such camera fluidity, is carried forward into *Fool for Love*.

Once Eddie arrives, it is apparent immediately that May and Eddie's relationship is volatile as they bicker and argue like an estranged couple. But the truth is eventually revealed to be that they are not just ex-lovers, but they also share a father. The trauma of their experiences, how they discovered their sibling relationship after falling in love, forms the central focus of the piece. Hanging about the motel complex, on the lookout for alcohol to steal, is the 'Old Man', an enigmatic character who, it gradually becomes apparent, is their shared father. In the original play, he sits to the side of the stage on a rocking chair and is only seen when the lights go up on him as he speaks. He is a spectral presence, who seems to haunt the protagonists, described by Shepard in the original text as existing 'only in the minds of Eddie and May, even though they may talk to him directly and acknowledge his physical presence'.[130] In the film, his role is still the same but Altman gives him a physical presence in the diegetic world by having him drunkenly wander about and ensconcing him in a barely habitable caravan to which he periodically returns to oversee the goings-on. The fourth character is Martin (Randy Quaid) who arrives half way through to take May out on a date; it is his presence that provides the catalyst for all the revelations about the family's shared past, as they are revealed to him, and to us.

Armed with an increased budget courtesy of Cannon, Altman not only opens out the play but employs the increased resources to instigate significant (non-textual) changes to the original production. As Frank Caso identifies, Altman's adaptations 'exhibit a progressive awareness of the power of his medium to alter the "text".'[131] Altman's assertion that 'the only real difference from the play was my decision to illustrate the monologues' understates the degree and effect of his own interventions.[132] Just as any new production of an existing play will provide a new perspective, so Altman's approach to *Fool for Love* asks its audience to consider the play's meanings in a slightly different way. In the theatre, the past events that characters recall are heard about but not seen. So the illustration of monologues, to which Altman refers, first occurs when the Old Man tells May a story about her childhood and the images differ subtly from the words. Then, quite late on, when May is getting ready to go out with her date, Eddie takes Martin to the bar, where he tells him the story of the relationship between the father and *his* mother. Martin finds himself a baffled witness to Eddie's mind games in his relationship with his half-sister. Eddie tells Martin about his father, the Old Man, and his peculiar way of life. For years he had regularly disappeared and then re-appeared. Eddie tells how his mother 'was always glad to see him when he came back' but what we see is both mother and child greet his return with stony faces.[133] Eddie finishes his speech by describing the first time he met May, and the teenage May (Sura Cox) is shown looking straight ahead wearing a white dress. As the camera pulls back, young Eddie's face is shown in reflection through the window, alongside the younger May. The camera closes in on Eddie before a seamless cut to the adult May, staring ahead in a white dress exactly like her younger self. It is a striking moment and May now picks up the story and tells it from her, and *her* mother's side. Her story follows more closely the images but still there are differences. When May says about her mother, 'she was holding my hand so tight', we see her trailing behind her mother.[134] Later, she says that 'I was filled with this joy' but we see her looking distraught.[135] These two monologues are spoken according to Shepard's original text, but Altman transforms our understanding of their veracity with the discrepancy between words and pictures.

Altman's decision to portray events differently to narrated recollections explores the unreliability of memories, and how we edit our past to conform to what we wish had happened. These differences are also Altman visualizing the spirit of May's observation, after overhearing Eddie's version of events, that 'he's told me the same story a thousand times, always changes it'.[136] At the same time, it is imagery that gives some sense to the inherent instability in Eddie and May's relationship. Altman makes visual that which is implied in Shepard's dialogue, that the couple have spent their lives being unable to come to terms with their peculiar relationship. The unfeasibility of what is an incestuous relationship is expressed in the distortions of their memories of what might have occurred in their youth, fantasies they use to prolong their trauma. Altman implies it is not simply what they say that is unreliable, but that *any* memory of our distant past is inevitably unreliable as well. What we see is therefore not necessarily any closer to what *actually* happened.

Much of what occurs in *Fool for Love* would seem untenable in a more conventional film presented in a realist mode and with a linear, comprehensible plot, and Shepard's ambiguous narrative structures and unreadable characters seem to make him a natural fit for Altman's unconventional tendencies. As Keyssar comments, the characters Shepard created in *Fool for Love* 'could walk into any Altman film of the seventies with ease'.[137] Similarly, when Ross Wetzsteon argues that if Shepard's 'plays seem elliptical and disjointed, this is because ... he has abandoned the conventions of coherence – traditional means of characterization, narrative, dialogue, structure', this description could equally be made about Altman's usual cinematic style.[138] It is such difficulty in precise interpretation that even makes it possible to read the events of *Fool for Love* (the film) as being a visualization of May's dreams. The re-appearance of Eddie from her past could be as much a figment as the Old Man. Such a reading is encouraged by Altman's other significant change to the play.

Whereas the difference in visuals and words is mentioned in most discussions of the film of *Fool for Love* (although to only a limited extent), the other way Altman subtly expands the scope of the play seems to have been missed entirely. The play is a four-hander, but Altman adds some characters who initially seem merely to be background colour. In a series of long shots, a married couple and a young daughter arrive at the motel. Later, the father drives off and then returns to a joyous welcome from his wife and they leave the girl locked outside while they reunite 'properly'. An affecting and psychologically rich scene now occurs when May, left alone after Eddie had driven off, notices the small girl who is all alone in the playground, shivering in her pyjamas. After a trademark Altman zoom on the young girl, May goes to her and hugs her before the mother appears and she runs off. Like a child, May herself now falls asleep in the playground. The Old Man goes over to May and they observe the family driving off. We now see that the driver is a younger version of Stanton, the family echoes of the past and the little girl May's younger self. This would seem to be a manifestation of May's memories, dredged from her subconscious. The lonely girl, abandoned by her father, is offered succour by her adult self. This complex interaction of past and present interprets Shepard's play in new ways and is a pure example of Altman's authorship: 'it was my idea to bring back the family from twenty years ago into the motel and mix up the time periods'.[139] These traces of past events engage with the happenings described in Eddie and May's monologues about their past, integrating them with Altman's other main disturbance of the play's original structure.

One of the trademark characteristics of the Altman style, which had been subjugated, necessarily, by the restrictions of the mise-en-scène in the theatrical adaptations, was his predilection for using windows and mirrors as symbolic signifiers. As Keyssar puts it, they 'are metaphors for viewing and for self-reflection in most of Altman's films'.[140] The Mylar mirror in *Jimmy Dean* was both a tool and simultaneously a metaphor for a story that is a reflection on the events of the past. But one of the benefits of the opened-up set of *Fool for Love* was that it enabled Altman to shoot characters and action through windows, often in extended scenes, such as when Eddie watches May inside her chalet or when the bar's reflecting surfaces provide a myriad of broken images while the camera objectively observes the characters' lives shattering on the other side of the windows (Figure 3.6).

Figure 3.6 May's contemplative mood reflected in the motel's windows and neon signs.

92   *The Lost Decade*

Fool for Love's reception in the press was the worst of his adapted plays to date. In the United States particularly, many of the reviews were unhappy with the changes made to the original. There was a sense that Altman had not afforded the well-regarded play enough respect. For example, Andrew Sarris chastised Altman especially for his opening up of the play and, like many of the American critics, he also alighted on Altman's refusal to obey Shepard's 'relentless' instruction.[141] *Fool for Love*'s negative notices only confirmed Altman's marginalization and the lukewarm reception was matched unsurprisingly at the box office. Cannon's report from April 1987 shows the film still registering (after two years) losses of $7,193,202, a figure that even exceeds the original budget because of the cost of distribution.[142]

1987–1989

After *Fool for Love*, things got only worse for Altman and, in terms of cinematic releases at least, 1987 was Altman's annus horribilis. As well as the frustrations surrounding the *Nashville* sequel, the year also marked the release of two films that are habitually described as among the very worst of his entire career.[143] *OC and Stiggs* was finally, reluctantly, released by MGM and was resoundingly rejected by critics and public alike. Altman also directed his final theatrical adaptation for the cinema, *Beyond Therapy*, from a play by Christopher Durang. A farce that strives to address such contemporary issues as bisexuality, newspaper dating and the dubious benefits of psychotherapy, it is somewhat baffling as to why Altman took it on at all. He made considerable changes to the original dialogue and took a screenwriting credit. According to Durang, the two fell out early on:

> The only thing of mine in there is whatever remnants of the play remain, which is why I have a credit at all. Anyway, I wrote my draft of the script which I don't even know if he read. He stopped talking to me because he was so upset that I didn't like his version.[144]

Even before submitting his first draft, Durang had written a long letter to Altman giving his thoughts about the 'budgetary' script Altman had written. He lists in some detail his objections, most prominently that 'it is "opened up" far more than I expected' and 'what happened to the story and the characters?'[145] The original play, which has six characters who largely interact in long two-way conversations, seems decidedly uncinematic, and this may explain Altman's decision to reimagine the play by expanding its cast and by making alterations to the plot that amplify the story's more farcical aspects.[146] The film, arguably the very worst of Altman's long career, was slated mercilessly by the critics and performed poorly at the box office. Its domestic gross of just $790,000 barely made a dent in the film's $8.3 million budget provided by independent production company, New World Pictures.[147]

In 1987, Altman also accepted an invitation from ABC TV to choose a play to direct for their theatre slot. He suggested two short early Harold Pinter plays, *The Room* and *The Dumb Waiter* (both 1957). The two plays were presented on television as *Basements* in May. In *The Dumb Waiter*, John Travolta and Tom Conti play the two assassins and *The Room* has a cast including Donald Pleasance, Linda Hunt, and pop star Annie Lennox. Altman claimed that Pinter liked the adaptations apart from complaining about Conti not playing it as 'cockney'.[148] Altman's memory is extremely selective because, in September 1987, Pinter wrote to the director to complain how he was 'deeply disappointed in both films' and refused point-blank to allow any possibility of a theatrical release (as separately conveyed to his lawyers).[149] He seems to regard his plays' every word as sacrosanct as he objects to Conti's 'utterly disgraceful' use of 'more of his lines than of mine', even though any changes, in fact, are entirely superficial. In *The Room*, he is incandescent at Altman's decision to omit the play's final line 'without consultation [which] renders the end of the play quite incomprehensible'.[150]

After the nadir of *OC and Stiggs* and *Beyond Therapy*, 1988 saw Altman demonstrating his ability to keep moving forward. Firstly, he ventured into opera again with a segment, Jean-Phillipe Rameau's 'Les Boréades', in an anthology film, *Aria*. Next came the television film, *The Caine Mutiny Court-Martial*, an accomplished version of Hermann Wouk's play that is as faithful to its source as the earlier adaptations.[151] Altman uses his trademark mobile camera to convey the tensions and emotions of the trial and brings out once again the best from a distinguished cast including Brad Davis, Jeff Daniels and Michael Murphy. Murphy would be the eponymous star of Altman's next project, the ambitious and groundbreaking *Tanner '88* – an eleven-part political satire for HBO about a candidate for the Democratic Presidential nomination who interacts with real candidates and leading figures from the political scene, as the series follows the primary race in real time, with hilarious results. *Tanner '88* seems a natural progression from the fictional, unseen politician in *Nashville*, to the fictionalization of a real president in *Secret Honor*, and now to the placing of a fictional candidate into a real presidential race. According to Chuck Tyron, while the series 'should be understood primarily as a primer on how to watch political television', it also broke new ground with its naturalistic and improvisational approach that 'challenged televisual norms'.[152] Its influence can be seen in programmes that similarly make their fictional characters interact with celebrities appearing as themselves, such as *The Larry Sanders Show* (1992–1998) or *Curb Your Enthusiasm* (2000–).[153]

As this account has shown, Robert Altman's alleged 'lost decade' continued the prodigious rate of production established in the previous decade, but on a variety of smaller-scale films for television and cinema, as well as occasional detours into opera and theatre. The masterful, typically idiosyncratic Van Gogh biopic, *Vincent and Theo* (1990), a European independent production, began Altman's return to the mainstream, building on the acclaim afforded to *Tanner* and leading to the success of *The Player*. Altman never returned to the restricted environments of his 1980s work, but this account has shown that the image of 'a maverick reputation in disrepair' might be just about justified by the moderate returns his work generated. Yet, from an artistic standpoint, films as imaginative and compelling as *Fool for Love* and *Secret Honor* indicate that Altman in the 1980s should not be so easily dismissed by film history even if his very finest work will always be considered to be those made in his more typical style. The difference between Altman and almost all his peers is how he was willing to explore new markets and independent financing. In this way, the trajectory of his 1980s filmmaking seems to have more in common with young directors like Jim Jarmusch and John Sayles, who were in the vanguard for the successful 'indie' scene of the subsequent decade, than with the other New Hollywood auteurs. Tzioumakis makes a similar point when describing how Altman was 'ignored completely as a "1980s independent"' and locates him 'as an independent … filmmaker within very particular industrial and institutional configurations'.[154] Altman's experience in the eighties tells us that the available options for the Hollywood Renaissance directors were determined by the type of artistic compromises they were willing to make in an era of close studio control and the blockbuster – or indeed, by the efforts they were willing to make to avoid them. Altman's choices belonged firmly in the latter category, finding a way to keep working while still maintaining creative control. In doing so, he was denied – and denied himself – the option of giving in to the 'high concept' diktats of the Hollywood machine.

4

Francis Coppola: Post-apocalyptic adventures

Francis Coppola's career would seem to encompass a mass of contradictions. As he put it himself, 'the success of *The Godfather* went to my head like a rush of perfume. I thought I couldn't do anything wrong'.[1] So it was that he conceived of grand projects and spent bewildering amounts of money. Yet he still wanted to make films that were outside the mainstream with 'a little variety and variation'[2] and, repeatedly over the years, he has professed a desire to just make small, personal films that he would write himself from scratch. By 1992, when in the midst of directing yet another genre epic, *Bram Stoker's Dracula*, his journals reveal how this uncertainty continued to trouble him:

> To what do I apply myself? Am I a writer? If so, a novelist, a short-story writer or a dramatist? Am I a director, a mogul or a screenwriter? Am I a scientist, an entrepreneur? What am I good for? If I really total out on a big-budget picture, it's going to be difficult to get another comparably paying job for a while – maybe for ever. But then again, do I really want another one of those jobs? I hate doing them and that's probably the main reason why they don't work out.[3]

While noting that the 'jobs' that he thinks did not 'work out' include some of the most storied films in the history of cinema, this inherent contradiction, which finds expression in his films as well as in his actions, can also be discerned in George Lucas's observation that 'all directors have egos and are insecure ... But of all the people I know, Francis has the biggest ego and the biggest insecurities'.[4]

Coppola stands front and centre whenever commentators seek to identify the culprits for the studios' retreat from auteur filmmaking. As Geoff King puts it, 'Coppola and Michael Cimino are usually singled out most prominently for blame'.[5] Although *Apocalypse Now* eventually became profitable, the hysterical coverage of its troubled and costly production focused largely on Coppola's overdeveloped ego and grandiloquent ambitions. When he followed it with the much-derided *One from the Heart*, his centrality in the narrative of auteurs in decline became yet more firmly established. However, what has already emerged from this study is that while many of the reasons for Renaissance directors' commercial woes were similar, their responses were considerably more diverse. While Robert Altman fled Hollywood and remained extraordinarily busy making low-budget theatrical adaptations, Coppola's own 'lost decade' was also industrious: he directed seven features and one-third of an anthology film, plus a solitary excursion into television.

It all began with a singular response to industrial change that was, at best, counter-intuitive in light of the inexorable movement towards populist filmmaking. Coppola's solution to the majors' unwillingness to finance Renaissance-style filmmaking was to purchase his own studio, where he would instil an environment of fulsome creativity, offering a more benign and stimulating version of the classical era. As Lynda Miles puts it, 'he saw himself in a clear line of descent from the great moguls whose personalities dominated their studios'.[6] When Coppola managed to bankrupt himself following the purchase of the studio and the costly failure of *One from the Heart* in 1981, he was obliged to spend the rest of the decade working constantly to pay off his debts and avoid losing his property portfolio to his creditors.

The familiar narrative about Coppola in the decade is one of artistic regression as he laboured as a director for hire. David Breskin's analysis is a good example of how this period has been understood: 'By the end of the 1980s, Coppola seemed an irrelevancy: serious people didn't care enough about his movies to argue about them, or even see them. Indeed, in that decade of disappointment and disaster, Francis Coppola lost his artistic instincts and his confidence.'[7] This chapter examines Coppola's 1980s *oeuvre* in a way that shows how such generalizations are inaccurate or at least incomplete. The dominant discourse about him as *the* superstar-director brought down by his own hubris has tended to overwhelm a more film-focused understanding of Coppola as a visual stylist. Whereas his confidence may have fluctuated, it is by no means certain that his 'artistic instincts' deserted him (as Breskin claimed). Not only that, some of his 1980s films were, in fact, fairly successful, particularly *The Outsiders* and *Peggy Sue Got Married* while *The Cotton Club* was also seen by reasonable numbers, if not enough to offset its extravagant budget.[8] Even in the films in which he was least engaged, there is still plenty of evidence of Coppola's artistic agency and his keen attention to visual style. However, to understand Coppola's authorship at this time, extra-textual factors cannot be completely elided in favour of a close textual approach because the industrial context and its inherent external pressures inform and problematize the idea that these films are the personal creative statements of a single auteur-director. The financial strictures alone that attached to Coppola after *One from the Heart* make certain that the films cannot be entirely separated from the circumstances of production. For Timothy Corrigan, Coppola at this time represented the peak of a new tendency where 'the auteur-star is meaningful primarily as a promotion or recovery of a movie or a group of movies, frequently regardless of the filmic text itself'.[9] Jeffrey Chown makes a similar point when describing Coppola as the epitome of the director as 'superstar'.[10] As Corrigan implies, such a focus on the auteur-director as a marketable commodity, however, tends to obscure the consideration of form, style and content in the films themselves.

As a correlative to this focus on Coppola as commercial auteur, my concern here is with how, and to what extent, Coppola's authorship is expressed in the films and how this manifests itself in terms of his particular approach to visual style. The flitting across genres and the lack of a consistent ideological positioning mean he is difficult to classify as an auteur who maintains a thematic consistency across the body of work. This has not entirely stopped some writers from expressing contradictory opinions about Coppola's political standpoint. Michael Ryan and Douglas Kellner state that Coppola may be modernist but he is not progressive, illustrating how 'modernist forms can be welded to quite conservative thematics'.[11] Carl Freedman does not see him in these terms at all, talking about 'the deeply political nature of Coppola's filmmaking'[12] and then going on to say that 'though one might hesitate to describe Coppola as a Marxist ... the *Godfather* series dramatizes processes of capital accumulation in ways that irresistibly invite the implementation of Marxist categories'.[13] Rather than searching for ideological consistencies, in order to pinpoint Coppola's authorial identity, it is the way that his films' style reflects their subject matter that is a better marker of his particular approach. This is my focus although certain other commonalities will be noted such as Coppola's concerted interest in family dynamics. As with the other single director-focused chapters, the analysis of specific films will be contextualized with a description of Coppola's career arc during the decade.

1980–1981

Before *Apocalypse Now* had even been released, at a time when Coppola might have been wise to keep a low profile, he was instead making grand statements about the future direction of the industry. In a notorious speech at the 1979

Academy Awards, an over-excited Coppola used his position as a presenter to inform the audience that he foresaw 'a communications revolution … it's going to make the masters of the cinema, from whom we've inherited the business, believe things that they would have thought impossible'.[14] Cowie suggests this display of arrogance may have been the precise moment that the industry turned its back on its former favourite *wunderkind*.[15] At the same time, he was in the process of taking his overarching ambitions to another level altogether. On 25 March 1980, he paid $6.7 million to acquire a Hollywood facility of his own, a 10.5 acre site, formerly known as Hollywood General Studios.[16] When Coppola employed one of his heroes, the British filmmaker Michael Powell, as 'senior director in residence' at the new studio, it is surely not entirely coincidental that Powell, a somewhat forgotten figure at this time, had co-directed one of Coppola's personal favourites, *The Thief of Baghdad* (Powell, Ludwig Berger, Tim Whelan, 1940) at the very same location.[17] Coppola's intention in running his own studio seems to encapsulate some of the contradictions that run through the whole of his career. He wanted to direct inexpensive films, the costs of which would be controlled by his technological innovations, yet he still anticipated being able to compete on equal terms with the other studios. Jon Lewis is very keen in his book about this period to absolve Coppola of most of the blame for his financial downfall. He argues that its main cause was the disavowal of auteur directors by the studios, but especially of Coppola because of his ambitious plans to fundamentally change filmmaking practice.[18] Lewis offers a compelling rationale for the dice being loaded against the director, but his premise is undermined by a number of factors, many of which he elucidates himself, not least Coppola's naivety about what was required to raise finance.[19] The complex nature of the filmmaker's experiences means the allocation of blame should not be reduced to a simple opposition between the system (Lewis) and Coppola's over-developed ego (most other accounts). It is certainly true that Paramount and Columbia should take much of the responsibility for the fact that *One from the Heart* was barely seen, their respective withdrawals of support meaning that the film stood little chance. Indeed, according to David Thomson, Coppola was convinced that 'none other than Lew Wasserman put out the word that he was not to be helped'.[20] However, this tells only a fraction of the story of the making and distribution of the film, which is apparent from Lewis's own work, as well as from Lillian Ross's extensive investigation into *One from the Heart*'s troubled production for *The New Yorker*.[21] In any case, even if the motivation behind the studios' decisions on this film was opaque, this was a new

Francis Coppola

era and Coppola was not alone among the Renaissance filmmakers in failing to understand how much the landscape in Hollywood had changed post-*Star Wars*. Much like Cimino and Friedkin before him, he was culpable in allowing a modestly budgeted film to become a $20 million-plus behemoth. *One from the Heart*'s reputation and visibility has suffered as a result of the perception that it was a grandiloquent folly.

Now renamed Zoetrope Studios, the problem for the nascent enterprise was that it did not have a sufficient credit line to fully finance *even one* film all the way from development to release.[22] Coppola seemed to imagine that he would be able to generate his own projects unhindered by external interference; acclaimed European auteurs like Hans-Jürgen Syberberg, Werner Herzog and Dusan Makavejev visited him to talk about possible collaborations.[23] Yet, during its short timespan (1980–1983), Zoetrope Studios was perpetually looking for distribution from one studio or another. As well as films directed by Coppola, there were difficulties securing distribution for all the other Zoetrope productions, particularly *Hammett* (Wim Wenders, 1982), but to a lesser extent, *The Escape Artist* (Caleb Deschanel, 1982) and *The Black Stallion Returns* (Robert Dalva, 1983) as well.[24] The idea of *One from the Heart* as an inexpensive, small film was quickly forgotten when Coppola began spending. Future director, Michael Lehmann, who was on the crew on *One from the Heart*, observed that 'Francis always talked about it as being a contained movie … I'm not exactly sure what happened … he kept building more sets. Before too long every stage on the lot had a set under construction.'[25] Coppola, without any deliberate intent to do so at the outset, effectively 'bet the house' on *One from the Heart*, risking not just the studio but his personal wealth as well. His behaviour in spending money he did not have, which he has replicated (if not to such a ludicrous extent) at other times during his career, resembles that of a compulsive gambler. At times, he seemed to believe he was operating in a different marketplace to everyone else and it was the epitome of optimism to conceive of building a dream studio at this time. For this reason, Jon Lewis's statement that 'one can hardly blame Coppola for going ahead with his studio project' does not entirely stand up to scrutiny.[26] Coppola himself has rarely been consistent over the years about what type of cinema he wants to make. Yet even though he has repeatedly returned to the idea that he really just wants to write and make personal films like Bergman or Antonioni, most of his long-cherished projects (that he also talks about *a lot*) seem quite the opposite: high-flown, grandiose and possibly unfilmable concepts.[27] Some thirty-plus years later, Coppola is still insisting that he envisaged *One from the*

100   *The Lost Decade*

Heart as 'something surefire that would be entertaining and popular', an antidote to the disastrous fate that he anticipated would befall him once *Apocalypse Now* was released.[28]

One from the Heart

The reputation of *One from the Heart* largely rests not on the film's intrinsic qualities but on its infamous and decisive contribution to Coppola's financial collapse, and its continuation of the kind of auteurist excess associated with the likes of *Sorcerer* and *Heaven's Gate*. Its initial critical reception cast the film in terms of Coppola's rampant ego before it had even been released and set in stone a negative perception from which it never recovered. The result has been that subsequent considerations have elided the film itself in favour of foregrounding its contribution to the failure of Coppola's romantic but doomed ambition to recreate the Hollywood studios of yore. In the United States, the film was screened only briefly at the time of its initial release, appearing on only forty-one screens on 11 February 1982, grossing $804,000 against a budget of about $28 million, before Coppola rapidly withdrew it from circulation.[29] Looking back at the decision to pull the film so quickly, Coppola recently observed that it 'involved some stupidity on my part', his ability to act rationally affected by his depressed state of mind as bankruptcy loomed.[30] *One from the Heart*'s initial reputation was largely based on hearsay and a vituperative press response (although there were some rare exceptions) but not on the actual opinions of actual audiences.[31] Therefore, to dismiss the film's artistic value by dent of its commercial failure is not an argument easily made because it is a film that was given little opportunity to find an audience. Nevertheless, Coppola's determination to make the film exactly as he wanted, predicated on the creative freedom the purchase of his own studio allowed, resulted in a film that challenged the stylistic norms of Hollywood filmmaking in such a way that it is likely that it would only ever have found a niche audience. In many ways, it is appropriate to think of it as an art film, in the way it offers a difficult blend of a simple, but contemporary, love story that borrows from Hollywood's past with a surfeit of visual style that functions, as Jeffrey Chown observes, 'as contrapuntal commentary on the film's substance'.[32] With the exception of Chown, and some brief but frequently positive assessment in the biographical accounts of Coppola's career, the filmic content of *One from the Heart* has rarely been considered.[33]

The following discussion takes some account of the film's production and use of groundbreaking technologies, but my principal interest is how these inform the content, form and style of the film itself.[34] *One from the Heart* is the 1980s film over which Coppola enjoyed the highest degree of artistic control, in the sense that he was able to work entirely without external interference and with a (fatally) unrestricted budget. Coppola employs classical narrative forms to tell a fairy tale about an ordinary couple who have relationship problems, but in terms that are reflective of specifically contemporary societal norms. Unlike in many of the revisionist films of the Renaissance, his approach to Hollywood genre here seems nostalgic and without irony. What made this approach challenging to mainstream tastes is how Coppola marries this combination of the classical and contemporary with an expressive, exaggerated and determinedly self-conscious visual design.

Narratively, *One from the Heart* uses structures that recall the traits of not only the Hollywood musical but the romantic comedy as well. The story is a simple one, what Coppola called 'a little musical Valentine'.[35] As the film opens, it is the night before the 4th of July holiday; Hank (Frederic Forrest) and Fran (Teri Garr) will celebrate their fifth anniversary living together the next day. Each has bought the other a gift that, in combination, functions as symbols of the problems in their relationship: he has bought the deeds to their house while she has bought tickets for an exotic holiday. Both have used each other's money to buy what they want for themselves and this duality, that they have different desires, is the problem in classical fashion that the film's narrative must resolve. They argue, make up and make love, and then argue again before Fran storms out. The remainder of the film follows their adventures over the course of the holiday weekend. Their paths keep nearly intersecting, as each conducts a fairy-tale-like romance, with Ray (Raul Julia) and Leila (Nastassja Kinski), respectively. The happy reunion that ends the story comes only after Hank's protracted and increasingly desperate attempts to win Fran back. The conclusion leaves the protagonists reconciled, Fran rejecting the fantasy life that is encapsulated in the travel agency shop window she decorates at work.

The couple are not married, and their modern living arrangement is the first indicator of how *One from the Heart* employs past narrative structures to tell a contemporary story. The distinction is apparent with the manner in which the film begins. After a brief opening scene on the vibrant Las Vegas streets, that evokes the spectacular first shots in *Les Enfants du Paradis* (Marcel Carné, 1946), the camera finally settling on Fran at work on its fringes, there is a cut to her arriving home, struggling unsuccessfully to balance a huge pile of shopping and laundry, and dropping half of it on the street. Hank now arrives and grumpily picks up what she has left behind. The song that plays over this scene is a duet that riffs on the silent on-screen events and establishes some sense of their relationship before they even speak. As the male singer (Tom Waits) observes, 'looks like you spent the night in a trench / And tell me, how long have you been combin' your hair with a wrench', the female comeback (Crystal Gayle) is, 'the roses are dead and the violets are too / And I'm sick and tired of pickin' up after you'.[36] This is a contemporary couple who live in a house that resembles their relationship: in need of some loving attention. The makeshift furniture itself is illustrative of their essential differences, as well as the impermanence of their relationship. Hank sits on a battered old car seat like he is still at work, while Fran is on a deck chair as if on holiday. These are contemporary representations of a couple's incompatibility, an updating of a simple but effective mode of storytelling. This contemporaneity becomes even more pronounced in how the couple's adventures play out, with their sexual desires more frankly expressed than would have been ever possible under the strictures of the Production Code, as when Fran has to break the mood to fetch her birth-control device (although the more traditional Hank wants to start a family).

In structural terms, however, the narrative is not contemporary at all, conforming, in many ways, to the basic form of the Hollywood musical where, according to Rick Altman, 'each separate part of the film recapitulates the film's overall duality'.[37] Coppola makes the parallel between what happens to each protagonist unmistakeable and 'the partners' separation provides an excuse for still more parallel scenes'.[38] So when Fran leaves Hank, she escapes to her best friend Maggie (Lainie Kazan) and we see Fran telling her about the break-up. At the same time, Hank goes to see Mo (Harry Dean Stanton) and does the same. Coppola uses a theatrical device to make the parallel even more blatant. In a ten-minute take (of which more later), Coppola makes the transitions from Mo's house to Maggie's apartment (and back and forth) using painted scrims, thin gauze screens that, when lit from the front, resemble a painting but from behind become transparent. There is a parallel here with Altman's use of the Mylar mirror in *Jimmy Dean* with both directors employing devices from the theatre to toggle between settings, creating illusions through light. Carrie Rickey calls the use of the scrim here as like 'a movie screen receiving emotional projections from each side' and they enable Coppola to seamlessly show what is happening with each of the dislocated pair.[39]

Coppola calls *One from the Heart* 'a musical fairy tale', but it is one without the characters singing diegetically.[40] Instead, the lyrics provide narration, often in place of dialogue, with songs written specifically for the film by Waits. Coppola's tendency to improvise and spend more and more money extended to the music as well, with Waits commenting to a Zoetrope employee that Coppola 'was the most indecisive man I have ever met'.[41] Excepting a few instrumental fills, the distinctively gruff vocals from Waits accompany Gayle's graceful tones, duets that comment and underscore the events happening on screen. Although, as in the integrated musical, the songs tell the story as much as the dialogue, the use and style of music are of a more contemporary hue. A suite of songs, derived from modern popular music styles, that provides a narrational voice, is a strategy that had been used during the Renaissance period, as with the Simon and Garfunkel music that provided *The Graduate*'s soundtrack or Altman's use of Leonard Cohen songs in *McCabe and Mrs Miller*. Their prominence is much greater here and Waits' particular and idiosyncratic style was not, perhaps, ever likely to appeal to a wide demographic, even if here he is at his most accessible and melodic.[42] While the songs often function to elide the need for dialogue, they do not disturb the narrative flow by having characters burst spontaneously into song. The film does use extravagantly staged scenes that seem primarily to function as spectacle, but they are integrated smoothly into the diegesis. For example, in the extravagant dance number that develops as Fran and Ray spill out onto the Las Vegas strip, the scene begins as a seduction by dance in Fran's travel agency. Although the singers often seem to closely resemble Hank and Fran, they are not simply expressing the couple's feelings. Coppola compares them to 'Zeus and Hera somehow peeking through the clouds and commenting on the action'.[43] From Gayle's 'old boyfriends lost in the pocket of your overcoat / like burned out light bulbs on a Ferris wheel' to Waits' advice that 'you can't take back the things you said man / cause you can't unring a bell', the musical narrators do often seem more perceptive about human behaviour than their earthbound counterparts.[44] Reviving the style of classic musicals was not enough, according to Justin Wyatt, for *One from the Heart* to be able to sell itself to a general viewership. If successful 'high concept' films rely on three ways to promote themselves, 'the look, the hook, the book', then *One from the Heart* illustrates how just having 'the look' cannot sell a film alone.[45]

One *from the Heart* has traces of another favourite Hollywood genre, the romantic comedy. More specifically, with the pair having been together for five years and the manner in which the narrative proceeds, it is reminiscent of what Stanley Cavell called the 'comedy of remarriage'.[46] Cavell identified commonalities in a series of 1930s and 1940s Hollywood comedies; Hank and Fran not being married only emphasizes how *One from the Heart* is a modern re-imagining of classical forms. Although *One from the Heart* is not a comedy per se, it is light-hearted and frequently comic, and its structure can persuasively be compared with Cavell's ideas. Hank's final desperate act to try to get Fran back, when he attempts valiantly but tunelessly to sing to her as she boards a plane with Ray, recalls how comedies of remarriage position their heroes as virtuous when they are willing to suffer 'a certain indignity' to win back their estranged partner.[47] His extreme act of self-effacement is the catalyst for Fran to realize how much she loves Hank. Another way *One from the Heart* resembles a comedy of remarriage is how the action moves from 'a starting place of impasse' to a 'green world, a place where perspective and renewal are to be achieved'. Cavell is citing here Northrop Frye's work on Shakespeare's comedies, and Coppola's 'green world' is, as in Shakespeare and Hollywood comedies, a 'mythical location' where Hank and Fran can disappear into fantasy, a space that eventually offers them the opportunity for 'renewal': it is a studio-bound, extravagant but pointedly artificial version of Las Vegas.[48] The Vegas of *One from the Heart* is shown as even more hyperreal than the real thing, and building it entirely on studio lots was, according to Coppola, 'our own fantasy of Las Vegas, which for me is a metaphor for America itself'.[49] The sets are lavish, a panoply of neon, their overblown absurdity most strikingly realized in the backlot of Hank's breaker's yard where retired motel and casino signs bestride an otherwise barren landscape (Figure 4.1).

The difficulties of marrying an uncomplicated story with a complicated style might point us towards why the film attracted such critical opprobrium. The film is dominated by its production design of artificial excess and by its dazzling use of symbolic colour. Vittorio Storaro, the director of photography, made extensive use of a modern lighting board used in the theatre to make intricate adjustments to lighting levels and to facilitate his expressive use of colour.[50] Storaro uses unnaturally vibrant colour washes to indicate emotion and character: he told Cowie that he 'had the idea to use the physiology of the colour itself to establish the mood of the film'.[51] The duality between the protagonists is enhanced by giving them colour motifs that reflect their characters: Fran in red

Figure 4.1 Hank's backlot of retired neon signs and assorted detritus symbolizes Las Vegas' absurdity.

and Hank in green. So Hank's scenes with Leila are bathed in a blue-green glow whereas Fran's romantic adventures are characterized by a profusion of red, in the lighting at moments of high passion and with a series of dresses. Coppola's use of scrims, rear-screen projections that are comically artificial and these outlandish lighting patterns all contribute to a film that overtly acknowledges its own sense of theatricality. Although theatricality could be said to be generic in any self-reflexive musical, its use here takes it in a rather unusual direction.

Coppola conceived of Zoetrope Studios as a creative hub of actors, technicians as well as other artists and visionaries. These included three of his heroes, who all worked on *One from the Heart*, and their contributions and inspiration can be glimpsed in the film's text and textures. Employed as head of Zoetrope's musical division, Gene Kelly advised Coppola on the spectacular dance number mentioned earlier. The scene's sheer exuberance, the Las Vegas streets seemingly peopled by thousands dancing, evokes Kelly's much-loved MGM musicals, particularly *On the Town* (Kelly, Stanley Donen, 1949).[52] Then there is the scene in Hank's scrapyard when the couple wake up in the morning and Leila is wandering about when she happens on a giant ruby ring which she tells Hank is the 'all-seeing eye'. This is a *homage* to Michael Powell, an overt reference to the 'all-seeing eye' from *The Thief of Baghdad*.[53] Powell's bold, experimental 1940s films in Technicolor also seem to be an influence on the look and style of *One from the Heart*, not least the luscious colours of the similarly studio-bound *Black Narcissus* (1947). The two scenes where Hank fantasizes about Leila before his date with her also display a Powell-like visual exuberance and ambition. Hank imagines Leila dancing in a giant cocktail glass in the reflection of a bar (Figure 4.2); a few minutes later, he is gazing up at an enormous neon sign of a woman's face when it magically transforms into Leila's face, lit in deep blue, singing Waits's song, 'Little Boy Blue'. What follows is an extravaganza of dazzling effects and rapid editing that resembles, and arguably prefigures, the style and ebullience of an MTV pop video (the influential channel having only just been launched in August 1981). Lastly, Jean-Luc Godard, who fascinated Coppola because of 'his resolute rejection of traditional studio methods', assisted Coppola on background process plates of Vegas scenery.[54] It is Godard's unwillingness to compromise as well as his innovative use of music and colour that can be

Figure 4.2 A Michael Powell-like visual exuberance as Hank dreams about Leila before their date.

perceived in the film's idiosyncratic style. The accumulation of influences and references to favourite films and filmmakers indicates both how *One from the Heart* was a personal experiment, but also how it harks back towards the films of the Renaissance which were often similarly allusive.

Costs surged when Coppola kept building more and more sets, yet over thirty-five years later he is still insisting his actions were justified by his original idea to make the film in a radical way that he calls 'live cinema', a method that necessitated the elaborate construction of interconnected sets. Coppola has fairly recently returned to this concept, conducting workshops for a semi-biographical project, *Distant Vision*. The idea follows the example of television from the late 1950s, with the work of John Frankenheimer particularly influential, with live performances shot on sets arranged in order of the scenes' progression.[55] Coppola wanted (and still wants) to recapture the immediacy and vibrancy of these early television plays. Coppola built the sets to facilitate this methodology but a decision – 'one of the few regrets in my long life' – to abort this plan was made largely because Storaro begged Coppola to reconsider because he felt unable to adequately light a film made in this way.[56] The inherent problems with making a feature-length film according to these methods were considerable in the early 1980s, not least because of the limits imposed by having to change reels, meaning that ten-minute takes would place restrictions on Coppola achieving the immediacy of 'live' performances.[57] This initial idea can still be discerned in the film's aesthetics. In those scenes where Coppola takes advantage of his elaborate set construction, there is a fluidity to the progress of the action. The scene described earlier, which flits from Mo's place to Maggie's and back again, is shot in a continuous ten-minute take. Coppola directs the actors to use the space flexibly, their movements within elaborately constructed homes accompanied by a camera in constant movement. The 'live cinema' concept ran alongside the other advanced technological methods used in the making of all the Zoetrope Studio productions during its brief existence. Various pre-visualization techniques, the use of electronic storyboards and the use of 'video assist' were all ahead of their time. Indeed, in both Brooks Riley and Raymond Fielding's contemporaneous examinations of Coppola's 'electronic cinema', grand claims are made about how pre-visualization systems would save 'millions of dollars'.[58] Such assertions now seem absurd considering how the budget spiralled wildly out of control. However, these alleged benefits of 'electronic cinema' do, perhaps, give us some indication of why Coppola felt able to continue spending money with such conviction.

The implications of Coppola's experiments with technology discouraged the studios from supporting it – or even, as Lewis alleges, led them to sabotage it – and the difficult circumstances of its adverse critical reception, well before a general release, played a significant part in its failure. However, when trying to understand the ongoing value of the film itself, and its place in Coppola's body of work, this does not tell the whole story. This discussion has shown that, even if the film's journey onto cinema screens had been smoother and more conventional, it was always going to divide audiences – after all, we have to give the contemporary critics *some* credit for their opinions. However, what also has been seen is how *One from the Heart* was a personal experiment that featured what Cowie called 'some of the most imaginative special effects ever seen in a Hollywood movie'.[59] Coppola's romantic dream of an idealized version of an 'old' Hollywood was insufficiently grounded in the harsh realities of 1980s filmmaking in the 'new' Hollywood but it is important that this does not blind us to the aesthetic qualities of the film and the ambition of Coppola's personal vision.

1982–1983

The fallout from *One from the Heart* led Coppola to agreements to repay his debts at roughly 30 cents on the dollar so that he could keep his homes and his production company (the original American Zoetrope in San Francisco).[60] To make his payments, Coppola was obliged to keep working and he concluded that what was needed next was something simple and inexpensive. In March 1980, Coppola had received a letter, accompanied by a petition signed by anywhere between 30 and 108 students from Jo Ellen Misakian, a high school librarian at the Lone Star Junior High school in Fresno, California.[61] She requested that Coppola consider making a film of her students' favourite book, *The Outsiders*, a novel for teenagers that had become a publishing sensation. Written by Susan Hinton (who published as S. E. Hinton) in 1967 when she was only sixteen, the book has sold 10 million copies in North America alone.[62] His decision to escape Los Angeles for Oklahoma to work on a project for which he was not obviously suited was based, according to the director, on 'the idea of being with half a dozen kids in the country and making a movie seemed like being a camp counsellor again … I'd forget my troubles and have some laughs again'.[63]

The Outsiders

When Hinton requested a mere $5,000 dollars for the rights to the book, such was the perilous financial situation at Zoetrope that they had to persuade her with a down payment of only $500, a percentage of future profits and a role in the film.[64] Coppola intended to make the film on location in Tulsa, Oklahoma, where the novel is set but, even with a relatively modest projected budget of $10 million, Coppola's reputation for financial irresponsibility and Zoetrope's problems meant funding the project was not simply achieved. When Coppola left for Tulsa on 1 March 1982 to begin pre-production, he still had not got the finance in place but nine days later, he managed to secure a distribution deal with Warner Brothers. On that basis, Coppola was able to borrow about $10 million from Chemical Bank, but only if he secured a completion guarantee. Completion bonds are a guarantee to provide the funds, if required, to complete a film's production and to satisfy banks and distributors that it will be completed on schedule. The company charges a fee (usually 5 per cent of the film's total budget) in exchange for their promise. They have no interest in the film's commercial success, so their risk is not about marketability and often not about distribution as well (if it will be sold on a pick-up basis); their abiding concern is simply to ensure that the film is made on budget and on time. *The Outsiders* was financed by Chemical Bank on the basis of the guarantee provided by Film Finances Limited, a private British company who specialize in completion bonds (not the National Film Finances Corporation that Lewis and others cite).[65] Film Finances' decision to approve support for Coppola was part of a strategy to raise their profile in the United States. Indeed, when principal photography was completed, they took out their own advertisements in the trade press which congratulated Coppola, cast and crew for completing principal photography on schedule and on budget.[66] However, they put in place severe restrictions on Coppola to mitigate the risk in allying themselves with such a notoriously reckless director and Coppola was obliged to agree to their terms to get the funds he needed from the bank. Film Finances' archives reveal the extent that their strictures restricted the director's actions. The important point here is that Film Finances had no interest in the nature of the film's content only in the director's efficiency in the timely completion of each stage of filming. Although Lewis argues that *The Outsiders* was a Zoetrope film in name only and claims that Warners controlled the production, in fact (until post-production) it was rather that Film Finances' conditions controlled

Coppola's spending but the arrangement still enabled him to make the film his own way.[67] The restrictions included Coppola deferring his directing and writing fee ($1.5 million), script and cast approval and an obligation to provide daily progress reports by telex (that reported on whether the film remained on schedule) as well as weekly cost statements.[68] Coppola had commitments to meet in terms of managing his debts and could only earn anything at all from *The Outsiders* by completing it in a timely and efficient manner. Coppola recognized his perilous situation and maintained a tight control over the production, coming in largely on budget and on schedule (as he would also do with his next film, *Rumble Fish*).[69]

By the time the film was audience-tested, Warners did make their presence felt and encouraged Coppola to reduce the two-hour running time, place more emphasis on the melodramatic elements and foreground Matt Dillon's (the notional star) character arc by editing out scenes that concentrated on the characterization of the Curtis family. In 2005, Coppola restored these scenes in a new version for DVD, now called *The Outsiders: The Complete Novel*, and much closer to Hinton's book. It now ran to 114 minutes compared with 90 in 1983. Making a qualitative comparison between the two is largely outside my purview here but, suffice to say, there are merits in both versions. What is important is that Coppola, under pressure admittedly, made the original decisions himself and for his own reasons as well (even if he claims to regret them now). He excised those scenes that produced an adverse reaction at test screenings, particularly those that attracted giggling at the more potentially homo-erotic scenes.[70] His decision to second-guess himself (remembering that he had final cut in 1983) and blame others seems characteristic of his restlessness and suspicion about his own commercial successes. As well as placing culpability on Warners for the edit, he reluctantly now questions the value of his late father's melodramatic score, replacing it with rock n'roll music from the time the story is set, the presence of which is sometimes overbearing in a way that the original score is not.[71] In fact, his father's traditional score seems more appropriate to a film that strongly evokes the 1950s teen drama. Coppola's denial of his father's contribution is certainly not what he thought in 1983 when he told Thomson and Gray that 'the key in *The Outsiders* is the score; the fact that it's this schmaltzy classical movie score indicates that I wanted a movie told in sumptuous terms, very honestly or carefully taken from the book without changing it a lot'.[72] In this frequent re-visiting of his past, Coppola seems to showing a constant need for (self) affirmation of his talents.[73]

Figure 4.3 Some of *The Outsiders*' cast of future superstars (from left to right: Estevez, Dillon, Cruise, Lowe, Howell, Macchio).

When *The Outsiders* is remembered today, it is usually for its remarkable casting, a 'who's who' of Brat Pack actors and future superstars. In varying degrees, Tom Cruise, Patrick Swayze, Matt Dillon, Ralph Macchio, C. Thomas Howell, Emilio Estevez, Rob Lowe and Diane Lane would all go on to have significant careers, an ensemble that Jonathan Bernstein calls 'a platform that would introduce an entire stud farm of fresh young acting talent into the national consciousness'[74] (Figure 4.3). But when Lewis talks about a "number of bankable young male stars" and Justin Wyatt argues that *The Outsiders*' key high-concept marker was its 'cast of teen idols', this somewhat misrepresents the situation at the time.[75] Before *The Outsiders*, only Dillon could be said to have any 'star' status, having appeared in five films already, including the lead in the just-completed Hinton adaptation for Disney, *Tex* (Tim Hunter, 1982). Cruise, who only has a small supporting role, was cast in his breakthrough film, *Risky Business* (Paul Brickman, 1983) while making *The Outsiders*. Swayze, Macchio and Lowe, who would all become leading actors in a few years' time, were making their feature film debuts after just a few appearances in television movies. Howell, the main protagonist in *The Outsiders*, was the youngest but had at least appeared in a small role in *E.T.* Coppola then can take some credit for his prescience in gathering such a talented ensemble (rather than the cast as representative of an overt commercial strategy).[76] His use of an extended rehearsal period, which formed part of his pre-visualization video methods, enabled the teenagers to form bonds that are reflected in the relationships depicted on screen. Admittedly the cast were already bankable enough to have featured prominently in the pages of teen magazines, presumably because of

112 *The Lost Decade*

their appearances on children's television, and this appeal to its target audience may provide a small clue to the film's success.[77]

The story was inspired by Hinton's own experiences growing up in Tulsa, Oklahoma, but she portrays a male-dominated milieu where mothers are significant characters by dent of their absence. That Hinton was so young is usually seen as a strength, informing her realistic portrayal of teenage experience, although one literary critic, Cynthia Rose, claimed that the film adaptation 'points to Hinton's misrepresentation of masculinity as the key failure of the work.'[78] *The Outsiders* focuses on the Curtis household, three brothers who live together in a small rundown house on the north side of an unnamed town where the well-off live on the south side.[79] The Curtis boys are orphans whose parents were both killed in a car accident some years ago. Darrel (Swayze) is a twenty-year-old who had to give up the opportunity to go to college to look after his brothers.[80] The good-natured Sodapop (Lowe) dropped out of school and works at a gas station and Ponyboy (Howell) is fourteen, an intelligent, intense boy who, as Darrel remarks in exasperation, spends all his time thinking about movies and books. There is little possibility that the Curtis family will ever be able to transcend their environment and *The Outsiders* tells a melodramatic, overheated story based on a novel written by a sixteen-year-old for a teenage audience. Coppola's presentation of such melodrama in a hyper-stylized setting appealed to audiences but was not always well received by critics, many expressing a view that such over-dramatized emotion belonged to an earlier era. The subsequent discourse surrounding the film has been dominated by the cast and the origins of the project, but it is at its most interesting when considering how its visual style is attuned to the protagonist and to its generic roots.

The film portrays teenage lives with barely an adult to be seen, where adolescent experience becomes overwhelming for these troubled young men. The film's visual palette is a reflection of these lives and is filtered through the prism of Ponyboy's imagination. Hinton wrote all her young adult novels with a first-person narrator and it is Ponyboy in *The Outsiders*. Coppola recreates this perspective, by depicting the story, as Hinton also does in the novel, as a school assignment Ponyboy is writing.[81] The film begins with him sitting at his desk and picking up his pen to describe the events that comprise the film and the audience experiences the events of the past through Ponyboy's eyes. Coppola also employs a circular structure that brings the story to a close by taking us all the way back to the beginning. By the end of the dramatic story, that culminates with the death of two of the Curtis's closest friends, it is the act of recalling the events that led to this tragic conclusion that prompts the proto-novelist, Ponyboy, to set down his story – which, in turn, forms the narrative that has just concluded. It is this structural frame that identifies how we see the film's events through Ponyboy's eyes. Alongside the deprived familial environments and societally determined poverty is a world of dramatic sunsets and sunrises, and of evocative landscapes, that exaggerate and foreground the expressive beauty of the natural world. These can be read as visual expressions of Ponyboy's romantic imagination. When Darrel tells him, 'You don't ever think and you've always got your head in a book', we can see how Ponyboy is very different from his peers and that he sees the world differently. How Ponyboy's poetic inclinations make him stand apart from his peers is reflected in one of Hinton's central messages, that the world is equally beautiful for the deprived and the privileged alike. This notion is expressed in Ponyboy's conversation with Cherry (Diane Lane) when he asks her, 'can you see the sunset from the south side?' When she replies, 'sure', he says that 'you can see it from the north side too'. The division between the rich kids who include Cherry – the 'Socs' (pronounced 'Soshes' and short for 'socialites') – and the Curtis brothers and all their friends – 'Greasers' who live on the wrong side of town – necessarily alienates them from each other. It comes across as a bit corny, but Ponyboy instinctively recognizes that Cherry is the type of person who looks at sunsets. They have much in common but can never be friends, and their relationship is governed by the tribal and elitist behaviour that is encoded in their social environment. In fact, it is Cherry and a friend chatting with Ponyboy and Johnny at the drive-in (after Cherry has fallen out with her very drunk boyfriend, Bob (Leif Garrett)) that prompts the Socs to attack the two boys later in the evening. Johnny kills Bob with a knife because he believes the Socs are about to drown Ponyboy. With the help of their doomed older friend, Dallas (Matt Dillon) who has been in prison and will be killed by the police by the end, Johnny and Ponyboy go on the run and hide out in the Oklahoma countryside.

During the boys' adventure in rural surroundings, there is a connection established that resonates both visually and textually. As a representation of Ponyboy's imagination, *Gone with the Wind* is a key reference point for the style of the film, Coppola drawing inspiration from the book's plot. Ponyboy and Johnny pass the time in their rural hideout reading a battered copy of the novel to each other. Among a number of scenes that visually recall the earlier film is when they set off and a train (carrying the boys) traverses the breadth of the screen. Captured in silhouette, behind the train is the first of a number

Figure 4.4 Sunsets in *The Outsiders* evoke both the perfection and the fleeting nature of youth.

of spectacular sunrises and sunsets. For Coppola, they represented the perfect metaphor for the film, 'even as we look at a sunset, we are aware that it is already starting to die. Youth too is like that: at its very moment of perfection you can already see the forces that are undoing it'[82] (Figure 4.4). The centrality of *Gone with the Wind* as a symbol of their formative experience together in alien surroundings is underlined later when Johnny is dying in hospital after having rescued some children from a fire (that he probably caused) and he asks Ponyboy to get the book for him. When Johnny dies, he leaves the book and a note for Ponyboy telling him to finish it. Coppola promoted the film, with his customary penchant for high-flown lyricism, by calling it '*Gone with the Wind* for 14-year-old girls' which, although ignoring his potential *male* audience, does make sense in the way *The Outsiders* evokes an epic grandeur in its aestheticization of the Oklahoma countryside.[83]

As Coppola did in *One from the Heart* (and would do in *Rumble Fish* and *Tucker* as well), *The Outsiders* borrows stylistically from other forms of cinema, using such influences not as pastiche or ironically but reverently as a jumping-off point for aesthetic experimentation. *One from the Heart* evoked the Hollywood musical and the height of classicism, employing an Academy ratio (an almost square 1.37:1) to evoke the glorious past and to give emphasis to vertical planes and detail. In *The Outsiders*, Coppola turns towards the 1950s melodrama, and its combination of widescreen ratios and Technicolor. Because Coppola wanted to imbue the characters with a certain heroic dimension, he decided to film in a

Francis Coppola

wide-screen anamorphic format (a ratio of 2.35:1).[84] Stephen Burum, the film's cinematographer, described what they were trying to do by using the wider ratio:

> It's how you play the borders ... We have to get beyond the idea of the frame as a proscenium arch and feel free to tilt the camera if that's more organic to the subject matter ... We composed from the character's point-of-view; everything is distorted though somebody's eyes but geared to Ponyboy since it's his story.[85]

The teen drama's hallmark text is *Rebel without a Cause* (Nicholas Ray, 1955) and Coppola's use of Panavision and an expressive, often unnaturalistic, colour palette invokes that film. Coincidentally or not, Macchio also bears a certain facial resemblance with Sal Mineo's character in the earlier film and both actors play the well-intentioned but fated 'best friend' role. Yet it is the prevalent sunsets and sunrises that remain the most obvious marker of a visual sensibility influenced by 1950s Hollywood, for all the *Gone with the Wind* allusions. They also epitomize the visual style of the same director as *One from the Heart*, one that is not geared to an obviously naturalistic mode. Whereas Jon Lewis may insist that it was 'a calculated and very conservative attempt to make a commercial picture',[86] such a perception of *The Outsiders* as a conventional teen drama peopled by a profusion of Brat Pack stars has undermined consideration of what is unusual and interesting about the film. In terms of critical legacy, it now inevitably suffers from the understandable comparisons made with Coppola's next film, *Rumble Fish* (shot back to back with *The Outsiders* in Tulsa) because on the one hand they are both Hinton adaptations, and on the other, they are so completely different. *The Outsiders* is not as conventional as it seems when it is compared directly with *Rumble Fish's* dazzling adventure in stylistic experimentation, a European art film in all but name.

✶✶✶✶✶✶✶✶✶✶✶✶✶✶✶✶✶✶✶✶✶✶✶✶✶✶✶✶✶✶✶✶✶✶✶✶✶

While shooting *The Outsiders*, Coppola was encouraged by Matt Dillon to read Hinton's later, more complex book, *Rumble Fish*, written in 1975 when Hinton was twenty-seven. He immediately decided to make it by shooting it back to back with mostly the same crew in the same location (and with Hinton on set as well). This ability to make two such different films so quickly in this way was facilitated by the sophistication of his electronic equipment. Coppola followed the same route regarding finance, getting a completion guarantee from Film

Finances, funds from Chemical Bank but, of course, he again struggled to secure a distribution deal. The budget of $10.5 million for *Rumble Fish* was also similar to its predecessor but Warners was disinclined to support another teen film, thinking it might crowd the market at the expense of *The Outsiders*.[87] They also had other issues with Zoetrope over their involvement in *Hammett*. In June 1982, after the production had marked time for almost six weeks in Tulsa, Coppola obtained a distribution deal from Universal as part of a two-film agreement with Abel Gance's silent epic, *Napoleon* (1927) for which Zoetrope now owned the rights.[88] *Rumble Fish* is the one Coppola 1980s film that has seen its reputation gradually improve over the years. Largely derided for its self-conscious artiness on release, it has since allegedly become a staple of university film courses.[89] The ubiquitous Matt Dillon played Rusty-James, the slightly dim narrator of the novel, with the other central role played by Mickey Rourke as Rusty-James's older brother, only ever known as the Motorcycle Boy.[90] Supporting actors included Dennis Hopper, who plays the boys' alcoholic father, and Diane Lane, returning from *The Outsiders*, as Rusty-James's on-off girlfriend.

As befits a novel that is very different from *The Outsiders*, albeit still with similarly excluded, working-class protagonists, deprived surroundings and lack of parental role models, it is a very different sort of film. It is an even more extreme exercise in self-conscious stylization, one that is in complete contrast to its predecessor: a black-and-white, expressionistic and dystopian view of a city and its inhabitants. The world portrayed in *Rumble Fish* is yet bleaker than *The Outsiders*, a colourless mise-en-scène used as a reflection of both the social environment and the existential angst of the Motorcycle Boy, a character we learn is unable to see colours. *Rumble Fish*'s continuing position as a text worthy of academic study probably derives mostly from its most particular aesthetic palette. Indeed, for Cowie, it has 'more technical experimentation (and more visual imagination) than in any American movie of the decade'.[91] Whereas *The Outsiders* seems to have been consciously constructed to attract a similar adolescent audience to its literary source, *Rumble Fish* is a more adult interpretation of teenage experience, its arthouse stylings not necessarily conducive for mainstream appeal. Whereas influences from Hollywood's past were predominant in the earlier 1980s films, here Coppola turned far more to earlier European cinema for inspiration. The black-and-white imagery, the use of canted angles and the predominance of shadows all recall the German Expressionist films of the 1920s although Thomson and Gray sense other slightly later influences, observing that 'it looks and feels like Welles and Cocteau'.[92] This stylization results in a starker representation of teenage life than in *The Outsiders*. For Molly Lewis, by comparison with Coppola's first Hinton adaptation, it is *Rumble Fish*'s black-and-white photography that 'imbues the film with a sense of pastness (or nostalgia)'.[93] Yet the expressionist leanings of the later film serve as distancing devices, and it is the richly coloured widescreen imagery of *The Outsiders* that carries a far greater nostalgic charge. *Rumble Fish* failed to find much of an audience, making barely $1 million in its first year of release.[94] In stark contrast to *The Outsiders, Rumble Fish* provided Coppola with no relief at all from his financial woes.

1984–1986

By the time Coppola completed his Oklahoma sojourn, his financial situation had become yet more perilous and it all came to an ignominious close when, on 10 February 1984 and less than four years since its purchase, the studio lot was auctioned off to the highest bidder for $12.3 million.[95] Coppola, under pressure to maintain payments to service his debt, now began the first of three films originated by others.

The Cotton Club reunited on paper the team behind *The Godfather*: producer Robert Evans, writer Mario Puzo and Coppola. However, the collaboration was an illusion; by the time the film wrapped, only Coppola still retained an active role. Evans, who had been in charge at Paramount when making the *Godfather* films, was now an independent producer. He had been developing the drama about Harlem's famous jazz club for some years and planned to direct the film himself. By the time Evans contacted Coppola begging him to rewrite Puzo's screenplay for $500,000, pre-production had already been underway for about six months and the whole enterprise was in trouble.[96] Once on board, it was not long before the other producers, and the star Richard Gere, were lobbying for Coppola to take over directing duties. By the time, the film was eventually completed for a conservative estimate of $47 million; it stood little chance of turning a profit.

The entire production from start to finish was a soap opera, involving Machiavellian subplots, the involvement of shady gangster figures and a real-life murder enquiry with (tenuous) links to the production and numerous court hearings.[97] Although Coppola can be absolved of much of the blame for the overspend, once he came on board, he brought his own brand of organized

118   *The Lost Decade*

chaos to the project. Coppola used the production's many issues to finesse a $2.5 million fee, 10 per cent of the adjusted gross and final cut.[98] He dispensed with Puzo's version and enlisted novelist William Kennedy to co-write. They ended up producing something like forty or fifty drafts (so many they lost count).[99] Despite his late arrival, there is much in the film's style that does seem distinctly 'Coppola-esque'. The musical numbers are spectacular and imaginative, the direction is sure-footed, and the film is grounded in a historicized and complex web of racial oppression and violence. However, the film struggles to marry the extravagance of the club scenes with a narrative that the scriptwriters, for all their many drafts, never really managed to work out satisfactorily. Given the troubled nature of its production, it can only be regarded as a compromised enterprise for the errant auteur.[100]

The next for-hire film Coppola directed, *Peggy Sue Got Married*, was his most successful of the decade and the director's involvement in the production was considerably less dramatic, as he came in both on time and under budget.[101] *Peggy Sue* is, however, also the 1980s film in which Coppola seems to have had the least personal investment. Chown contends that 'the point is we are not in auteur territory with *Peggy Sue*, however entertaining the film finally is or whatever similarities it may have to other Coppola films. We cannot categorically ascribe whatever is in a film to its director'.[102] Coppola only came on board as third-choice director (after Jonathan Demme and Penny Marshall), and only after casting and script were complete.[103] When Ray Stark, the veteran producer, approached him in the autumn of 1984 to rescue the troubled production for his usual fee of $2.5 million, Coppola accepted because he needed the money. He remarked in a radio interview in 1987 that *Peggy Sue* 'was not the kind of film I normally would want to do' but that he was due to pay 'millions of dollars' shortly.[104] Waiting for Kathleen Turner, shooting eventually began in late August 1985 and was completed near the end of October, ahead of schedule.[105] As with *The Cotton Club*, there is still evidence that indicates the presence of a dedicated stylist: the film's sense of fantasy is bolstered by moments of surreality that recall his earlier 1980s work. Although any cohesion across Coppola's career is more stylistic than thematic, the exploration of family dynamics is an abiding concern (emphasized even more forcefully in *Tucker*). *Peggy Sue*'s final message about the importance of family values, then, is unsurprising: according to Lee Lourdeaux, he often concludes his films with 'an idealized Italian sense of natural beauty and family unity'.[106] *Peggy Sue* was Coppola's most successful film of the 1980s generating returns of $41 million domestically alone. Tri-Star

Pictures, the company behind *Peggy Sue*, had seen enough that they immediately offered Coppola the opportunity to direct *Gardens of Stone*, based on a novel by Nicholas Proffitt. The subject matter brought the director back to the subject of the Vietnam War and, although bearing no other similarity to *Apocalypse Now*, it seems likely that they chose Coppola for this very reason.

In the break between agreeing to direct *Peggy Sue* and Turner becoming available, Coppola made a brief (and his only) foray into directing for television. In this regard, Coppola was different to Altman and Friedkin who both began in television and returned there in pursuit of work in the 1980s. Coppola was approached by Shelley Duvall in November 1984 to direct *Rip Van Winkle* for her 'Faerie Tale Theater' series on HBO.[107] He was attracted by the opportunity to use videotape (which formed an essential component of his pre-visualization techniques) to experiment with his ideas for the type of 'live' shooting he had originally envisioned for *One from the Heart*. He recruited the Japanese designer, Eiko Ishioka, who had just done some radical work on Paul Schrader's *Mishima* (1985), which Coppola and George Lucas had co-produced, to build a theatrical mise-en-scène that foregrounds surreal imagery and playful means of exposition. *Rip Van Winkle* is an idiosyncratic and charming piece and, as ever with Coppola's more *outré* enterprises, it sharply divides opinion: Goodwin and Wise call it 'Coppola's first unqualified artistic success since *Godfather II*' while Cowie insists that it is 'a prisoner of its artifice, a perfunctory scribble in the margins of Coppola's career'.[108] Coppola's comment, made apparently without irony, that he enjoyed the miniscule budget ($650,000) and tight schedule and that 'the bigger the budget, the less freedom you have', once again reminds us of the irresolvable dilemma of choosing between artistry and ambition that seems to haunt Coppola.[109]

1987–1989

Gardens of Stone is part of a late eighties cycle of Vietnam films but differs from films like *Platoon* and *Casualties of War* because it does not depict the horrors of combat directly. Comparing Coppola's film to the others, William Palmer suggests that '*Gardens of Stone* is the most austere and symbolic in its representation of the nihilism of the Vietnam War'.[110] In fact, rather like Altman's *Streamers*, the film deals with the war in the Far East as an overbearing background presence, a place of dread from which both films' young soldiers are unlikely to return.

120   *The Lost Decade*

Whereas most films about Vietnam (including *Apocalypse Now*) tend to be both anti-militarist *and* anti-war, *Gardens of Stone* is shot through with a respect for the army as an institution while simultaneously rejecting the Vietnam conflict as an unspeakable folly.

Once again, Coppola accepted the job because he needed the money. However, he seems to have also discovered an affinity with the subject matter: he had been fascinated by army ritual since attending military academy as a teenager.[111] As noted earlier, many of Coppola's films revolve around themes of familial loyalty and he related to Gene Phillips that he wanted to portray the army as a quasi-family where its 'members are bound together by a traditional code of honor and by mutual loyalty and affection'.[112] The film tells the story of the Old Guard who perform the ceremonial burials at Arlington National Cemetery and Coppola had to accede to various script changes demanded by the army in return for their permission to film at the genuine locations. Coppola's regular editor, Barry Malkin, recounts that, 'in the end, [the army] relaxed their demands and we were allowed to skip over certain parts of the ceremonies because it took too long … It's a different kind of film in total. It's brooding, purposefully so'.[113] The spectacle of the burial ceremonies is indeed the most striking aspect of *Gardens of Stone* and there is a grace in their ritualistic precision enacted in strikingly beautiful settings. *Gardens of Stone* is a somewhat forgotten and undervalued film, one that was received rather indifferently by critics and performed limply at the box office. If remembered at all, it tends to be because of the tragedy that occurred during its making.

During a break in filming to celebrate Memorial Day, Gio, Coppola's eldest son who had been working with his father since he was sixteen, was killed in a speedboat accident. Coppola carried on filming almost immediately, telling others that 'Gio would have wanted it that way' and principal photography was completed in only eight weeks, and only a mere 7 per cent over budget.[114] Such was the eerie parallel between the tragedy and the film's narrative that Coppola was filming funeral scenes only three weeks after his son's death. For all Gio's tragic death inevitably distorted the film's reception; it is, in any case, a sombre story and is particularly lacking in action for a film about soldiers. Any evidence of a lack of focus from the grief-stricken director can only really be seen in an occasional jarring transition: it would be entirely unsurprising if Coppola's usual close control of the edit was compromised by his personal circumstances. In any case, the film which opened to little fanfare in early 1987 did not do fare well at the box office, making only just over $5 million (against a budget of $13 million).

Francis Coppola 121

Following *Gardens of Stone*, Coppola returned to an idea that had been gestating since at least 1976 when he had acquired the rights to the story of Preston Tucker, an automobile pioneer who, immediately after the Second World War, manufactured a revolutionary car, the 'Tucker Torpedo', but whose radical plans for change were thwarted by the established Detroit manufacturers. When he was a child, Coppola had been excited when his father had put his name down for a Tucker but remembered his subsequent disappointment when the car never materialized and he was told Tucker was a 'crook'.[115] Over the years, the project had mutated: according to Coppola, it was originally conceived as 'a dark kind of piece ... a sort of Brechtian musical in which Tucker would be the main story, but it would also involve Edison and Henry Ford and Firestone and Carnegie'. Leonard Bernstein even agreed to write the score.[116] The project stalled as the Zoetrope debacle unfolded. By the mid-1980s, it occurred to Coppola that his former *compadre*, George Lucas (who, like Coppola, also owned one of the rare Tucker cars) might be interested in collaborating to make Tucker's story. Their relationship had soured over the years, but Lucas admitted he was unable to resist his old friend: 'he has charisma beyond logic'.[117] Lucas agreed to produce the film, the project thus becoming the mirror image of *THX1138* (1971) and *American Graffiti* (1973) with producer and director's roles reversed, and Lucas now the one seemingly more likely to be able to raise the finance.

Tucker: The Man and His Dream

Possibly the most frequently made observation about Coppola's *Tucker* is how closely the eponymous hero's story resembles the director's own. Stéphane Delorme insists that it 'is clearly a self-portrait' and Jill Kearney reported from the film set how the parallels between the two men were being discussed on set by both cast and crew.[118] However, it is also true, as Lewis insists, that the project existed long before many of the biographical similarities had 'taken shape'.[119] Lewis, however, fails to take account of how little we know of the earlier conceptions of the project. Many of the parallels may have only come through in the final version of the story. After all, as with the Brechtian musical concept, earlier iterations of the project may have borne little similarity to the completed film. However conceived, the biographical echoes and the personal resonances are undeniable and make *Tucker* seem, arguably, Coppola's most personal film. He may have long regarded Preston Tucker (Jeff Bridges) as a kindred spirit, an impulsive gambler who was unafraid to reach for his dreams and there are both real-life biographical similarities, as well as others that come through more in the characterization and relationships as enacted on screen; on both levels the similarities pile up. Tucker was an innovator whose ideas anticipated many of the components of car design that are used routinely today. Seatbelts, fuel injection, shatterproof glass and rear motors were first used in the Tucker car. Coppola's ideas for his 'electronic cinema' were certainly not as obviously influential as Tucker's, arguably only because of the advances made in digital technology which rendered his video-based systems redundant. However, in 1988 at least, it might be said that Coppola was, much like Tucker, ahead of his time. As the film tells it, Tucker was thwarted by the might and influence of Detroit's 'Big Three' (Ford, Chrysler and General Motors). They worried that his innovations were sufficiently inventive, as the hostile senator (Lloyd Bridges) says in the film, 'to cost billions to keep up with them'. This seems close to Lewis's assertions about how the Hollywood studios operated to ensure the failure of *One from the Heart*.

Coppola's familiar theme of the importance of familial unity is ever present throughout *Tucker* and there are discernible similarities between the Coppola and Tucker family dynamics. Tucker's eldest son, Junior (Christian Slater), nervously tells his father that he wants to turn down a chance to go to Notre Dame and learn how to build cars instead. Gio, Coppola's son for whom he was still grieving, had said almost exactly the same thing when he told his father he would not go to college but be a filmmaker instead.[120] To this request, Tucker tells his son, 'Sure you can stay with me. I'm gonna depend on you', and hugs him: the scene is moving anyway, even before one considers the personal resonances. A further connection between *Tucker* and Gio is that it was when the latter was washing one of his father's Tuckers that it occurred to Coppola (senior) to revive the project in the first place and the film ends with a dedication to his son 'who loved cars'. The Tucker family is a solid, loving family unit where the others revel in their father's eccentricities. The portrayal of Vera, Tucker's wife (Joan Allen), could even be read as a tribute to Coppola's long-suffering wife, Eleanor. Not only is Vera tolerant of her husband's eccentric, wild decisions and recklessness with money, but she punctuates his vanity as well, as when she chastises him for admiring himself in the mirror. At one point in the film, when Tucker is on the road promoting the car and the board try to cancel most of the innovations, Vera confronts the elderly members to good comic effect. The chairman, Bennington (Dean Goodman), the epitome of stuffiness, tries to fob her off, telling her that she should contact his wife who 'deals with all social arrangements'. It is the way she stands up for herself that resonates as something Eleanor might have done as well.[121] The Tucker family all seem to be involved in some way with the family business and Coppola, too, always involved as many of his family as he could in his films. On *Tucker*, this extended to others' families as well. Susan Landau, co-star Martin's daughter, was the unit publicist, and according to Kearney, 'most of the camera crew seem to be nephews of Vittorio Storaro'. Cynthia Tucker, Preston's granddaughter, also worked on publicity.[122] In fact, the familial harmony of the Tucker family is idealized to an extent that may seem rather *too* perfect for some tastes, but it does add to the sense that the film, as many have observed, is a type of 'Capra-esque' fable.[123]

It is the manner of the film's conclusion with the triumph of the little man against the system, as well as its relentless optimism, epitomized by the effusive Bridges, that makes *Tucker* most resemble a Frank Capra film. The film rarely allows the darker forces bearing down on Preston to have much effect on his sunny demeanour. Nonetheless, as Cowie observes, it does manage largely to avoid Capra's 'whimsy and folksiness'.[124] The film's climax ends in a courtroom with our hero allowed (somewhat implausibly) to make the final statement himself in his own defence.[125] He has been charged with defrauding dealers into investing in a car that did not exist. Like James Stewart in *Mr Smith Goes to Washington* (1939), Tucker makes an impassioned appeal for the ordinary working man and evokes the spirit of the 'American Dream' when he exclaims 'rags to riches ... that's what this country's about'. When he says, 'if Benjamin Franklin was alive, he'd be arrested for flying a kite without a licence', it is not difficult to discern Coppola's own beliefs about Hollywood stifling creativity reflected in Tucker's words. In reality, although Preston was, indeed, found not guilty of fraud, his story is not really about success at all. As with *One from the Heart* and the debate about culpability between Coppola and the studios, it is questionable how much it was Tucker himself and how much it was the Detroit manufacturers that were responsible for the failure of the enterprise.[126] Only fifty cars were ever built and when Tucker arranges for them all to be driven to the courthouse, Coppola provides us with the final showpiece sequence of the film as the cars (mostly the nineteen real Tuckers borrowed for the film) are depicted gliding serenely through the traffic in formation, their iridescent colours gleaming in the sunshine[127] (Figure 4.5). The film ends with a caption that tells us that forty-six of the fifty cars made are still running but that Tucker died six years after the court case. The parallels with Coppola's story fortunately end there but the wayward optimism of Jeff Bridge's portrayal, of a man with

Figure 4.5 Coppola used nineteen of the surviving Tucker cars which are driven to the courthouse at the end of the film.

too many ideas and a reckless disregard for money, makes the comparison with the film director irresistible.

Tucker is an unconventionally stylized film and bears little similarity to a traditional biopic, providing a snapshot, a small segment of a man's life, as well as of post-war American society and the corrosive power of big business. The film begins with a certain panache, the viewer plunged into the late 1940s as the credits play out across a promotional film for the Tucker car that Coppola uses as a means of introducing the protagonist. A narrator helpfully fills in some of the early details of Tucker's life prior to the events of the film. The use of an off-screen voice, who describes the proto-hero as a 'dreamer, inventor, visionary, a man ahead of his time', is accompanied by a flurry of montage in a manner that recalls the style of another 'larger-than-life' director Orson Welles with whom Coppola has frequently been compared. The montage sequences evoke *Citizen Kane* but an astute and more persuasive comparison is made by Cowie about *The Magnificent Ambersons* (1942) when he observes that both films revel 'in the nostalgia for vanished times and the notion of an auto inventor being spurned'.[128] It is a distinctive marker of Coppola in the 1980s that his films offered a self-conscious surfeit of style that is keyed to the subject matter and through which he made frequent allusions to past films and filmmakers. *One from the Heart*, *The Outsiders*, and *Rumble Fish* all share with *Tucker* a theatricality, a sense of experimentation and a denial of a literal realism that aligns Coppola's approach to visual style with that of Welles. As Cowie puts it, both Coppola and Welles 'adhered to the tradition of Méliès, rather than Lumière – the fantasy rather than the realistic, documentary approach'.[129] Today, Coppola continues to bemoan Hollywood's dependency on naturalism wryly observing that 'there are any number of styles one is able to choose in the movie business – as long as it's *realism*'.[130]

The self-conscious theatrical devices that Coppola used liberally in *One from the Heart*, many of which were initiated as part of Coppola's original conception of that film as 'live cinema', are occasionally employed in *Tucker*. Both films foreground this theatrical tone from the beginning: as *One from the Heart* opens with a pair of stage curtains parting, so *Tucker* starts with an advertisement declared as being courtesy of 'the Public Relations Department of the Tucker Corporation'. Three-sided sets built adjacent to each other are used to facilitate long takes that travel across different diegetic locations. In one scene on Preston's promotional tour, he is in black tie at a formal function as he passes a column but when he appears on the other side of it, in a continuous shot, the setting has changed to daytime and Tucker is now in a bright grey lounge suit, maintaining his high-wattage grin as he strides purposefully through the sequence. In another scene, by dollying the camera between two sets, Coppola shows Tucker talking to his wife on the phone with both in the same frame, depicting events taking place hundreds of miles apart. Preston is captured in a medium shot that allows reaction shots of his adviser, Abe (Landau), to be seen, but Coppola privileges Vera's reaction by filming her in profile and in close-up. It is a striking and stylized moment that underscores the pair's instinctive harmony (Figure 4.6).

Figure 4.6 Coppola uses his 'live cinema' techniques to film the Tuckers on either end of a telephone call.

126   *The Lost Decade*

An important link to the visual style of *One from the Heart* comes from both films sharing the same cinematographer, Vittorio Storaro. A key collaborator, who also shot *Apocalypse Now* and Coppola's segment of *New York Stories* (1989), Storaro's approach to distinctive colour patterning is apparent elsewhere in his work including the renowned films he made with Bertolucci (notably *The Conformist* in 1970) and especially in the expressive primary colours of *Dick Tracy* (1990) for Warren Beatty. On *Tucker*, he and Coppola do not go as far as they did on *One from the Heart* with that film's hyperreal expanses of colour-coded symmetry that function to symbolize character. Nevertheless, this expression of meaning by means of colour washes and stylized palettes is employed much more subtly in *Tucker*. When Preston and Abe visit Bennington at his office, everyone is dressed in various shades of brown, matching the wood-panelled offices and leather-bound furniture, giving the setting an atmosphere of quiet affluence but also a serenity, an entitlement that is borne out of indolence and unchallenged power. Earlier when Abe and Preston hatch their plans for the first time, they chat in the semi-darkness and a diffused blue light – the moonlight is very blue – pierces the gloom, an appropriate, almost magical setting for the creation of a magical enterprise. Storaro's attention to colour design is matched with Dean Tavoularis's production design that gives the 1940s fashions and set decoration an effervescence that complements the ever-smiling Tucker's unbridled energy.

Because this examination is about Coppola's authorship and his personal relationship to the content, it is worth concluding on *Tucker* with a brief examination of the nature of Coppola's relationship with Lucas in making the film and how the way it was understood at the time may has distorted a balanced understanding of the film's authorship. Most writers have tended to accept at face value the narrative that Lucas and Coppola themselves promoted about the making of the film. Lucas, although notoriously publicity-shy, spent considerable time alongside Coppola publicizing *Tucker* and there was a consistent theme in their interviews: that Lucas had reined in Coppola's wilder tendencies and that Coppola allowed himself to be led by Lucas towards a more populist approach because the latter had a better sense of what an audience wants.[131] When Coppola declared that Lucas 'wanted to candy-apple it up a bit, make it like a Disney film', Lucas was telling the same interviewer that 'Francis needed someone to hold him back. With *The Godfather*, it was Mario Puzo, with *Tucker* it was me'.[132] The nature of their collaboration was repeatedly promoted like this, but we really have only Lucas and Coppola's word for how their respective influences manifested themselves in the film. Their assertions have been jumped on with alacrity by

Francis Coppola 127

critics and biographers, as they retrospectively uncovered 'evidence' in the film to support the pair's claims. It was remarkably easy to find it superficially but is much harder to substantiate definitively. One point certainly runs contrary to this discourse: Lucas, who provided the initial funds, was unable to secure distribution from several studios before Paramount (after production had begun) agreed to get involved. According to Jill Kearney, Paramount's overriding motivation was because they were courting Coppola to make a third *Godfather* instalment.[133] It reflects the industry's fickle and short-term memory that studios seemed to remember the Lucas who had produced the infamous *Howard the Duck* in 1986 (Willard Huyck), rather than the one who made *Star Wars* and its sequels. Another aspect of *Tucker*, that is often attributed to Lucas's influence, the film coming in on budget, does not take account of how Coppola had managed to do so on all but *The Cotton Club* since *One from the Heart*. In fact, this budget was a generous $25 million, giving Coppola plenty of licence, even though such an amount spent on this type of film was unlikely to yield a profit in the 1980s marketplace. It is not necessarily certain then that Coppola's creative agency was subjugated by Lucas's involvement. It was certainly a personal film, one largely unhindered by studio interference, and it is possible to argue that the expansive director of *The Godfather* and *Apocalypse Now* is a discernible authorial presence in the quite different but equally idiosyncratic stylings of *Tucker: The Man and His Dream*.

****

Immediately following *Tucker*, Coppola contributed a short film, 'Life without Zoe', to the 1989 anthology, *New York Stories*, with the other segments directed by Scorsese ('Life Lessons') and Woody Allen ('Oedipus Wrecks'). Starring and co-written by his daughter, Sofia, it is a slight but charming fable, a gently fantastical children's story in the vein of *The Black Stallion* and *The Escape Artist*. Malkin recalled that something was lost in the edit: 'I think [Coppola] yielded to commercial demands, and I was sorry that a number of things wound up on the floor.'[134] From the set of *New York Stories*, Coppola told Robert Lindsey that not only was he now financially secure because of recent property inflation but that *Tucker* would be his last Hollywood movie as from now on and he would finance his projects himself: 'I'm really quite wealthy and can afford to do what I want.' Asked if his net worth exceeds $20 million, he replied, '[T]hat would be conservative.'[135] Around the same time, he also told Cowie that he would not, under any circumstances, contemplate making a third *Godfather* film for Paramount.[136] Yet, only a few months later, Coppola's grand statements came back to bite him. He was sued for $3 million by Jack Singer, who had loaned him this sum to help finance *One from the Heart*.[137] His wealth was tied up in his five homes and his vineyards, so he was obliged once again to accept Hollywood's dollar and earn a fortune making *Godfather Part III* (released in 1990).[138] It was not until 1997 and *The Rainmaker* that Coppola did bid farewell to Hollywood. After a ten-year hiatus, his long-standing desire to make inexpensive films in his own way was finally realized in the first decade of the new century when he returned with three idiosyncratic, inexpensive, somewhat uncommercial and rather brilliant films that were released to little fanfare: *Youth without Youth* (2007), *Tetro* (2009) and *Twixt* (2011).[139]

The ability of Francis Coppola to keep working in the 1980s, while still remaining largely within the Hollywood system, seems to indicate that the industry still saw some occasional value in his ability to attract publicity, a commercial auteur who retained some degree of marketability and might even provide a modest hit like *Peggy Sue*. Their nervousness and reluctance to support him most of the time were occasionally set aside because he seemed the best available option at the time. In some ways, the studios' behaviour towards Coppola seems as conflicted as his own ongoing personal battles between artistry and power. This tension between ego and aesthetics continually haunted his decision-making. What has become apparent from this discussion is that it not sufficient to characterize the 1980s Coppola as, in Stephen Prince's words, 'a journeyman director for hire, compelled to craft less audacious works'.[140] Not only that, but Coppola's use of new technologies was at the time genuinely innovative: the benefits resulting from his exploitation of the latest advancements in electronics foreshadowed many of the advantages that the rapid development of digital cinema made commonplace. In terms of his overall career, the 1980s stand as significant because, despite all the external pressures that disturbed his authorial voice, he still used the decade to experiment and develop his style. These ten years of filmmaking provide us with an opportunity to learn how such a director was able to function in Hollywood in the 1980s, what were the limits imposed on him by the system, but also how and what he somehow managed to force Hollywood to allow him to produce on his own terms.

5

William Friedkin: Ambiguity and anti-heroes

William Friedkin's career has been largely defined by the fame and influence of two films, *The French Connection* and *The Exorcist*, which he made consecutively in 1971 and 1973. In a 1995 article that pointedly asked 'Whatever Happened to William Friedkin?', Larry Gross observed that 'it's tough now even to grasp how completely Friedkin's two early successes helped create the idiom of serious/popular Hollywood filmmaking over the last twenty-five years'.[1] His work has never again reached anything like this level of importance and, like Coppola, Altman and Cimino among others, his reputation and subsequent ability to get films made in Hollywood were seriously undermined by a single catastrophic failure. *Sorcerer*, a remake of Henri Clouzot's *The Wages of Fear* (1953) made in 1977, preceded both *Apocalypse Now* and *Heaven's Gate*, and the difficulty of marketing Renaissance-style filmmaking in the late 1970s was brought into sharp relief when *Sorcerer* was released within a week of the first *Star Wars* film. Moving forward into the 1980s, Friedkin's filmography seems to indicate that he found it more difficult than either Coppola or Altman to keep working because he directed only four films for the cinema in the decade. In addition, he did also direct two feature-length television films, an episode in a television series, and was involved in a handful of prestige music videos. In any case, Friedkin was never as prolific as Altman and Coppola, and his output in the 1980s is broadly comparable with the amount of work he completed in other decades (in the 1970s, for example, he only directed five feature films[2]). It was the type of work available to him that was different for Friedkin in the 1980s as he contended with reduced choices, limited budgets and a lack of box-office success. Friedkin observed in 1982 that 'a filmmaker who wants to do other than just entertain in some very superficial way has got a lot of problems today. He's got to disguise his themes'.[3] Such a notion relates directly to contemporary audiences' preferences in the 1980s for simple narratives and unambiguous heroism.

Many Renaissance filmmakers suffered in the post-Renaissance period because of a breakdown in their relationships with decision-makers at the major studios. Those who remained steadfast (and often obstreperous) about being allowed to work without interference were no longer tolerated by the profit-focused conglomerates. When Walon Green said, about the studio executives, that 'they hated Billy ... really hated him. They were thrilled when he started bombing'[4], he was only echoing the director's own observation that 'I burned a lot of bridges ... Those people I snubbed on the elevator going up, were the ones I met going down. There was a lot of resistance to my doing films at some of these studios'.[5] Friedkin's problems with the majors were further exacerbated by a determination, like Altman, to work (if possible) on projects that he had generated himself. Friedkin's solution to the problem, however, was neither as practical nor as drastic as Altman's exile and willingness to work with micro-budgets. He remained in Los Angeles and strove to carry on working much in the manner of his career to that point. Like Altman though – and, to a lesser extent, Coppola as well – he turned to the burgeoning independent sector to enable him to make films on his own terms. Of course, this meant that he had to manage with more limited financial resources. At the same time, he did still, to some degree at least, have to repair relationships with the majors in order to secure distribution. In the 1980s, as Friedkin discovered himself, when the collapse of the Dino De Laurentiis Group scuppered *Rampage* in 1987, independent film production and distribution was an inherently risky business.

Friedkin's creative agency was, arguably, at its greatest in the 1980s because in three of the four films, he wrote the scripts himself (and without collaborators).[6] This period was the only time in his career where Friedkin took any screenwriting credit although this is not to say that he was not closely involved in the screenwriting process on other films, it being notoriously difficult for a director to be given any writing credit from the Screenwriters Guild. Justin Wyatt directly connects Friedkin's lack of commercial success in the 1980s to his scriptwriting when he argued that his poor box office was 'in part due to the narrative ambiguity of films such as *Cruising* and *To Live and Die in L.A.* which both carry the high concept style without the linear, recuperable genre narratives'.[7]

I will be paying some attention to this narrative ambiguity because it is a manifestation of an unwillingness to conform to expected norms while still operating in familiar Hollywood genres. For example, *Rampage* manages to blend a serial-killer horror narrative with a courtroom drama, while bearing almost no resemblance to any other slasher film or legal thriller ever made. It is this difficult engagement with conventionality that makes Friedkin's 1980s work both interesting *and* seemingly uncommercial. He seems psychologically disinclined to conform because of what Gerald Petievich (the novelist of *To Live and Die in L.A.*) called 'his self-destructive bent ... where he is almost pathologically incapable of offering an uplifting ending ... Billy loads his films with a really dark side of human nature'.[8] This chapter discusses these films as expressions of Friedkin's particular approach to thematic content and visual style, as well as how he developed both subject matter and form that is reflective of the era in which they were made and of the director's personal beliefs at the time. Some of the more persistent attributes can be discerned throughout his career such as the morally compromised protagonists who frequently seem to challenge audiences to try to identify with them in spite of – not because of – their behaviour. These exclusively male anti-heroes (unfortunately Friedkin, like so many of his peers, tends to relegate women to supporting roles) all feature in present-day settings as Friedkin, who started out in documentaries, explores contemporary issues with a cynical eye, in contrast with Coppola (and to a lesser extent, Altman) whose work tended more to the fantastic or historical. At the same time, I also use mostly untapped sources to offer a fresh perspective, using Friedkin's papers lodged with the Academy's Margaret Herrick Library in Los Angeles, to contextualize the circumstances of production within 1980s Hollywood filmmaking. They allow a deeper understanding of Friedkin's thought processes as he underwent the writing of different drafts of his screenplays.

1980–1982

After *Sorcerer*'s commercial and critical failure, a dejected Friedkin accepted a 'for-hire' assignment in 1978 to direct *The Brink's Job*, a relatively conventional comedy about a famous real-life heist. Although the film only performed moderately, according to Nat Segaloff, it helped to re-establish Friedkin's reputation for bringing in a project on budget and on time, so that 'as usual, he had his choice' of new projects, indicating that the reputational fallout from *Sorcerer* was relatively limited.[9] One indicator of this relative freedom was that, between *The Brink's Job* and *Cruising*, he turned down the opportunity to direct an adaptation of William Peter Blatty's *Exorcist* sequel, *Legion*.[10] It was not until a few years later, following the release of the highly controversial and

132   *The Lost Decade*

divisive *Cruising*, along with the studios' accelerated withdrawal from auteur filmmaking after *Heaven's Gate*, that Friedkin found his options becoming significantly reduced.

For a while, Friedkin had been considering making his first foray into theatre. An odd coincidence in terms of this book, in late 1977 Friedkin preceded Altman's interest in David Rabe's play, *Streamers,* when he agreed to direct it at the Westwood Playhouse in Los Angeles. Nothing came of it, but he went on to work with Rabe developing Thomas Thompson's true-crime book, *Blood and Money*, either as a stage production or as a possible mini-series for CBS.[11] The seeds of what would become his next project were sown on a trip to Houston to research *Blood and Money.* On the flight, Friedkin was captivated by the stories told to him by Randy Jurgensen, a former policeman who had advised him on *The French Connection*, about his experiences working undercover in New York's gay leather clubs.[12]

Cruising

Some years previously, Friedkin had been approached by *French Connection* producer, Philip D'Antoni, about making a film from Gerald Walker's 1970 novel, *Cruising*. The somewhat unpalatable story, inspired by a series of unsolved murders in 1969, was about a policeman who becomes a murderer himself when overwhelmed by his own homosexual urges after going undercover in New York's affluent gay community to investigate a serial killer. Friedkin has said, 'I didn't think much of it … I wasn't compelled to make it into a film at that time.'[13] D'Antoni then managed to get Steven Spielberg interested but this came to nothing, so he sold the property to Jerry Weintraub (who had produced Altman's *Nashville*). In 1979, Weintraub returned to Friedkin again who now had some fresh ideas about how he could combine the novel with the stories Jurgensen had told him. Jurgensen had gone undercover in the 1960s to investigate uniformed men, possibly police officers, who were blackmailing, and in all probability murdering, homosexuals.[14] Friedkin had also just read a January 1979 piece by Arthur Bell in *Village Voice*, 'Another Murder at the Anvil', which described two murders in four months at a gay club in New York's meat-packing district.[15] Yet another factor was the rumours circulating about mysterious deaths in the gay community that turned out to be the beginning of the AIDS epidemic.[16] He reversed his earlier decision because he could now see how he could transpose Walker's novel to the underground leather scene, as depicted in both Jurgensen and Bell's accounts.[17] Warners were interested but dropped out when Al Pacino was cast, put off by his $2 million fee. Weintraub now secured backing from Lorimar, an independent company known more for television production (including *Dallas* and *The Waltons*) who were in the process of trying to make inroads into feature film production (also backing Hal Ashby, as discussed in Chapter 2).[18] Pacino and Friedkin seem to have worked well together up until the former saw the completed film. Pacino was incensed because he said he would have played the role differently if he had known that Friedkin would implicate his character as a possible murderer.[19] In subsequent years, Pacino would effectively erase the film from his career and Friedkin seemed to be getting his own back when he said, 'I feel, in retrospect, that the addition of Pacino meant nothing … He was too old for the part.'[20] Both views are, of course, highly partial and a more objective assessment might be that Pacino was eminently suitable for a role that matches the intensity of his similarly obsessive character in *Serpico* (Lumet, 1974).

Cruising is a disturbing story of violent murder among a gay subculture based around leather and sado-masochism, practised in specialist clubs and the dark corners of Central Park in New York. According to Mark Kermode, the film 'broke all the existing taboos of mainstream cinematic sex with its frank, tactile portrait of an exotic, erotic underworld.'[21] To understand this scene's febrile atmosphere, Friedkin carried out extensive research and even went 'cruising' himself. He observed of his experiences: 'I wasn't bothered that much … I was just another fat Jew in a jockstrap.'[22] His Bacchanalian depiction of this life was always likely to be controversial, but the filmmakers never could have anticipated the extraordinary level of opprobrium that the film attracted. Nevertheless, its extremely frank depiction of the highly sexualized scene seems a deliberate act of provocation. While Friedkin has, on occasion, expressed incredulity at the controversies the film generated, he still admitted to Linda Ruth Williams that *Cruising*'s graphic depiction of sado-masochistic practices was calculated to 'get away with stuff most people weren't getting way with – I wanted to see how far I could push the envelope'[23] (Figure 5.1).

Cruising's portrayal of one small section of homosexual society as an environment that fosters murderers attracted a range of objections from homophobes and homosexuals alike but, of course, for very different reasons. It achieved notoriety even before principal photography was complete when protests dogged the filming on the New York streets. Reports of demonstrators filled the pages of broadsheet newspapers for days on end on both sides of the

Figure 5.1 Friedkin's depiction of sado-masochistic practices in the leather clubs was deliberately provocative.

continent.[24] It seems that the protests did have some impact on the film itself: a few lines were clearly intended to mitigate any impression that the subculture depicted is representative of gay society. The detective in charge, Edelson (Paul Sorvino), tells Pacino's character, Steve Burns, when sending him undercover, that both victims 'were not in the mainstream of gay life. They were into heavy leather, S & M. It's a whole different way of life'. A more obvious attempt to appease protesters was to begin with an ill-advised disclaimer (subsequently removed from videos and DVD versions): 'The film is not intended as an indictment of the homosexual world. It is set in one small segment of that world, which is not meant to be representative of the whole.' Once completed, the film managed to still appear regularly in the press because of a very public, protracted row after the film's initial run between Weintraub and Friedkin on one side and the censors on the other. On 4 January 1980, just before its release date and after protracted negotiations, the film had been given an R-rating ('under-17s must be accompanied by an adult').[25] The film's extremely frank depiction of graphically sexual acts in the club scenes was pushing against the limits of acceptability of that time and a number of theatre chains objected to the film's lenient rating, either refusing to show the film at all or explaining to their customers that it contained X-rated content. These included the country's largest chain, General Cinema Corp (GCC), who refused to show *Cruising* because their policy was to never show X-rated films.[26] The objections of a group as powerful as GCC may

William Friedkin

135

have prompted the row, largely conducted in the press, between Richard Heffner, the Chairman of the Classification and Ratings Administration (CARA), and Friedkin and Weintraub. Heffner claimed that the print of *Cruising* in cinemas was not the same as the one which had been rated, arguing that the required cuts had not been made.[27] Friedkin and Weintraub went on the offensive after Heffner implied, in a piece by Dale Pollock in the *Los Angeles Times* on 4 May, that they had 'mislead [*sic*] the board'.[28] On 17 June, they took to the press directly publishing a statement that concluded:

> Members of the MPAA have charged that we agreed to make certain changes in *Cruising* … to obtain an 'R' rating, and then did not make the changes. This is false … we did not release a different version (other than to delete scenes) than the one that was submitted for rating.[29]

Eventually, Friedkin made the minor cuts that Heffner demanded for subsequent releases with about two minutes being excised at a cost of about $200,000.[30] But, for all the public debate, Stephen Prince's assessment that the board's reaction was cursory and that the changes 'were cosmetic rather than substantive' seems accurate. He is also the only one to suggest a causal link between the reactions from major exhibitors and the censors' belated response.[31]

Feelings ran high about the film and Arthur Bell, whose work had provided one of the inspirations for the story in the first place, regularly attacked the film in his 'Bell Tolls' column in *Village Voice*. Vito Russo in his 1981 survey of homosexuality in cinema was equally disdainful of *Cruising*'s representation of gay life, arguing that 'the audience is left with a message that [Pacino] is not only contagious but inescapably brutal'.[32] This wave of negativity dominated the film's public discourse at the time, but this obscures how more balanced views were also expressed. The February 1980 issue of gay magazine, *Mandate*, pointed out that the 1,600 gay extras in the film was a significantly larger number than those who had protested about its making.[33] The palpable enjoyment of these extras on-screen is reflected by a number of grateful letters to Friedkin from those who worked on the film: one particularly effusive example praised the way the film represented 'freedom of artistic expression'.[34] Support for the film also came, in the face of all the protests, from the New York authorities including Mayor Koch, who Friedkin wrote to personally to thank him 'for the support … [that was] not necessarily the most politically expedient'.[35]

Reviews were almost unanimously negative, frequently tending towards to the hostile. For example, Vincent Canby called it 'exceptionally unpleasant, not necessarily because of the subject matter but because it makes no attempt to comprehend it'.[36] The tone of the reviews was so extreme that a college professor, George Grella, who doubled as a film critic for his local paper, was prompted to send Friedkin his extremely positive review in which he concluded that *Cruising* 'constructs some of the harshest, subtlest, and most complex metaphors for our life and time that I have ever seen'.[37] Grella told the director that 'I wanted you to see that at least *someone* reviewed *Cruising* as a movie instead of as some sort of perverse ideological statement'.[38] Friedkin took the trouble to write back, telling Grella that 'I'm grateful to you for going against the grain'.[39] The virulent nature of the film's reception is aptly illustrated by its nominations for Worst Film, Worst Director and Worst Screenplay at the first ever Golden Raspberry Awards.[40] Largely unavailable for years, it was only in 1998 with a brief re-release in cinemas, and in 2007 with a DVD version, that the film began to enjoy something of a critical rehabilitation.[41] In recent years, the film has attracted positive academic attention, examining *Cruising*'s sexual politics with twenty-first-century sensibilities, as well from other perspectives such as Gary Needham's historical analysis of United Artists' involvement in the film and R. Barton Palmer's argument for the film's rehabilitation from its 'bad film' reputation (although one might now question his overall premise given the positive attention afforded to the film in the intervening period).[42] Of course, societal attitudes towards homosexuality have changed immeasurably in the last twenty-five years and this has contributed to this re-appraisal. According to Paul Burston, 'the film is now part of queer film history and a testament to how a frightened Hollywood treated a disenfranchised minority ... reactions to *Cruising* say as much about the time when they were written as about the film itself'.[43] Although this aspect of the film, and how it was received, plays an important part in understanding *Cruising* in its historical context, the film is much more than a *cause célèbre* because its complexities make it an especially interesting example of Friedkin's particular authorship. With the partial exception of Bill Krohn (see below), I diverge from other analyses of the film in using the various draft scripts lodged in the archives to explore this aspect of *Cruising*.

Of all the contemporaneous responses, the most learned came from Robin Wood. In 'The Incoherent Text: Narrative in the 70s', a 1980 article for *Movie* (reprinted in his 1986 book), he avowed 'to do some justice to *Cruising* ... it has received none so far'.[44] Wood finds *Cruising*'s 'interest lies partly in [its] incoherence' but also credits Friedkin with 'a certain level of distinction' because he 'exhibit[s] a large degree of involvement'.[45] Wood's deconstruction of the film's incoherence is one way of beginning to make sense of *Cruising*'s many ambiguities and confusing narrative progression. Both Bill Krohn and Adrian Martin have followed Wood's example by focusing on incoherence with much of the recent work on the film also offering some analysis of this aspect of the film.[46] Martin aligns Friedkin through *Cruising* with other directors such as Oliver Stone and Ken Russell whose work can be placed 'within a certain *cinema of hysteria*' which Martin explains as 'a mode of filmmaking that actively cultivates incoherence'. For Martin, not only is *Cruising* 'a masterpiece of '80s cinema' but it takes 'Friedkin's style to the furthest reaches of disorientation and ambiguity'.[47] Krohn builds on Wood's analysis but goes further by reaching for a definitive explanation to make sense of the film's many inconsistencies. Whereas Wood seems happy to accept the incoherence as intentional but not necessarily explicable, Krohn insists that 'ultimately, only a supernatural interpretation … can resolve those contradictions'.[48] Although this does (sort of) make credible that which seems impossible, this is certainly outside of the author's intention. Friedkin has said himself that 'all the films I've made are enormously ambiguous … I make a film to explore something, and in the course of that exploration, my attitudes get formed'.[49] The development of what would eventually become the completed film, through various drafts of the script and the director's impulsive, contradictory divergences once on set is such that Friedkin's 'exploration' became progressively more uncertain and puzzling.

The basic premise of *Cruising* is of a policeman going undercover into an alien environment to catch a serial killer. Before this occurs, the film begins with an arm being pulled from the Hudson River, which is revealed, promptly, as one of a series of unsolved so-called torso murders. Only the police lieutenant, Edelson, makes any connection between the discovery of body parts and the killings linked to the leather scene that provides the film's main plotline. It is one of a number of ways that *Cruising* fails to match generic expectations as, by the end, no further evidence is offered to gather these two killing sprees together. When Friedkin chooses to make the very last shot of the film match up to the first, with a trawler once again making serene progress along the river, there is a sense that any minute, the trawler might find another body part because the city's effluence, a symbol of a degenerate society, will inevitably rise to the surface. The film moves swiftly onto the first murder when the victim is picked up in one of the leather bars and is taken back to a hotel and murdered by a man in sunglasses who speaks in a distinctive deep voice. At this point, Edelson calls

138   *The Lost Decade*

in Pacino's Burns to go undercover into the gay scene. Burns is told that this is the second such murder and that he has been chosen because he bears a resemblance to both victims. Another murder, apparently committed by the same person, is then depicted. By the time we get to the end, after Burns has traced and caught the supposed killer, Stuart Richards (Richard Cox), the solution of these murders has ostensibly been solved, Stuart's fingerprints supposedly found on the knife that killed one of the victims. But this pleasing solution, one that would conform to convention where the detective always catches the killer, is undermined by yet one more murder. The film ends with the putative hero apparently achieving his goal and returning in triumph to his girlfriend, Nancy (Karen Allen) – yet many questions remain, not least of which is, has Burns become a killer himself?

Cruising then is far from an easily digestible genre piece and Friedkin adopts a series of unsettling strategies that undermine any notion that the film can be easily explained or understood. In the various drafts of the screenplay written before filming, the killer's identity is clear, unambiguously identified in murder scenes as Stuart.[50] By the time, Friedkin had completed principal photography, the script (as shot) now describes both murders seen on screen as being committed by 'The Killer'.[51] The first point of confusion in the film comes with the actors playing the roles. Richard Cox, as Stuart, appears a couple of times in the first half but appears to be more an observer than participant until his identity is revealed later. However, in both cases, the murderers, faces hidden behind dark glasses, are clearly *not* played by Cox. Even more confusingly, the second victim, Eric, appears to be played by the actor who committed the first murder (Larry Atlas). The whole identity issue is deliberately disorienting. Whereas thrillers often confuse and provide more questions than answers as they proceed, conventionally all will be satisfactorily resolved by the end but in *Cruising*, the situation becomes progressively more confusing. Once Stuart is in custody, although he denies murdering anyone, another violent death, of Burns' neighbour when he was undercover, Ted Bailey (Don Scardino), further muddies the water. One suspect is Ted's roommate, Gregory (James Remar), who is extremely jealous but there is also a suggestion that the killer might be Burns. The viewer is keyed to this possibility by his violent reactions when confronted by Gregory but particularly by Edelson's reaction when he learns the victim is Burns's neighbour. Cutting straight from this scene, Friedkin completes the pattern of confusion by inserting a single unscripted shot, a repeat of one from near the beginning which apparently showed the killer on the way to pick up his victim. A man in the full leather uniform and sunglasses (probably played by Larry Atlas) crosses a deserted street and enters the club where the first victim is picked up.

The killer/killers may look different, but he/they always sound(s) the same and the voice seems to provide irrefutable evidence of Stuart's guilt. The final versions of the script identify this as the 'Voice of Jack' (Stuart's father's name is Jack) and Friedkin endorses one with a hand-written remark that 'killer's voice to be the voice of the father throughout'.[52] This distinctive voice seems to definitively link the two murders depicted and, when we learn that this is the voice of Stuart's dead father, surely he must be the killer. Yet even here, while unnoticed by most commentators, it is worth noting that the 'Voice of Jack' is *not* provided by the actor playing the father (Leland Starnes) but by another actor (James Sutorius). Maybe, this was simply a practical solution regarding actor availability; on the other hand, in a film in which Adrian Martin estimates that 80 per cent of the voices are post-synchronized, Friedkin may have chosen to offer yet another layer of ambiguity or confusion in post-production.[53] One scene seems to make the father's role apparent: Stuart meets him in the park and appears to be receiving his instructions to carry out the murders, with his father telling him, 'you know what you have to do'. Stuart's father sounds like the murderer and the screenplay notes that 'his most striking feature to us is his voice'.[54] As Stuart talks to his father, Friedkin chooses to intercut point-of-view shots of the murders happening, as if Stuart is recalling his actions. The message seems clear: that he is motivated by unresolved father issues to become a murderer. When Burns breaks into Stuart's flat, he finds dozens of unopened letters to his father whom we later learn has been dead for ten years. In the second draft, Friedkin inserted Stuart's father into the story for the first time but at this stage, he was alive. In this version, Stuart is unable to perform in a sexual encounter with an older woman (Barbara) followed by a scene in his father's office where it becomes clear Barbara is his father's mistress.[55] Stuart is trying to exact revenge, but his sexual failure implies he is in denial about his homosexuality, his feelings confused by his dysfunctional relationship with a controlling father. But in a revised fourth draft of the script, Friedkin moves the encounter to the park, excises Barbara and makes the father a fantasy.[56] As he developed the story, Friedkin made the narrative yet more oblique during both the shooting and editing of the film. The switching of identity, the different actors, the Ted Bailey murder at the end and the way that all the victims and killers seem to resemble each other seem to suggest that Stuart is not the murderer at all and, in fact, seems to indicate the presence of *at least* two killers. The perplexing repeat shot of the putative killer crossing the street certainly indicates that the murders will continue.

As will also be seen in *To Live and Die in L.A.*, the changes Friedkin made on set (to his own scripts and original conception), that confuse and confound, appear to reflect the director's inclination to sabotage his own work's commercial appeal in favour of a more auteurist tendency to give audiences the opportunity to interpret the material in different ways. In *Cruising*, while various explanations have been proffered in various forms, there is rather too much inconsistency to be able to make complete sense of its progressively confusing aspects. Friedkin's oft-repeated preference to avoid easily digestible solutions may offer some explanation, not least for the film's enigmatic ending. The final scene is in Burns and Nancy's apartment. Burns tells her the job is finished and he is back for good before going to shave off his disguise in the bathroom. Meanwhile, she finds his leather gear and tries on the cap and sunglasses for herself, yet another simulacrum of the killer's image. The last shot (before the trawler on the river) is of Burns staring at himself in the mirror nonchalantly before his gaze moves to the left and he appears to see something in the mirror (Figure 5.2). Presumably this is Nancy in her new attire and his closing expression is perplexing, unreadable, leaving the audience to speculate what he is thinking. Wood and Krohn each offer an alternative reading. Krohn's is all about what Burns sees in the mirror: 'it could be his own image as a bisexual man, or as The Killer, or it could be an image

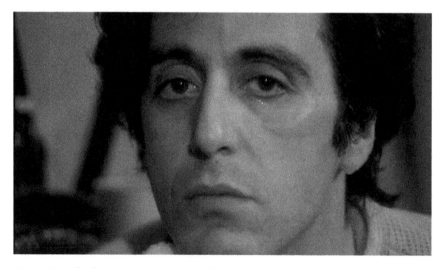

Figure 5.2 The final ambiguous shot of Pacino looking in the mirror has invited a range of interpretations.

signifying that his relationship with Nancy has been irrevocably contaminated with the S&M games he has been playing.[57] Wood's analysis is more apocalyptic: 'Burns, now irredeemably disturbed, is about to murder Nancy when he sees her dressed in leather, *her* body will be found in the river. Or less specifically ... while the culture continues as it is, the patterns of violence will continue, spreading everywhere.'[58] Stephen Choe has a third explanation: 'the final shot [of Pacino] also places the viewer in the position of being his next possible victim.'[59] All of these readings have some merit, and the presence of such diverse views indicates the elusiveness of the scene's meaning. Friedkin's impulses towards the ambiguous seem an attempt to achieve the type of complexity that characterizes the type of cinema he most admires, from directors such as 'Fellini, Godard, Truffaut, Kurosawa, H. G. Cluzot [*sic*], especially'.[60] He has also often discussed the influence of the 'unpredictable' work of Antonioni and one of the striking features of much of the Italian auteur's work is his penchant for enigmatic, unknowable endings.[61] *Cruising*'s final scene, with a glance that seems freighted with meaning, but which cannot be easily explained, or even understood, recalls the way Antonioni concludes his most famous film, *L'Avventura* (1960): in both films, the question of what will transpire in the respective lovers' relationships is left to the viewers' imagination. In mainstream Hollywood in 1980, such a lack of resolution was now anathema, unlike earlier in the previous decade where the influence of European art cinema, and its fondness for equivocal conclusions, had been more welcome.

There are different accounts of *Cruising*'s final cost: Alexander Wilson claims that the film came in 60 per cent over budget but a more reliable source is Dale Pollack's contemporaneous report in *Variety* that the film came in on budget at $7 million and, despite the disruption caused by the protests, the New York principal photography was completed on time in forty days.[62] Stimulated by a strong opening presumably resultant of the swirling controversy, the film actually ended up performing moderately well, earning just under $20 million domestically. Ercolani and Stiglegger consider this return a 'flop', but this seems unjustified given the film's budget and the unrelenting negativity of its critical reception.[63] Its returns certainly look favourable when compared with the less than $4 million realized by the notoriously expensive *Heaven's Gate* in the same year. *Cruising*'s long-term chances were not helped by its persistent morbidity that went against the grain of Hollywood cinema at this time as well as the swirl of unwelcome publicity it attracted – how difficult it was to understand also undoubtedly played its part. As the new decade dawned, *Cruising* indicates that the Renaissance auteurs were still (with difficulty) able to impose their particular artistic sensibilities on their work but now had to rely on the independent sector for their seed money. Distribution from the major studios continued to be available but as Coppola's experiences also showed, it was not granted on the basis of the commercial auteur's allure alone. In the case of *Cruising*, the money followed the star not the director: once Pacino was on board, the film became much more marketable. Friedkin's final downbeat summation of *Cruising* in his own book has considerable resonance with one of this book's central themes that Renaissance directors, in the 1980s, were pushing back against the prevailing tide:

> My timing was off. It was the beginning of the Reagan era, a feel-good period. The ambiguous films I revered and the ones I made were passing out of vogue. It happened quickly ... Audiences wanted reassurance and superheroes, not ambiguity. *Cruising* was another defeat, on a par with *Sorcerer*.[64]

****

The relative failure of *Cruising* was put into perspective when, on 6 March 1981, Friedkin suffered a serious heart attack. Remarkably, he was back in work by June when he accepted a chance to finally make his debut directing for the theatre. Seemingly rejuvenated by the novelty, he told the *New York Times* that 'I feel excited as though I was just starting out'.[65] The play was Tom Kempinski's *Duet for One* with Anne Bancroft and Max von Sydow, which opened at the Royale Theatre on Broadway in December 1981 but closed after only twenty performances and twelve previews.[66] In the summer of 1982, Friedkin signed up to direct *Deal of the Century* with a script by Paul Brickman, who had just written and directed *Risky Business*. It was deemed a 'hot' property with Hollywood insiders apparently deeming it 'the funniest and most erudite screenplay anyone had read since Preston Sturges'.[67] A comedy that satirizes the arms trade was a complete change of pace for Friedkin after the dark and downbeat *Cruising*; he might also have considered it a relatively calm way to return to the stressful business of directing a feature film following his heart attack.

1983–1985

Deal of the Century, eventually released in November 1983, was Friedkin's only studio production in the decade and the only time he did not write the screenplay. It is a bit puzzling that Warners chose Friedkin for such a project, given his previous relatively uninspired track record on comedies with *The Night They Raided Minsky's* (1968) and *The Brink's Job*. In any case, it was a sign of the reduction in creative control for directors when Friedkin's autonomy was quickly undermined by Warners insisting on their under-contract actor, Chevy Chase, for the main role. Jack Nicholson had been mooted to play the role and the original idea was a black comedy in the vein of Kubrick's *Dr Strangelove* (1964), but the casting of Chase meant that such a tone clashed with his trademark 'madcap' style.[68] Friedkin's hopes to achieve his customary authenticity were undermined when the loan of aircraft failed to materialize.[69] An internal memo reveals that the production had proceeded under a false impression because of 'a misquote about approval by Department of Defence and Department of Navy. Neither did in fact'.[70] In the end, neither Chase nor his co-stars Sigourney Weaver and Gregory Hines could rescue a film that is an uneasy mix of satire and the broadest of broad humour. Its domestic box office of just over $10 million was underwhelming for a big-budget, star-led studio picture, and its release was largely restricted to North America. No one seems to have had anything good to say about *Deal of the Century*. Brickman complained that 'Friedkin didn't make the movie I wrote' and Chase called it 'a piece of shit'.[71] Friedkin himself told Segaloff that 'at a certain point, I realised how sick the whole arms business was and it no longer seemed funny to me'.[72] Such is his apparent disregard for the film, he ignores it completely in his autobiography.

After *Deal of the Century*, Friedkin became involved in what was a burgeoning art form, the pop music video, when he directed a film to promote Laura Brannigan's 'Self Control'. Friedkin proudly described it as being 'like an X-rated video … it was censored all over the world'.[73] The filmmaker then made a return to the small screen following an approach from Philip DeGuere, who was resuscitating *The Twilight Zone*, the series created by Rod Serling about the supernatural from the late 1950s and early 1960s. Friedkin had started his career in television and at this time, it was considered a rite of passage – and a one-way street – for directors to progress from television to the cinema. It was a sign of the times, therefore, when Friedkin joined Altman (and on one occasion, Coppola) in seeking employment in television. Friedkin chose 'Nightcrawlers' from the available options, a story that is more horror than science fiction. The affecting twenty-minute episode tells the story of a guilt-ridden Vietnam veteran whose nightmares about his experiences come to life, resulting in a neighbourhood diner being attacked by troops conjured up from the soldier's imagination. DeGuere valued the prestige of having secured the participation of Friedkin and allowed him greater freedom than his other directors: Friedkin boasted that

144   *The Lost Decade*

the head of network television's Standards and Practices was impressed enough to give the go-ahead to 'the most intense television he'd ever seen'.[74] Another assignment accepted by Friedkin was a video for Barbra Streisand's version of *West Side Story*'s 'Somewhere' for her 1985 *Broadway Album*. The co-producer of the video, Cindy Chvatal, recalled how the pair, both famously controlling and stubborn, surprisingly indulged in 'a charm contest' when they met to decide how the film would be made.[75]

Sometime in 1984, Friedkin was sent the galleys for a new novel, *To Live and Die in L.A.*, that fictionalized the experiences of its author, Gerald Petievich, who had worked for the US Secret Service, a division of federal law enforcement charged at the time with the incongruous dual duties of providing security for the nation's leaders (including the President) and ensuring the integrity of financial systems.[76] This included the investigation of the trade in counterfeit currency that formed the novel's main plotline. Friedkin was particularly interested in 'the kind of surrealistic life of a Secret Service agent, about which almost nothing is really known'.[77] This quest for fiction grounded in real-life experience, as his earlier exploits in New York's leather bars attested, is a thread that runs through most of Friedkin's work and can be traced back to his background in documentaries. On this occasion, the thoroughness of his research was enough to worry the actual Secret Service, who insisted on interviewing everybody involved with the film and unsuccessfully demanded to pre-screen the film.[78]

To Live and Die in L.A.

When Friedkin was approached in July 1984 by Irving H. Levin, who had previously distributed *The Boys in the Band*, about making a film for his new enterprise, SLM Productions, he chose *To Live and Die*.[79] The recently formed company comprising Levin, Sam Schulman and Angelo Marquetti, had secured a ten-picture distribution deal with 20th Century Fox worth some $100 million. However, when Fox was bought by Rupert Murdoch, SLM took against the newly installed executives and took the deal to MGM. Initial budgets for the project, marked as 'Tentative' and 'Proposed', from late 1984, were only between $5.6 and $5.8 million.[80] A 'Cost Summary' for the completed production reveals it was actually finalized at $7,133,189 and, in the end, this was considerably exceeded with the final cost listed as $10,333,796.[81] Even taking account of the overage, this still seems surprisingly inexpensive given the large number of expensive locations, the seemingly extremely high production values and a technically complicated car chase sequence. The most obvious explanation for this lies in the modest above-the-line costs. Friedkin's fee was only $407,498 but he retained 50/50 ownership of the project with Levin, who acted as line producer, so the film had the potential to be extremely lucrative for him – but only if it was a success.[82] Its domestic return of about $17 million, while not disastrous, failed to meet Friedkin and SLM's expectations, although overseas sales, as well as an extended afterlife on video, DVD and Blu-ray, will have presumably now reaped a reasonable return. The film's lack of star names was even more of a budgetary factor. Even though Friedkin claimed at the time, 'if I'd been offered the biggest stars in America, I wouldn't have changed one member of our cast', there were clear financial restrictions that influenced his decisions.[83] The two male leads, William Peterson (Secret Service agent, Richard Chance) and Willem Dafoe (counterfeiter, Rick Masters), both secured roles immediately afterwards that established their reputations: *Manhunter* (Michael Mann, 1986) and *Platoon* respectively. Not only that but according to Philip Lopate, despite his character's villainy, it was Dafoe's 'mysteriously spiritual aura' in *To Live and Die*, and not his saintly character in *Platoon*, that led Scorsese to cast him as Jesus in *Last Temptation of Christ*.[84] Before *To Live and Die*, however, both Peterson and Dafoe were complete unknowns with only a handful of bit parts between them. The other main part was taken by John Pankow, as Chance's partner Vukovich, another fledgling film actor recommended to Friedkin by Peterson. Peterson and Dafoe were each paid only $50,000 (for ten weeks), Pankow just $35,000.[85] The eventual total for the cast amounted to a modest $946,767.[86] To understand this in context, on *Cruising* Pacino alone was paid more than double this amount. The budget was mostly expended on filming and on post-production. So, for example, the expenditure on locations was more than $200,000 above estimate at $812,531 and the total cost of post-production of $1,884,655 was more than two and a half times over budget.[87]

To Live and Die in L.A. was marketed as a Los Angeles *French Connection*, an idea that Friedkin at one time rejected, observing that it was only the theme of 'the thin line between the policeman and criminal' that was similar.[88] It is not just at a thematic or narrative level, however, that there are interesting points of comparison, but neither is *To Live and Die* simply a West Coast version of the earlier film. While Choe argues that Friedkin 'clearly attempts to model key elements of the later film upon the earlier',[89] a better way to understand the relationship between the two is as a series of dichotomies. Firstly, both are set in December which immediately points to the settings' inherent differences. The

146 *The Lost Decade*

hard-bitten, scruffy New York policemen follow suspects on the streets, clad in heavy coats and shivering in the winter cold; in *To Live and Die* everyone drives and dresses in light, elegant clothing, and the city is depicted, in Friedkin's words, 'as a violent, cynical wasteland under a burning sun'.[90] Masters, *To Live and Die*'s antagonist, appears to take great pleasure in his counterfeiting craft and boasts about its exceptional quality to his clients. He is somewhat urbane, like Charnier (Fernando Rey) in *The French Connection*, qualities that mask their ruthless natures. Both of these villains' behaviour away from crime is in stark contrast with the unreconstructed protagonists who oppose them. The elderly Charnier eats at nice restaurants on the waterfront and is solicitous towards his chic wife while the younger Masters is a more Californian form of sophisticate, a painter apparently so sensitive and dedicated to 'art for art's sake' that he burns his paintings once they are completed. Friedkin foregrounds this artistic side when Masters is introduced for the first time immediately after the credits, performing what appears to be a sort of ritualistic, quasi-religious ceremony when he destroys his latest work. Even the spectacular car chases, the most obvious and least subtle way the two films are similar, are representative of the different cities. In New York, the cop uses a car to chase a man escaping on the over/ underground railway, whereas in Los Angeles, where everyone drives, it has to be a pursuit along the absurdly busy four-lane freeways (the spectacle enhanced by Chance and Vukovich escaping their pursuers by going against the traffic). In fact, Friedkin's attempt to outdo the spectacle of *The French Connection*'s most iconic scene is, according to Sharon Willis, specifically attuned to its different location by being 'an explicit excess, based on commuter anxiety, that rehearses the pleasure of seeing traffic entirely disrupted, while one is not involved'.[91] A final dichotomy is one of time frame as *The French Connection* and *To Live and Die* are both firmly grounded in their respective decades in terms of both mise-en-scène and style. *To Live and Die* sees Friedkin adapting his style towards an aesthetic that seems very much of its time. The contemporary chic and rapid pacing are complemented by what now feels like its most distinctively 1980s characteristic: the synthesizer-dominated soundtrack from British electronic duo, Wang Chung, could only be from that decade. They were very much a personal choice of Friedkin's, who had heard the group at an obscure venue in Twickenham and liked their 'interesting hip sound'.[92] As he had done on *Sorcerer* with Tangerine Dream, Friedkin asked the group to write a soundtrack, of which they had no experience at all, based only on the script and then used what he liked from the sixty minutes of music that they sent him.

It would therefore seem, at first glance, given the obvious comparisons, that Friedkin must have partly been attracted to Petievich's novel because he saw it as an opportunity to return to the same themes and character types as *The French Connection*.[93] However, this presumption is not borne out by the available evidence. The various drafts of the screenplay, and their relationship to the source novel, indicate that Friedkin came to many of the similarities between the two films through a process unrelated to duplicating aspects of his early hit. Early drafts use the novel's basic narrative structure that differs in significant ways from the finished product. In the film, Jim Hart (Michael Greene) is Chance's partner and friend and is on the verge of retirement when he is murdered by Masters. Chance swears revenge and along with his new partner, Vukovich, sets about catching Masters. By the end, Chance is shot dead before Vukovich kills Masters. The source novel has a different basic set-up where Hart investigates Masters separately from Chance and Vukovich (who are already partners at the beginning) and Hart is still alive at the end.[94] Given nominative determinized names by Petievich that make more sense in the novel and early scripts, Hart is positioned as 'good-hearted', and Chance is a real 'chancer' who is certainly more immoral than in the final film. The original conclusion in the book sees Chance shot by his informant, Ruth, for the money stolen from an FBI agent earlier; Hart arrests Masters and Vukovich goes to jail.

Friedkin initially stayed reasonably faithful to the novel with two separate lines of investigation of the same criminal by different agents.[95] At some point, presumably between April and October 1984, Friedkin contacted William Peter Blatty, the writer of *The Exorcist*, asking for his advice about the screenplay and Blatty's undated reply offers his help because 'I see you floundering and uncertain of your judgements' and 'it is the least I owe a man who … made me a multimillionaire'.[96] By the time of the third draft, it appears that Blatty's advice has influenced the changes to the story and contributed to a leaner and more conventional structure.[97] Blatty, who offers his services in an unofficial capacity, tells Friedkin that 'if you want a commercial hit, major work must be done' and is most concerned with Chance's character.[98] He suggests quite forcefully that Friedkin 'must narrow Chance's motivations to putting Masters away and Masters, ideally … should be a truly bad motherfucker'. By repositioning him as the main protagonist, by giving him a clearer and singular goal, he suggests the audience will then feel some affinity with Chance despite his dubious behaviour.[99] Blatty makes no reference to precise specifics, but Friedkin's reaction seems to have been to adopt a more familiar Hollywood-style structure where the hero is motivated by revenge for the murder of his partner or family member. Had the film concluded with Chance exacting his revenge by capturing or killing Masters, it would have been yet more conventional and Friedkin's final draft, indeed, does have Chance surviving the shoot-out with Masters and his accomplice (Vukovich perishing in this scene instead).[100] On set, Friedkin changed his mind and killed off Chance in a manner that mirrors Hart's violent demise as he is blasted by the shotgun of Masters' silent accomplice. The film's editor, Bud Smith, recounts how Friedkin came up with the idea of killing Chance rather than Vukovich 'on the spot'.[101] Vukovich confronts and shoots Masters as he is engulfed by the flames from the fire that he lit himself. The final scene, where Vukovich visits Ruth (Darlanne Fleugel), Chance's informant and occasional lover, and appears to have inherited his partner's immorality and demeanour, was written while Friedkin was already in principal photography. This ending with the (anti-)hero violently killed was vehemently opposed by Levin. To appease him, Friedkin shot an alternative, light-hearted ending although it was only ever a ploy to appease SLM without ever intending it to be used. In this version, Chance and Vukovich, both heavily bandaged from their injuries, are shown to have been transferred to Alaska and are watching their former boss on the television, taking credit for the counterfeiting arrests. Although it tested much better, the happy ending that Levin wanted was not supported by MGM's management and Friedkin's preferred version prevailed.[102]

The film, in its final form, comprises many scenes, some present in the original source material, which have been liberally moved around, firstly at script level and then further juxtaposed in post-production. This methodology recalls how Friedkin played around with the structure of *Cruising*. A particularly striking example is how each draft begins differently, all with scenes that appear in the final film that ended up placed elsewhere. In the undated handwritten early draft, it is the printing of the counterfeit currency sequence that comes first but in the next version, it begins with Hart at the airport watching Falcone (later renamed Cody), an associate of Masters.[103] The final draft starts with Masters destroying his painting, eventually the scene that follows the credits.[104] Finally, the film itself has an unscripted pre-credits sequence that fulfils two purposes. Firstly, the Secret Service's dual responsibilities, which fascinated Friedkin, are illustrated through a sequence with Hart and Chance on Reagan's security detail, ending with them confronting a Muslim bomber who is trying to assassinate the president. This scene places the film firmly in its historical context as Reagan can be heard, in the background, declaring 'death and taxes may be inevitable but unjust taxes are not'. At the same time, this successful but stressful assignment establishes both Chance and Hart's close friendship and Hart's imminent retirement. This enables Friedkin to enact a slightly hackneyed story of a detective (or similar) needing to crack that one last case before he retires. This idea is carried forward into the next scene in which the pair feature, when Hart tells Chance he is doing this last 'small' job alone. All this set-up is different to the novel (excepting Hart's love of fishing and coming retirement) and Friedkin is playing on generic expectations. When Hart refuses Chance's help because it is a straight-forward job, the viewer is likely to surmise it is not going to end well. This set-up conforms to Blatty's advice to Friedkin to give Chance a more identifiable reason to break rules so flagrantly. As Krohn explains the director's methods, 'every shot, scene, sequence in a Friedkin film is a module which can be potentially displaced, eliminated, added or even duplicated'.[105] In *To Live and Die*, it is apparent that Friedkin switches scenes around in this manner, but the process does not have the effect of stimulating incoherence as it does in *Cruising*. There are only occasional small inconsistencies that arise from this technique such as when Masters brings Serena home as a sexual gift for his girlfriend Bianca (Deborah Feuer), yet a few scenes earlier, Serena and Bianca were seemingly already involved. While Friedkin retooled the narrative to make Chance's character and motivation more identifiable, his changes to the ending conform to a preference for leaving audiences with as many questions as answers. Some years later, Friedkin said that 'the ending in the book is much better ... I don't know why I changed it, I was going toward some metaphysical horseshit that didn't come off'.[106] Robert Arnett argues that this denouement shows how the law enforcers' obsession and corruption (formerly Chance's, now Vukovich's) have become 'transcendent and self-perpetuating' while Ian Mantagni similarly sees it as 'a spectral transference of Chance's corrupt spirit on to the personality of Vukovich'.[107] These enigmatic last shots make for a typically downbeat conclusion with Vukovich perpetuating his former partner's sins. Doyle may have been left frustrated and morally bankrupt in *The French Connection* and, in *Cruising*, the audience suspects Burns may be a murderer; in *To Live and Die*, Friedkin serves up the ultimate punishment for his anti-hero: only the ghost of Chance's former self survives.

Friedkin's films usually have a strong sense of place, from the grubby New York streets in *The French Connection* to the same city's leather bars and parks in *Cruising*, the Georgetown district of Washington in *The Exorcist* or the south American jungle of *Sorcerer*. In *To Live and Die in L.A.*, this tendency is at its

Figure 5.3 The filming concentrated on rundown, industrial parts of Los Angeles rather than the usual fashionable views of downtown and Beverly Hills.

most pronounced (as foregrounded in the title) because Friedkin chooses to portray the city as a reflection of the false and duplicitous characters who 'live and die' there. There was a conscious attempt to portray the city in a different way to the predictable and familiar way it is usually seen. According to Bud Smith, their approach was influenced by a book called *24 Hours in Los Angeles*, with the expanses of downtown and 'chichi' Beverly Hills eschewed in favour of the rundown and industrial areas of Wilmington and San Pedro, as well as the arid landscapes to the east in the Mojave desert (Figure 5.3).[108] Michael Wilmington aptly describes it as 'a Darwinian world, dogged with trash hard as brick, soaked with evil'.[109] The film's very first shot, before the prologue, is unmistakably Los Angeles, the Hollywood hills in the background and a row of palms trees in the fore with the sun just rising above the horizon casting the hazy image in an orange glow. Just before the film closes, Friedkin and cinematographer, Robbie Müller, offer a near-repeat of the same shot but now the sun appears to be setting, about to disappear below the horizon as if the events of the film have comprised but a single day.

This doubling of the image, two different shots which seem identical but are not, is at one with the film's dominant theme. *To Live and To Die* is essentially about betrayal and illusion: no one can ever be really trusted, and nothing can be taken at face value. The central presence of counterfeit money (Masters' specialism) is a persistent reminder of this theme, and the fake currency's resistance to the rule of the law, according to Choe, functions as an 'allegory' of the 'postmodern condition'.[110] At any given point, someone is betraying someone else. The levels and degrees of deceit are pervasive so that the only really sincere relationship, between Hart and Chance, can only last long enough for Hart to be swiftly dispatched. Masters is ripped off by a client whom he immediately murders. Cody (John Turturro) betrays Masters who tries to have him killed, while Cody also deceives Chance by escaping from his custody. Grimes (Dean Stockwell), the lawyer, betrays his client Masters, and Chance and Vukovich also double-cross Masters. Deception as a motif begins with the counterfeit trade, what Segaloff calls the film's 'constant illusion', which functions, in essence, as a continuous doubling of an image.[111] The pervasiveness of illusion as a motif is seen early on when Bianca appears for the first time. Shot from the back, she is in masculine attire, so Masters appears to be passionately kissing another man. Only when she turns around and takes off her wig does it become clear it is a woman. Nothing and no one can be taken at face value, even the director himself who cheated by using a male stand-in for the rear angle (Figure 5.4).

When Richard Lippe and Florence Jacobwitz examine the film in terms of its relationship to contemporary representations of masculinity, the motifs and codes they identify also underscore this dominant theme. When they observe how 'the code of rage/violence is all-pervasive' in articulations of masculinity in contemporary cinema, in *To Live and Die* it is betrayal that provides its fuel.

Figure 5.4 No one in the film can be trusted including Friedkin who 'cheats' with a male stand-in.

152   *The Lost Decade*

They also show the importance in the film of the 'Buddy Honor Motif [where] male bonding/love/eroticism is legitimized through male "friendship" in the personal realm and "partnerships" in the professional'. However, the film pushes back against this tendency much more than Lippe and Jacobwitz allow because the honour code is repeatedly shown to be untenable. Chance must kill Masters to avenge his 'buddy' yet, in the final confrontation, he fails miserably as he is killed himself – and not even by his nemesis. When Lippe and Jacobwitz use Cody refusing to inform on Masters as a prime example, they miss that in the very next scene, he has reversed his decision.[112] The final scene puts the seal on the theme of deceit as endemic in contemporary America. Chance's manipulated informant, Ruth, who has been effectively prostituting herself in exchange for her freedom, suffers the final betrayal as she is denied an escape from her degradation as a vessel of institutional and patriarchal power. Vukovich visits her (as Chance had done before) and informs her in no uncertain terms that she is now *his* informant; whether she will be expected to continue her sexual favours is left unanswered.

To Live and Die is a fascinating exercise in genre manipulation that is also, aesthetically, very much of its time. It played some part in launching the careers of its unknown lead actors and its reputation has gradually improved. Why it failed to make much of an impact in its time is less clear although perhaps a clue can be found in its critical reception. It had its admirers, but the ever-acerbic Canby thought it 'so relentlessly nastily trendy that it comes close to self-parody'.[113] David Denby in *New York* magazine said it 'is a sleek piece of trash with dispensable heroes thrown onto the garbage heap with everything else'.[114] This suggests that it was its cynicism, its portrayal of a world without hope, that caused the film to be out of step with audiences and critics. Once again, it seems, Friedkin's tendency to explore the darker side of humanity had resulted in a film too cynical to be embraced by a mainstream mid-1980s audience.

1986–1989

After *To Live and Die*, Friedkin was increasingly finding it difficult to generate new projects which may be why he gravitated back to television again, making two feature-length films about an elite squad of law enforcers that had its origins in a real-life unit organized by Gerald Petievich. Continuing the relationship established on *To Live and Die*, Petievich is the credited writer of the first film, *C.A.T. Squad*, which Friedkin directed in late 1985 for NBC. Budgeted at £4 million, about twice the usual cost for a made-for-television film, it aired on 27 July 1986 and tells a well-worn story of a gang of specialists and outcasts, like a cross between *The Dirty Dozen* and *The A-Team*, who carry out dangerous and difficult missions.[115] The dialogue is hide-bound by cliché and if Petievich was the sole writer as credited, this seems to support Friedkin's claim that he wrote *To Live and Die*'s screenplay *without* Petievich. Ratings were sufficiently strong for Friedkin to direct a sequel, *C.A.T. Squad: Python Wolf*, shot in autumn 1987 and aired on 23 May 1988.[116] The second film, with a different writer, Robert Ward (and story credits for both Friedkin and Petievich), is better written and benefits from a more complex narrative than its predecessor. The *C.A.T. Squad* films are among the most predictable work of Friedkin's career and anticipate his more decisive move towards mainstream action filmmaking with *Rules of Engagement* (2000) and *The Hunted* (2003). Between directing these two television films in 1986 and 1988, Friedkin wrote and directed his most obscure work, the largely unseen *Rampage*, which might seem to be a return to his fascination with horror and the nature of evil, yet remains, in many ways, his most unusual and uncharacteristic film.

Rampage

Friedkin's first film was *The People vs. Paul Crump* (1962), a documentary about a man on Death Row, made at a time when he was vehemently opposed to the death penalty. Crump was reprieved but since has admitted his guilt and by the 1980s, Friedkin's own views about the death penalty had become less certain. This was the background to his decision to option the rights to William Wood's 1985 novel, *Rampage*, a polemic about the death penalty and the fault lines in the American, and specifically the Californian, legal system. It was based on both personal experience, Wood having served as a Deputy District Attorney (like the book and film's protagonist) until 1981 and on a real-life case.[117] With his background in documentaries, Friedkin was particularly attracted to Wood's inside knowledge, as had previously been the case with Petievich and Jurgensen. The book was not an obviously commercial prospect because it relegates the serial killer himself mostly to the role of spectator in a procedural about the vagaries of the Californian approach to questions of legal sanity, and its impact on a possible capital verdict. The making of such a film became a possibility when Dino De Laurentiis, who had produced *The Brink's Job* and

154   *The Lost Decade*

(as we have already seen) seems to have been fond of employing Renaissance auteurs, approached Friedkin about making another film for him. As he tells it in his autobiography, Friedkin wrote an initial draft in four weeks and took it to De Laurentiis who expressed the view that, 'if made inexpensively', the film might attract a similar audience to his recent, offbeat hit, David Lynch's *Blue Velvet* (1986).[118] On paper, at least, the comparison makes some sense because both stories depict the evil lurking behind the white picket fences of small-town America.

For its lack of obvious commerciality, it is not surprising that *Rampage's* budget was initially agreed at only $5 million.[119] Eventually, it was set at $7 million but it was probably Friedkin's personal stake in the film's fiscal arrangements that focused his mind sufficiently to bring it in for just above six ($5,184,239 on production and $1,050,120 on post).[120] The financing, in a similar arrangement to Coppola's on *The Outsiders* and *Rumble Fish*, was a reflection of the times with a $7 million loan from European American Bank contingent upon the provision of a completion guarantee. This was provided by Film Finances' new branch, located on Sunset Boulevard in Los Angeles, who provided their services on condition that the Dino de Laurentiis Group (DEG) and Friedkin each provided a contingency of $250,000.[121] Friedkin's overall fee was $1.5 million (plus a writer's fee of $175,000) but the structure of the project's ownership reflected the perilous prospects for this type of low-concept filmmaking.[122] DEG and Friedkin (Rampage Productions) owned the property equally, on a 'negative pick-up arrangement whereby Friedkin ... was responsible for the budget until its delivery to DEG'.[123] Shot in only thirty-six days, *Rampage* had a largely unknown cast much like *To Live and Die* (although this is confused by hindsight because of the subsequent success of the earlier films' stars). Neither of the actors playing *Rampage's* principal characters, Michael Biehn (as Deputy District Attorney Tony Fraser) and Alex McArthur (as the killer Charles Reece) became stars subsequently. Friedkin had initially wanted William Peterson for the lead, but, in fact, it was Biehn who was the most famous of all the actors on *Rampage* or *To Live and Die* because of his major supporting role in *The Terminator* (James Cameron, 1984). This is apparent in his remuneration, $200,000 for eight weeks, compared with the $50,000 that McArthur (as well as Peterson and Dafoe) earned.[124] The most significant name attached to the project was the composer, Ennio Morricone, who was paid $137,500 for music that Friedkin imagined would be 'a similar high-energy track' to his famous Western scores for Sergio Leone.[125] In fact, what he provided was an understated score suited to the subject

William Friedkin

155

matter, which Friedkin acknowledged was 'haunting' although not what he had envisaged when he hired the famous composer.[126]

Rampage was screened on the last night of the 1987 Boston Film Festival on 24 September at the USC Coliseum on 19 November and then received an extremely limited release in Europe.[127] In the United States, the release date kept being pushed back before it disappeared from the schedule altogether. De Laurentiis's company was in trouble and in August 1988 they filed for bankruptcy.[128] It was only in 1992 that *Rampage* finally achieved a domestic release when Miramax stepped in and provisionally agreed to distribute the film. After a year-long negotiation including a disappointing preview, Friedkin made changes that not only responded to commercial concerns to make the film more easily understood but also reflected his ongoing, malleable opinions about the death penalty. *Rampage*'s box-office return, when it was released domestically in November 1992 to a mixed reception, was only $796,368. The film had little impact on public consciousness and is now largely forgotten. Friedkin's conclusion in his autobiography was 'that it was *too* serious, not what audiences expected from the director of *The Exorcist* and *The French Connection*'.[129] In most other countries, including the UK, it was never released at all, perhaps because the vagaries and complications surrounding the question of legal sanity and its impact on the possibility of a capital sentence remain peculiar to non-American audiences. The sight of expert psychiatrists with opposing opinions, who are used to shore up both the prosecution and defence, is familiar from cinema and television. What *Rampage* does that is more unusual is expose the machinations and corrupt practices that determine their behaviour.

Friedkin's negative portrayal of these 'experts' in the courtroom was personally motivated because he was in the middle of a bitter custody battle for his son with ex-wife, the British actress, Lesley Anne-Down. Friedkin observed about the case: 'I feel our case was decided by psychiatrists and not the courts, and that this shrink's methods were no more valid than a witch doctor's.'[130] Friedkin's anger about this state of affairs fed directly into *Rampage* where all the practitioners are venal and self-serving. The first expert seen in the film is a weasely type employed by the prosecution to support their contention that Reece, the murderer, is legally sane and therefore able to receive the death penalty. He declares unconvincingly after meeting Reece that 'it's possible' that Fraser can make a case for legal sanity. The defence's psychiatrist is more confident but also more callous and immoral. He confronts his opposite number and persuades him to change his testimony to avoid being charged with malpractice because his clinic had released Reece on

156   *The Lost Decade*

an earlier occasion. To persuade his colleague, he cites the real-life recent case of John Hinckley, Reagan's failed assassin, where a psychiatrist was prosecuted 'for failing to predict future violence'.[131] When the first psychiatrist reneges on his original opinion, Fraser employs another practitioner who seems, at first, to be plausible when presenting his evidence. He confirms the audience's inclination, having borne witness to the horrific crimes, to side entirely with the prosecution but this is immediately undercut: when cross-examined, it is revealed that he has appeared on fifty occasions for the prosecution and supported their case in every instance, earning him the nickname of 'Doctor Death'. This seems to be an allusion to the real-life psychiatrist, James Grigson, also known as 'Doctor Death', who similarly testified in 'at least fifty' cases and always sided with the prosecution.[132] For all Friedkin's personal bias, these portrayals only reinforce what is written in the novel. Friedkin does not, though, confine his criticisms to psychiatrists and the legal system; in the opening scene, he starkly exposes the absurdity of identity checks and waiting periods that govern Californian gun purchases. When Reece tries to buy one, he is told there is a fifteen-day waiting period. He asks if he needs ID and the response is 'no, just a Californian driving licence'. Reece only has to answer 'a couple of questions' before the shopkeeper is satisfied, completing the transaction by telling Reece, 'I'll see you on December 21st and Merry Christmas.' Reece has to merely wait until that date to collect his Christmas present and begin his killing spree.

Once Reece is armed, the film moves swiftly to the first murder which is cross cut with Fraser and his wife, Kate (Deborah van Valkenburgh) receiving communion. The couple have lost a child whose death is shown to haunt Fraser's thoughts (although Friedkin set aside from early drafts a subplot about their marital problems).[133] The action in the film is mostly observed from an objective distance in medium shots but in these early scenes that jump between protagonist and antagonist, the viewpoint is more subjective with Reece's second victim seen in close-up just before death, making apparent the true horror of Reece's murderous acts before a rapid cut to a medium close-up of Reece bathed in blood, inside a cage with a tiger prowling behind him in the enclosed space. This brief foray into fantasy, into Reece's mind, that seems to imply his bloodlust is connected to a compulsion to behave like a wild animal, is uncharacteristic in what is largely a sober film unadorned by ostentatious camerawork. While the crime is discovered and Fraser attends the scene, Reece moves rapidly onto his second murder. A family bury their dog which the father, Gene Tippetts (Royce D. Applegate), is convinced was carried out by their neighbour, Reece. When the father and older son go out, Reece enters their house and kills the mother and the younger son (whose body goes missing and turns up later, dumped by Reece in a nearby river). The horrific acts are not shown, only the aftermath when Reece is again shown bathed in blood. This is characteristic of the film's low-key approach where most of the violence takes place off-screen, which is in stark contrast with *To Live and Die*'s excess of style and action. Reece is caught and much of the later part of the film is taken up with his trial. However, one hour into the film (which lasts 107 minutes), there is a sudden burst of action when Reece escapes while he is being transported in a police van from court. He manages, in the time before he is re-caught, to commit some unseen act of depravity that leaves him yet again covered in blood (Figure 5.5). This interlude seems to have drifted in from another film; presumably its purpose was to add a dose of energy to a particularly downbeat film. Once Reece is re-caught, the trial proceeds and Reece is found guilty and likely to face the death penalty. Then, the defence demands further, more advanced brain scans which now identify Reece as insane and the jury reverses their verdict, sending him to a state hospital with a possibility of parole in the future. This conclusion was different from the 1987 version which ended after Reece is found guilty and, before the verdict, commits suicide in his cell. What would have been the final shot of Reece's body lying prone with a hint of dribble hanging from his mouth appears in the 1992 edit as part of a dream

Figure 5.5 When Reece is re-captured, he is covered in blood from some unseen act of depravity.

158 *The Lost Decade*

sequence in which Fraser imagines this fate for the murderer. This original ending conformed to both the novel and the real-life events on which it was based.

Wood's book was based on the case of Richard Chase who committed a series of horrific murders and mutilations in late 1977 and early 1978 before committing suicide in prison after his conviction in May 1979.[134] Friedkin, as he had done with *Cruising* and, to a lesser extent with *To Live and Die*, used the source novel as a jumping-off point for extensive research into the subject matter which he amalgamated with the original book. It was this mining for the small details that led Friedkin, once again, towards controversy, albeit on a much smaller scale than his difficulties with *Cruising*. On this occasion, it also seems Friedkin was not at fault. In a story in the January 1986 edition of *NewsRounds*, the monthly newspaper of the Rush-Presbyterian-St Luke's Medical Center in Chicago, it was reported that Friedkin visited Dr Jim Kavanaugh at the facility as research for a film that would 'show the world through the eyes of a killer who is also schizophrenic.'[135] The consequence of this small report in a publication with an extremely limited readership was a deluge of letters of complaint sent to Friedkin. In terms of an early intervention, the protests even outdid *Cruising*, occurring before a screenplay had even been written. Most of these letters, written between February and May 1986, said much the same thing: schizophrenics are no more or less likely to be killers than anyone else and the making of a film where a schizophrenic is a murderer will stigmatize them. The writers were a combination of health professionals and members of the public, particularly parents of schizophrenic children. The majority cited the *NewsRounds* article, and these included those which were part of a concerted campaign by the Alliance for the Mentally Ill (with a membership of thirty thousand).[136] Friedkin was sufficiently concerned to feel the need to respond in the June/July edition of *NewsRounds* in which he stated: 'In no way is it my intention to equate murder with mental illness ... the film deals with the death penalty in California and the arguments for and against it. My purpose ... is to *accurately* portray the role of forensic psychiatry in a murder case.'[137] There is a certain irony that it was the writer-director's determination to provide an accurate representation by making the visit to specialists in the field that should have caused the protest. Objections focused on a single quotation from which it was assumed that Friedkin would sensationalize the issues and the *Cruising* farrago may have prompted the complainants to fear the worst.

What was not said amidst all this pre-production uproar is that in the real-life case, upon which Wood and Friedkin based their narratives, Richard Chase *was* diagnosed as schizophrenic (although this does not necessarily undermine the complaints).[138] The extreme reactions certainly indicate Friedkin's uncanny ability to attract controversy. These visits to Kavanaugh's institution eventually fed into the final film in a specific way that allowed Friedkin to use more recent medical advances than in the novel. Advances in PET scan technology, which pinpointed evidence of schizophrenia in the brain, become a crucial plot point in the film's revised 1992 ending. After being found guilty, further tests show the use of technology from which the doctors conclude, '[A]bnormal patterns without a doubt ... consistent with schizophrenia. What it shows is a picture of madness.' Whereas the original version concludes with the suicide of Reece, the 1992 version finishes with a shot of him staring into the camera, clutching the prison bars, followed by a stark caption that informs us that 'Reece has served four years already and has already had one parole hearing. The next one is due in six months'. In the original version, the question of insanity as a reason to keep a murderer alive is not answered: Reece's premature death leaves open what his fate would have been. The new ending, on the other hand, adds a frightening coda that makes clear Friedkin's views. He said that it put the film 'firmly on the side of the death penalty. This version is more ironic and unsettling'.[139]

Friedkin's research extended beyond the visits to psychiatric clinics. He read up on Chase extensively and, in February 1986, received advice from a public defender in Sacramento about the veracity of the source novel.[140] In January 1986, he was sent copies of defence arguments against the death penalty by another lawyer, Colleen Grace.[141] All this research informed the film's script, adding layers of verisimilitude which can be seen most obviously in the details of Reece's horrible activities and in Fraser's closing arguments. However, it is not just the extent of the research or the determination to be accurate that recalls Friedkin's beginnings in documentary filmmaking but also the film's unvarnished imagery. Yet the director's observation that he 'tried to make the film without style ... no discernible visual style' does not seem entirely accurate.[142] The film's visual palette is understated – and to a considerable extent – but Friedkin's decisions *do* denote a specific style even if it is one determined not to draw attention to itself. In the exterior scenes, when Reece stalks his neighbourhood, or in the scenes that depict the domestic life of Fraser and his wife, everything appears drained of both colour and light (Figure 5.6). There is a restraint in the film's lighting schemes that makes Stockton's suburbs seem to be engulfed in a permanent haze. There is very little self-consciousness or overt flair in Friedkin's direction, but there *are* exceptions. When the police and Fraser search Reece's cellar, this

Figure 5.6 The killer stalks an ordinary neighbourhood seemingly drained of colour and light.

is both the film's most horrific and most cinematic scene. A swinging light illuminates the space fleetingly, as the music becomes steadily more ominous, revealing in glimpses, Nazi regalia, mice and rats scurrying, brains and dead animals in jars. Another example is when Reece makes his escape from custody and, here, Friedkin plays on Reece's blood-sucking pathology. He escapes from a church, in which he was hiding, in one dramatic leap straight through the ornate stained-glass window, like a vampire with supernatural powers.[143] These infrequent flourishes aside, the subdued tone of the film is underpinned by restrained presentational decisions, by the sheer ordinariness of a typical American suburb and by Morricone's subtly evocative music.

Friedkin was much more faithful to the source novel than in his previous 1980s work, with script drafts and revisions also less extensive. However, Friedkin still made last-minute changes on set that resulted in some interesting ideas, on paper at least, being discarded. He initially had plans to visualize Reece's thought processes. The first draft states, 'Reece separates from himself, and in a state of depersonalization is literally out of his body watching himself through the following action … [He] hovers above the scene like a Chagall figure.' There is also a hand-written note that states: 'Throughout the film, Reece's P.O.V. is transferred to video-tape, color-altered and re-transferred to film.'[144] Friedkin chose not to use these subjective visual effects because he reasoned that it would have encouraged the audience to feel some unearned sympathy for Reece.[145] By the time of the re-release by Miramax, Friedkin's later changes are documented in a revised continuity script dated 11 July 1991. One addition extends an olive branch of hope amidst the despair (perhaps as a correlative to the depressive new ending). In the penultimate scene, the only wholly sympathetic characters in the film, Gene and Andy Tippetts (the father and son of the family in the second murder), enjoy a visit to the fairground and Gene tells a rapt Andy a story while he carries him aloft.[146] This singular hopeful and redemptive scene is as positive as this 'too serious' film ever gets.

Steve Choe has argued that both the protagonist and antagonist in *Rampage* display echoes of characters from other Friedkin films. He notes the resemblance between Reece, in his leather jacket and shades, and the killer(s) in *Cruising* and also identifies how Fraser's obsessive nature recalls both Doyle in *The French Connection* and Chance in *To Live and Die*.[147] Despite such similar character traits, *Rampage* does seem an outlier in Friedkin's career, even though he has frequently dabbled in a range of different genres and styles. The film touches on topics that appear in serial killer thrillers and courtroom dramas but hardly ever relies on familiar generic tropes. It does examine contemporary issues that conceivably might have resonated with a 1980s or 1990s domestic audience but its mode of execution, and its troubled and deferred release, did not lend itself to attracting a wide audience. The film moved Friedkin further away from the Hollywood industrial power complex as he, like a number of his peers, sought finance and distribution from the independent sector. This did allow him a high degree of creative freedom but ended badly when DEG, like so many overreaching independents in the 1980s, was unable to fulfil its commitments. Although it is as obscure a film as any in Friedkin's career and was patently out of step with the marketplace at the time of its release, it still asks provocative questions about American society that seem just as relevant today because, some thirty years later, gun control and the death penalty in the United States continue to generate controversially strident and diverse opinions.

✳✳✳

Like so many Renaissance auteurs, William Friedkin's career in the 1980s was neither profitable nor prolific. He had never been as productive as some others such as Altman, but none of the four films he directed for the cinema made worthwhile money. Both *Rampage* and *Deal of the Century* are largely forgotten today, and both received only cursory theatrical releases in their time, with neither ever exhibited in the UK. *Cruising* and *To Live and Die*, although initially somewhat unsuccessful, have both, gradually, enjoyed a higher profile and enhanced critical reputation. What this examination of Friedkin's decade has revealed is how he shared with both Altman and Coppola a desire to carry on making the type of cinema that was now less welcome in the blockbuster-dominated Hollywood marketplace. In the 1990s and 2000s, Friedkin continued to make films at a similar rate but was no longer writing his own screenplays or generating his own projects. When he directed *Jade* in 1995, it was Joe Eszterhas, the in-demand writer of 1992's *Basic Instinct*, whose authorial signature seemed predominant. Studio fare like *Blue Chips* (1994), *Rules of Engagement* and *The Hunted* were films with generic plots and big stars, while *The Guardian* and *Bug* (2006) took him back into horror territory with mixed results. Nevertheless, in many of these post-1980s films, he still retained his penchant for morally ambiguous protagonists. Friedkin's work in the eighties, with the benefit of hindsight, now looks like a concerted attempt to make a last stand for his particular brand of filmmaking in an environment that now favoured more manageable subject matter.

Conclusion

The reasons for the decline in the fortunes of the Hollywood Renaissance auteurs in the 1980s have been seen to be much the same but their responses to the consequent challenges to their ability to work as they wished were diverse and nuanced. Although it is true that the prevalent marketplace conditions presented difficult challenges for these directors, sweeping generalizations about the progression of their careers provide an incomplete picture when the focus of study is shifted away from box-office performance or right-leaning ideology and towards the fortunes and films of those auteurs whose names still tend to dominate discussions of the acclaimed cinema of the previous decade. The extent that directors' career paths were not uniform is amply illustrated by how differently the three case-study filmmakers approached the difficulties of finding ways to express themselves satisfactorily. Each example has revealed contrasting aspects of 1980s filmmaking, their experiences and films allowing a variety of perspectives on the history of the period. For all this, it is still accurate to observe that the story of the Renaissance auteur in the 1980s still re-enforces, by dent of their films' poor box-office performance, some of the commonly held perceptions about the decade. It was always a challenge, even for those who achieved some measure of success, to achieve any consistency at the box office.

Coppola's experiences were unique, and his freewheeling decade featured both extravagance and foolhardiness, but also, contrary to reputation, surprising instances of discipline and restraint. He inscribed, particularly on the projects he originated, a visual style that reflected the thematic concerns of individual films and the extent that he was able to engage in innovative modes of filmmaking even when he was working for others is notable. He pioneered new video-assisted methods that allowed for the sort of pre-visualization and editing practices that would become common practice with the subsequent advances in digital technology. On the more personal projects, as we have seen, Coppola quotes from his influences but in a way that is distinctive rather than imitative. My examination of the films' aesthetics, and of Coppola's authorship, is a correlative to the way that his 1980s films have tended to be used as part of the wider saga of Coppola's financial demise and indefatigable hubris.

Coppola still managed to achieve more commercial success than either Altman or Friedkin, despite the latter's ostensibly more predictable attempts to maintain a career in Hollywood by operating in familiar genres and dealing with more contemporary subject matter. What is most interesting about Friedkin is how he seemed unable to resist undermining his own chances of success by demonstrating a perverse determination to register his individuality. He undermined the potential conventionality and commerciality of the work through his refusal to offer easily digestible narratives that conformed to viewers' expectations.[1] The ambiguity and incoherence, especially in *Cruising* but also in *To Lie and Die*, make the films difficult to understand and go some way to explain Friedkin's problems at the box office. What has been seen, perhaps even more than Coppola, are the surprising ways that Friedkin's 1980s films can be thought of as among his most personal work; my focus on the screenwriting in his case reflects the degree of creative control he was able to exert. In Hollywood, a director's authorial agency has always been challenged by producers and production companies' reluctance (in both studio and independent sectors) to allow them creative freedom. Friedkin suffered in this respect on *Deal of the Century* but on the other three films he directed in the decade, because he fulfilled the dual role of writer-director, this meant that he was able to exert a high degree of authorial control.

Altman undertook an entirely different route to keeping in meaningful employment and his sheer productivity is indicative of the fresh opportunities available in both cable television and low-cost filmmaking, if directors were willing to lower their expectations about budget, fees and audience reach. By taking himself away from Hollywood, he found novel solutions to the problem of maintaining his customary level of creative control. Operating with small budgets that bore no comparison even with Coppola's or Friedkin's reduced funding, Altman still managed to be innovative in the manner in which he expressed himself cinematically and we have seen the extent that his authorship can be identified in the staging and filming of ostensibly faithful adaptations of theatrical properties (although, as seen, the level of fidelity was not quite as high as the writing credits suggest). The low-key and low-cost nature of Altman's 1980s films has led to a perception that what followed in the 1990s represented a comeback, aptly illustrating the way that the diversity in auteurist filmmaking in the 1980s has been undervalued.

Conclusion

This project was conceived from the outset as a challenge to the homogeneity that routinely characterizes the story of the Hollywood Renaissance auteur in the 1980s. It is unsurprising, therefore, that any conclusions that can be drawn are not particularly simple or easily explained. In fact, the fortunes (or lack of them) for this diverse group, and the films they directed, have required ways to explain them that reflect the wide range of circumstances that make up their individual narratives. Industrial developments, changes in audience tastes, the difficulties of obtaining finance and distribution, as well as personal behavioural issues, were interconnected factors, which for each director impacted on their careers in varying degrees and produced a range of different outcomes.

At the outset, I noted that many of this book's aims aligned with the practice of 'New Film History'. In this regard, by offering a more nuanced perspective on a particular decade, aspects of film history, obscured by the conventional historiography that has codified the nature of the transition from the 1970s to the 1980s, have been enriched. In the study of this period, gaps have been revealed and problems highlighted in what are often generalized and occasionally problematic accounts. This is then a fresh perspective on what is conventionally considered to be a 'standard' period in Hollywood history.

Writing at the mid-point of the decade, Stephen Farber profiled five 'maverick' directors' gravitation towards the independent sector which he identified as being caused by the lack of opportunities now available from within the studio system. In doing so, he made an important point about the divergent nature of Renaissance auteurs' situations in the 1980s, observing that 'track records are neither guarantee nor curse, and having a bad one does not mean that a director, producer, can't continue making pictures for years'.[2] As Farber implies, for all the changes in the industry and the lack of support for maverick directors, it was not necessarily success in the immediate past that determined the amount, or type, of work they were offered and the reasons that directors were hired were often due to other project-specific factors. The reality in the 1980s for directors who wanted to carry on working at the sort of scale to which they were accustomed, was that maintaining high production values or attracting stars could usually only be achieved with studio backing. Justin Wyatt's argument about how adhering to the precepts of high-concept filmmaking was the route to attracting a substantial viewership seems particularly relevant here: Scorsese's *The Color of Money* is a particularly apposite example in this respect, where the director achieved his biggest hit to that point by moving into more conventional territory and harnessing some of the high-concept markers that Wyatt identifies

166 *The Lost Decade*

(the Newman-Cruise star package and a pre-sold property that was a sequel to the book and film of *The Hustler*).

It was the progressively increasing reluctance from the majors to venture much beyond the blockbuster model in the 1980s that led the Renaissance auteur towards independent finance but even then, a film was still reliant on the Hollywood studios for distribution if it stood any chance of becoming a hit. Even though a film might be independently funded, the freedom to make a film according to the director's wishes without outside interference was still dependent on a production company being willing to allow them such latitude: there were no guarantees that an independent would be less controlling than a major studio. At the same time, in an independent production that was only made for a modest sum, the scope of a director's creativity was often challenged by a lack of available funds.

Such difficulties were not, of course, confined to the Renaissance auteurs. Had this book's concern been about the viability of authorial creativity in 1980s Hollywood as a whole, it might easily have focused on a younger cadre of filmmakers who were in the vanguard of the growth in independent cinema in the post-Renaissance period (such as Sayles, Jarmusch or Lee). By concentrating instead on those particularly associated with the previous period in American cinema, and who were no longer considered to be bankable at the box office, it has been seen that the conventionally stated division between two eras can be perceived more fluidly than usual, at least in terms of authorial creativity. Yet in the 1980s, it is also clear that the Renaissance auteurs were all still subject to the same pressures and problems that derived from new industrial and societal determinants, as well as the technological developments that fuelled ancillary markets. These factors functioned to both underpin and accelerate the changes in audience tastes that led to a greater concentration on more populist filmmaking.

The characterization of the eighties as a 'lost decade' is persuasive as a means to describe the hiatus in innovative, unconventional and personal filmmaking in Hollywood, between the acclaimed films of the Renaissance and the successes in Indiewood cinema in the 1990s, and such a designation stands as a marker for a lack of both public and academic attention. The division between eras is also appropriate because the fate of the Hollywood Renaissance auteur has shown the extent that opportunities were diminished in the 1980s, not just for them but for those others who faced similar challenges. Not only that, but it should also be acknowledged that these filmmakers were no longer in the first flower of youth. While they had dazzlingly reflected the *zeitgeist* when they burst into public consciousness in the late 1960s, they no longer seemed to be culturally relevant to a populace in thrall to a Reaganite optimism.

The research into the three case-study directors then has revealed many differences in their filmmaking experiences in the 1980s but it also has suggested similarities that are indicative of the state of the American film industry at the time. The vaunted reputations of these three filmmakers, much like most of their peers as well, had already become more of a hindrance than a benefit. After *Heaven's Gate*, but particularly in their cases after *Apocalypse Now*, *Sorcerer* and *Popeye*, all three were no longer as attractive to the major studios in terms of their allure as 'auteur-stars'. The conglomerated entities were less inclined to use a critically acclaimed auteur to burnish their reputation but there were still exceptions under certain circumstances. The change of attitude was caused by the changing nature of the marketplace, but also by directors' individual behaviours. As we have seen, almost all of the Renaissance auteurs enjoyed the sort of relationships with Hollywood studio executives that could problematize their ability to get projects green-lit. Even when they did find work that involved the participation of the majors, they all struggled (frequently in vain) to retain a degree of authorial control. Studios were less forgiving and less indulgent than in the earlier decade because they considered, paraphrasing Biskind, that there was now less chance of these filmmakers' laying 'golden eggs'.[3]

What has also become apparent is how Hollywood's conglomerated environment of diminished opportunities led film directors towards other areas in which they could practice their craft. Today, forty years on, filmmakers considered to be auteurs are happily gravitating towards the opportunities and budgets offered in television by the new media behemoths of the twenty-first century, Netflix and Amazon (as well as all the others scrambling to get a slice of the new 'pie'). In the 1980s, however, it was still considered a step down in class to move from big screen to small. It was only because of the vastly reduced options available to them in cinema that directors like Altman, Friedkin and Coppola made forays into television. Altman, in particular, was prescient in identifying the opportunities that television might be able to offer enterprising filmmakers. The smaller budgets required to make a television film in the 1980s, even at feature length, meant far less risk for those providing the finance, but more significant was that new avenues were opening up due to the growth of cable and satellite channels in the States and the need for product to fill up the schedules.

Elsewhere, the arrival of MTV at the beginning of the decade was a boon for the production of extravagant and prestigious music videos designed to stand out on the nascent channel. Major pop stars, including Michael Jackson and Bruce Springsteen, sought the prestige of a director's authorial star image (and presumably also their skill set) with six of the Renaissance auteurs featured in this study (Ashby, Coppola, De Palma, Friedkin, Rafelson and Scorsese) hired to direct mini-features, expensive in terms of their per-minute cost but which still palled compared to the cost of making even the cheapest feature film.[4] Such work has rarely been noted in the scramble to characterize these directors' careers as in terminal decline but these opportunities, on television and in music videos, were one way to keep in employment. They certainly avoided the associated risks to auteur-directors when they were foolish enough to provide their own funds to get projects off the ground, as Bogdanovich and Coppola found to their cost.

Even if the relative neglect shown to the films made by the Renaissance auteur in the 1980s might be justified because they were mostly box-office failures, these directors still managed to offer up a range of cinema that ought to be taken into account when their legacy, both individually and collectively, is considered. They made a range of films that are particularly interesting as examples of the different ways that directors' authorship is inscribed in their work. This book suggests that many of the films featured might be overdue for some critical re-evaluation but they are also valuable because, collectively, they form a pattern of creativity that puts into question existing accounts that characterize the decade as being 'lost' for auteurist filmmaking and that deny the Hollywood Renaissance auteur any role in the history of 1980s American filmmaking. The circumstances of the marketplace at the time when examined through the prism of the selected directors have provided a new position from which to appreciate individual films, American film history, and the viability of sustained authorial creativity within post-studio era Hollywood. That the 1980s produced films that are as diverse, artistically ambitious, and formally and stylistically rich as *Fool for Love, One from the Heart* or *To Live and Die in L.A.* illustrates why the 1980s output of the Hollywood Renaissance auteur should not be so readily consigned to a dusty corner of film history.

Appendices

Appendix 1
Directors and their 1980s feature films:
Production and distribution by industry sector

Director	80s films	Production			Distribution		
		Major studios*	Mini-majors*	Indie	Major studios	Mini-majors	Indie
Robert Altman	8	3	1	4	4	1	3
Hal Ashby	4	0	0	4	3	1	0
Peter Bogdanovich	3	1	0	2	2	0	1
Francis Coppola	7	0	2	5	4	3	0
William Friedkin	4	1	0	3	3	0	1
Dennis Hopper	2	0	1	1	0	1	1
John Milius	3	2**	0	2**	2	1	0
Brian de Palma	7	5	2	0	5	2	0
Arthur Penn	4	1	1	2	3	1	0
Bob Rafelson	2	2**	0	1**	2	0	0
Martin Scorsese	5	3**	0	3**	5	0	0
Totals	**49**	**17**	**7**	**27**	**33**	**10**	**6**

* Majors: Paramount, Fox, Warners, Universal, Disney, Columbia, MGM/United Artists
  Mini-majors: Cannon, Filmways, Orion, Tri-Star.
** Includes one studio/independent co-production.

Source: *IMDb* (www.imdb.com).

170 *Appendices*

Appendix 2
Top grossing 1980s films directed by Hollywood Renaissance auteurs

Film	Director	Production	Distribution	US returns ($ million)
The Untouchables (1987)	Brian De Palma	Paramount	Paramount	76
The Color of Money (1986)	Martin Scorsese	Disney	Disney	52
Popeye (1980)	Robert Altman	Paramount/ Disney	Paramount	49
Mask (1985)	Peter Bogdanovich	Universal	Universal	48
Colors (1988)	Dennis Hopper	Orion	Orion	46
Scarface (1983)	Brian De Palma	Universal	Universal	45
Peggy Sue Got Married (1986)	Francis Coppola	Tri-Star	Tri-Star	41
Conan the Barbarian (1982)	John Milius	Universal/ DEG	Universal	39
Red Dawn (1984)	John Milius	United Artists	MGM	38
Dressed to Kill (1980)	Brian De Palma	Filmways	Filmways	31
The Outsiders (1983)	Francis Coppola	Zoetrope	Warners	25
The Cotton Club (1984)	Francis Coppola	Orion	Orion	25
Black Widow (1987)	Bob Rafelson	Fox	Fox	25

Source: *Box Office Mojo* (www.boxofficemojo.com).

Notes

Introduction

1 A few examples among many include Diane Jacobs, *Hollywood Renaissance* (London: The Tantivy Press, 1977); *The Last Great American Picture Show: New Hollywood Cinema in the 1970s*, ed. Thomas Elsaesser, Alexander Horwath and Noel King (Amsterdam: Amsterdam University Press, 2004); Glenn Man, *Radical Visions: American Film Renaissance 1967–1976* (Westport: Greenwood Press, 1994).

2 Now known as *Star Wars: Episode IV – A New Hope*, I use the original title throughout.

3 For example, see Geoff King, *New Hollywood Cinema: An Introduction* (London: I.B. Tauris, 2002), 49–84; Andrew Britton, 'Blissing Out: The Politics of Reaganite Entertainment (1986)', in *Britton on Film: The Complete Film Criticism of Andrew Britton*, ed. Barry Keith Grant (Detroit: Wayne State University, 2009), 97–154; Tom Shone, *Blockbuster: How Hollywood Learned to Stop Worrying and Love the Summer* (London: Simon and Schuster, 2004).

4 Quoted in Peter Biskind, *Easy Riders, Raging Bulls* (London: Bloomsbury, 1998), 408.

5 Justin Wyatt, *High Concept: Movies and Marketing in Hollywood* (Austin: University of Texas Press, 1994), 73.

6 Examples of those who use 'New Hollywood' as alternative to 'Hollywood Renaissance' are Peter Krämer, *The New Hollywood: From Bonnie and Clyde to Star Wars* (London: Wallflower Press, 2005) and Jim Hillier, *The New Hollywood* (New York: Continuum, 1992).

7 Thomas Schatz, 'The New Hollywood', in *Film Theory Goes to the Movies*, ed. Jim Collins, Hilary Radnor and Ava Preacher Collins (Abingdon: Routledge, 1993), 8–36; Kristin Thompson, *Storytelling in the New Hollywood: Understanding Classical Narrative Techniques* (Cambridge, MA: Harvard University Press, 1999).

8 King, *New Hollywood Cinema*.

9 For example, 'The American New Wave: A Retrospective', an international academic conference at Bangor University, 4–6 July 2017.

10 Nicholas Godfrey, *The Limits of Auteurism: Case Studies in the Critically Constructed New Hollywood* (New Brunswick: Rutgers University Press, 2018), 162.

11 Robert Kolker, *A Cinema of Loneliness: Penn, Stone, Kubrick, Scorsese, Spielberg, Altman*, 3rd edition (Oxford: Oxford University Press, 2000), xiv–xv.

12　For example, Elsaesser, 'American Auteur Cinema: The Last – or First – Great Picture Show', in *The Last Great American Picture Show*, 37; Krämer, *The New Hollywood*, 1–5.

13　*The Hollywood Renaissance: Revisiting America's Most Celebrated Era*, ed. Peter Krämer and Yannis Tzioumakis (New York: Bloomsbury Academic, 2018).

14　*When the Movies Mattered: The New Hollywood Revisited*, ed. Jonathan Kirschner and Jon Lewis (Ithaca: Cornell University Press, 2019).

15　Robin Wood, *Hollywood from Vietnam to Reagan*, 2nd edition 2003 (New York: Columbia University Press, 1986), 145–8.

16　David Thomson, 'Who Killed the Movies?', *Esquire* 126, no. 6 (December 1996): 56.

17　Britton, 'Blissing Out', 97.

18　Ibid., 106.

19　Stephen Prince, 'Introduction: Movies and the 1980s', in *American Cinema of the 1980s: Themes and Variations*, ed. Stephen Prince (Oxford: Berg, 2007), 1.

20　Wood, *Hollywood from Vietnam to Reagan*, 147.

21　Timothy Corrigan, *A Cinema without Walls: Movies and Culture after Vietnam* (London: Routledge, 1991), 115.

22　Jon Lewis, *Whom God Wishes to Destroy: Francis Coppola and the New Hollywood* (London: Duke University Press, 1997).

23　Wyatt, *High Concept*. 8. Emphasis in original.

24　Ibid., 21–2.

25　Stephen Prince, *A New Pot of Gold: Hollywood under the Electronic Rainbow, 1980–1989* (London: University of California Press, 2000), xv.

26　Biskind, *Easy Riders*, 434.

27　On society, for example: Alan Nadel, *Flatlining on the Fields of Dreams: Cultural Narratives in the Films of President Reagan's America* (New Brunswick: Rutgers University Press, 1997); William Palmer, *The Films of the Eighties: A Social History* (Carbondale: Southern Illinois University Press, 1995).

28　For example, see Geoff Andrew, *Stranger than Paradise: Maverick Film-makers in Recent American Cinema* (London: Prion Books, 1998); Emanuel Levy, *Cinema of Outsiders: The Rise of American Independent Film* (New York: New York University Press, 1999).

29　Examples include Susan Jeffords, *Hard Bodies: Hollywood Masculinity in the Reagan Era* (New Brunswick: Rutgers University Press, 1994); Mantia Diawara, *Black American Cinema* (New York: Routledge, 1993); Vito Russo, *The Celluloid Closet: Homosexuality in the Movies* (New York: Harper & Row, 1981, revised ed. 1987).

30　Appendix 2 lists the most successful films directed by my group of Hollywood Renaissance auteurs (thirteen that grossed over $20 million domestically).

Notes   173

31   Following *Heaven's Gate*'s losses, United Artists was sold off to MGM by its owners, Transamerica Corporation, in 1980. The merged entity struggled to compete in the 1980s with the other majors. For an insider's account of the *Heaven's Gate* debacle, see Steven Bach, *Final Cut: Dreams and Disaster in the Making of Heaven's Gate* (London: Pimlico, 1996).

32   Krämer and Tzioumakis, 'Introduction', in *The Hollywood Renaissance,* xviii.

33   Yannis Tzioumakis, *American Independent Cinema: An Introduction* (Edinburgh: Edinburgh University Press, 2006), 248.

34   Geoff King, *Indiewood USA: Where Hollywood Meets Independent Cinema* (London: I.B. Tauris, 2009).

35   Tzioumakis, *American Independent Cinema*, 253.

36   Scorsese continues to this day to talk about a dramatic downturn in the 1980s: in an interview promoting *The Irishman* (2019), he commented about the decade, 'at that time I really couldn't get anything made'. Philip Horne, 'Three and a Half Hours with Scorsese', *Sight and Sound* 29, no. 11 (November 2019): 27.

37   Maya Montañez Smukler, *Liberating Hollywood: Women Directors and the Feminist Reform of 1970s American Cinema* (New Brunswick: Rutgers University Press, 2019).

38   *Ishtar* returned about $14 million against a budget of $55 million. May only directed four films in her career, none after *Ishtar*. The others were *A New Leaf* (1971), *The Heartbreak Kid* (1972) and *Mickey and Nicky* (1976).

39   David A. Cook, *Lost Illusions: American Cinema in the Shadow of Watergate and Vietnam, 1970–1979* (Berkeley: University of California Press, 2002), 133.

40   Michael Pye and Linda Myles, *The Movie Brats: How the Film School Generation Took over Hollywood* (London: Faber and Faber, 1979).

41   For alternative selections of key directors of the period, see James Monaco, *American Film Now* (New York: New American Library, 1984), 139–387; Cook, *Lost Illusions,* 67–158; Hillier, *The New Hollywood*; Jacobs, *Hollywood Renaissance; The Other Hollywood Renaissance*, ed. Dominic Lennard, R. Barton Palmer and Murray Pomerance (Edinburgh: Edinburgh University Press, 2020).

42   Altman also made his debut in the 1950s with the relatively unknown *The Delinquents* (1957), but his case is different from Penn's because his commercial breakthrough took another thirteen years.

43   Although I am unable to justifiably include Paul Schrader, I still want to make special mention of *Mishima: A Life in Four Chapters* (1985), produced by Coppola and Lucas, and one of the most fascinating, formally inventive and complex films of the entire decade. Note also that neither George Lucas nor Terence Malick directed anything at all in the 1980s.

174   *Notes*

44   Peter Lehman, 'The American Cinema and the Critic Who Guided Me through It', in *Citizen Sarris, American Film Critic: Essays in Honor of Andrew Sarris*, ed. Emanuel Levy (Lanham: The Scarecrow Press, Inc., 2001), 76.

45   Corrigan, *A Cinema without Walls*, 105.

46   Andrew Sarris, 'Notes on the Auteur Theory in 1962', in *Auteurs and Authorship: A Film Reader*, ed. Barry Keith Grant (Oxford: Blackwell Publishing, 2008), 43.

47   Pam Cook, 'Authorship Revised and Revived', in *The Cinema Book*, ed. Pam Cook, 3rd edition (London: BFI Publishing, 2007), 479.

48   V. F. Perkins, *Film as Film: Understanding and Judging Movies*, 2nd edition (London: Da Capo Press, 1993), 168.

49   Ibid., 172.

50   James Chapman, Mark Glancy and Sue Harper, 'Introduction', in *The New Film History: Sources, Methods, Approaches*, ed. Chapman, Glancy and Harper (London: Palgrave Macmillan, 2007), 8.

51   Aaron Hunter, *Authoring Hal Ashby: The Myth of the Hollywood Auteur* (New York: Bloomsbury Academic, 2016), 7, 11. See also Godfrey, *The Limits of Auteurism*; Krämer and Tzioumakis, 'Introduction', in *The Hollywood Renaissance*, xix.

52   For example, see Robert Self, *Robert Altman's Subliminal Reality* (Minneapolis: University of Minnesota Press, 2002), 159–66; Helene Keyssar, *Robert Altman's America* (New York: Oxford University Press, 1991), 243–59; Sarah S. Sinwell, 'Fantasies and Fangirls: Gender and Sexuality in Robert Altman's Come Back to the 5 & Dime, Jimmy Dean, Jimmy Dean', in *The Later Films and Legacy of Robert Altman*, ed. Lisa Dombrowski and Justin Wyatt (Edinburgh: Edinburgh University Press, 2021), 159–71.

53   Peter Cowie, *Coppola* (London: Andre Deutsch, 1989); Michael Goodwin and Naomi Wise, *On the Edge: The Life and Times of Francis Coppola* (New York: William Morrow and Co., 1989); Ronald Bergan, *Francis Coppola* (London: Orion, 1998); Michael Schumacher, *Francis Ford Coppola: A Filmmaker's Life* (London: Bloomsbury, 1999); Gene D. Phillips, *Godfather: The Intimate Francis Ford Coppola* (Kentucky: University of Kentucky, 2004); Stéphane Delorme, *Francis Ford Coppola: Masters of Cinema* (Paris: Cahiers du cinéma Sarl, 2010).

54   Lewis, *Whom God Wishes to Destroy*.

55   Care always needs to be taken when considering the involvement of directors in the writing of their films. Directors were only granted a screen credit if they could satisfy the Writers Guild that they had written at least 50 per cent of the script. The clarification of the 'genuine' authorship of scripts is greatly assisted – as I am able to do with Friedkin – by consulting original draft screenplays in archives.

Notes 175

Chapter 1

1 Philip Drake, 'Reputational Capital, Creative Conflict and Hollywood Independence', in *American Independent Cinema: Indie, Indiewood and Beyond*, ed. Geoff King, Claire Molloy and Yannis Tzioumakis (London: Routledge, 2012), 141.

2 King, *New Hollywood Cinema*, 101.

3 Mark Crispin Miller, 'Introduction: The Big Picture', in *Seeing through Movies*, ed. Mark Crispin Miller (New York: Pantheon Books, 1990), 7.

4 Leighton Grist, *The Films of Martin Scorsese, 1978–99: Authorship and Context II* (Basingstoke: Palgrave Macmillan, 2013), 156. See also Chapter 2.

5 Tzioumakis, *American Independent Cinema*, 11. Emphasis in original.

6 For example, see Greg Merritt, *Celluloid Mavericks: A History of American Independent Film* (New York: Thunder's Mouth Press, 2000), xi–xv; Yannis Tzioumakis, '"Independent", "Indie" and "Indiewood": Towards a Periodisation of Contemporary (Post-1980) American Independent Cinema', in *American Independent Cinema: Indie, Indiewood and Beyond*, 28–40; Levy, *Cinema of Outsiders*, 2–9.

7 Levy, *Cinema of Outsiders*, 2 (although he spends another seven pages elaborating on this).

8 Richard Maltby, *Hollywood Cinema*, 2nd edition (1995; repr., Oxford: Blackwell Publishing, 2003), 223.

9 I take mini-majors to mean those companies that were not the eight majors but were able to distribute their own films. The relevant companies in terms of this book are Orion, Tri-Star, Cannon and Filmways.

10 Maltby, *Hollywood Cinema*, 220.

11 Drake, 'Reputational Capital', 142.

12 Richard Maltby, '"Nobody Knows Everything": Post-classical Historiographies and Consolidated Entertainment', in *Contemporary Hollywood Cinema*, ed. Steve Neale and Murray Smith (London: Routledge, 1998), 35.

13 Prince, *A New Pot of Gold*, 117.

14 Maltby, *Hollywood Cinema*, 219; Justin Wyatt, 'The Formation of the "Major Independent": Miramax, New Line and the New Hollywood', in *Contemporary Hollywood Cinema*, 74.

15 Peter Biskind, *Down and Dirty Pictures: Miramax, Sundance and the Rise of Independent Film* (London: Bloomsbury, 2004), 81.

16 Maltby, *Hollywood Cinema*, 221.

17 Miller, 'Introduction: The Big Picture', 5.

18 Maltby, 'Nobody Knows Everything', 37.

176 *Notes*

19 Stephen Prince, 'Hollywood in the Age of Reagan', in *Contemporary American Cinema*, ed. Linda Ruth Williams and Michael Hammond (Maidenhead: McGraw-Hill, 2006), 241.

20 Grist, *Scorsese*, 155.

21 Thomas Clagett, *William Friedkin: Films of Aberration, Obsession and Reality*, 2nd edition (Los Angeles: Silman-James Press, 2003), 240. The film's funding is discussed in Chapter 5.

22 Quoted in I-Lien Tsay, '"Let Me Love You": Ambiguous Masculinity in Michael Cimino's Melodramas', in *The Other Hollywood Renaissance*, 88. Dargis also points out how much the film is now also 'feverishly admired' and 'holds one of the most contested places in American movie history'. Ibid.

23 See for example, *The Verdict* (Lumet, 1982); *The Morning After* (Lumet, 1986); *Silkwood* (Nichols, 1983); *Working Girl* (Nichols, 1988).

24 Douglas Gomery, *The Hollywood Studio System: A History* (London: BFI Publishing, 2005), 198.

25 Prince, *New Pot of Gold*, 92.

26 A note on box-office returns quoted in the book. Unless otherwise stated, all box-office returns are US grosses from *Box Office Mojo* (www.boxofficemojo.com). More accurate figures are used where available and referenced individually.

27 Data extrapolated from figures quoted in Prince, *New Pot of Gold*, 41.

28 Gomery, *The Hollywood Studio System*, 199.

29 Ibid., 243.

30 Prince, *New Pot of Gold*, 63–4.

31 Gomery, *The Hollywood Studio System*, 282–4.

32 Prince, *New Pot of Gold*, 31.

33 Gomery, *The Hollywood Studio System*, 283; Prince, *A New Pot of Gold*, 26.

34 Ibid., 46–9.

35 Gomery, *The Hollywood Studio System*, 221.

36 Joel W. Finler, *The Hollywood Story* (New York: Crown Publishers, 1988), 278.

37 Prince, *New Pot of Gold*, 41.

38 Gomery, *The Hollywood Studio System*, 241.

39 Tzioumakis, '"Independent", "Indie" and "Indiewood"', 30–1.

40 John Pierson, *Spike, Mike, Slackers & Dykes* (New York: Hyperion, 1995), 126.

41 United Artists were ahead of the curve having already set up United Artist Classics in 1980.

42 Tzioumakis, '"Independent", "Indie" and "Indiewood"', 28. See also Geoff King, *Indiewood USA: Where Hollywood Meets Independent Cinema* (London: I.B. Tauris, 2009); Biskind, *Down and Dirty Pictures*; Wyatt, 'The Formation of the "Major Independent"'.

Notes

43 Prince, *New Pot of Gold*, 143.

44 The colourful nature of Golan and Globus's tenure is amply illustrated in the documentary *Electric Boogaloo: The Wild, Untold Story of Cannon Films* (Mark Hartley, 2014). See also Prince, *A New Pot of Gold*, 150.

45 Richard Lippe and Robin Wood, 'An Interview with Arthur Penn', in *Arthur Penn*, ed. Robin Wood with Richard Lippe, Barry Keith Grant (Detroit: Wayne State University Press, 2014), 223.

46 Prince, *New Pot of Gold*, 152.

47 William Friedkin, *The Friedkin Connection* (New York: Harper Perennial, 2013), 401. These films are discussed in Chapters 2 and 5.

48 Douglas Keesey, *Brian De Palma's Split-Screen: A Life in Film* (Jackson: University of Mississippi, 2015), 146–8; Lippe and Wood, 'An Interview with Arthur Penn', 218.

49 Pierson, *Spike, Mike*, 204.

Chapter 2

1 Barry Langford, *Post-Classical Hollywood: Film Industry, Style and Ideology since 1945* (Edinburgh: Edinburgh University Press, 2010), 207.

2 Prince, *New Pot of Gold*, xvi.

3 Ibid., 341–69.

4 See Appendix 1 for the most successful 1980s films directed by Renaissance auteurs.

5 Their successes included *Out of Africa* (Pollack, 1986) and *Down and Out in Beverly Hills* (Mazursky, 1986).

6 Drake, 'Reputational Capital', 142.

7 Kenneth Von Gunden, *Postmodern Auteurs: Coppola, Lucas, De Palma, Spielberg and Scorsese* (Jefferson: McFarland and Co., 1991); David Greven, *Psycho-Sexual: Male Desire in Hitchcock, De Palma, Scorsese and Friedkin* (Austin: University of Texas Press, 2013); Leo Braudy, 'The Sacraments of Genre: Coppola, DePalma, Scorsese', *Film Quarterly* 39, no. 3 (April 1986): 17–28.

8 *Cape Fear* (Scorsese, 1991); *Mission Impossible* (De Palma, 1996).

9 Mitchell Zuckoff, *Robert Altman: The Oral Biography* (New York: Alfred A. Knopf, 2009), 381.

10 David Thompson and Ian Christie (eds), *Scorsese on Scorsese* (London: Faber and Faber, 1989), 108.

11 Todd Berliner, *Hollywood Incoherent: Narration in Seventies Cinema* (Austin: University of Texas Press, 2010), 180.

12 Bach, *Final Cut*, 164–6.

13 Grist, *Scorsese*, 42.

14 Ibid., 88.

15 For example, see Christina Newland, '*Joker*', *Sight and Sound* 29, no. 11 (November 2019): 70.

16 Thompson and Christie, *Scorsese on Scorsese*, 97–101.

17 Ibid.

18 Grist, *Scorsese*, 156.

19 Thompson and Christie, *Scorsese on Scorsese*, 101.

20 Other examples include *Desperately Seeking Susan* (Susan Seidelman, 1985), *Into the Night* (John Landis, 1985) and *Something Wild* (Jonathan Demme, 1986).

21 Thompson and Christie, *Scorsese on Scorsese*, 97. In the latter part of the decade, Eisner and Katzenberg dramatically transformed Disney's fortunes (see Prince, *New Pot of Gold*, 41).

22 Ibid., 104.

23 Ibid., 108.

24 Ibid.

25 Berliner, *Hollywood Incoherent*, 149.

26 Grist, *Scorsese*, 156.

27 Thompson and Christie, *Scorsese on Scorsese*, 123.

28 Grist, *Scorsese*, 159.

29 Quoted in ibid., 158.

30 Thompson and Christie, *Scorsese on Scorsese*, 124.

31 Carl Freedman, *Versions of Hollywood Crime Cinema: Studies in Ford, Wilder, Coppola, Scorsese, and Others* (Chicago: Intellect, 2013), 63.

32 Darren J. N. Middleton, *Scandalizing Jesus? Kazantzakis's the Last Temptation of Christ Fifty Years On* (New York: Continuum, 2005); Thomas R. Lindlof, *Hollywood under Siege: Martin Scorsese, the Religious Right, and the Culture Wars* (Lexington: University Press of Kentucky, 2008); Robin Riley, *Film, Faith and Cultural Conflict: The Case of Martin Scorsese's 'The Last Temptation of Christ'* (London: Praeger, 2003).

33 Grist, *Scorsese*, 155, 161–2.

34 Ibid., 8. Spielberg was originally involved but dropped out and was replaced by Coppola.

35 Ibid., 154.

36 For example, *Kundun* (1995) and *Silence* (2016).

37 Paul Ramaeker, 'Notes on the Split-Field Diopter', *Film History* 19 (2007): 191.

38 Greven, *Psycho-Sexual: Male Desire*; Eyal Peretz, *Becoming Visionary: Brian De Palma's Cinematic Education of the Senses* (Stanford: Stanford University Press, 2007); Chris Dumas, *Brian De Palma and the Political Invisible* (Bristol: Intellect Books, 2012); Keesey, *Brian De Palma's Split-Screen*; Linda Badley, 'Brian de Palma's Embattled Red Period: Hitchcock, Gender, Genre, and Postmodernism', in *The Other Hollywood Renaissance* (Edinburgh: Edinburgh University Press), 100–16.

Notes 179

39 Robert Kolker, *A Cinema of Loneliness*, 4th edition (Oxford: Oxford University Press, 2011), 187 (all other citations are taken from the 4th edition unless otherwise stated); Wood, *Hollywood from Vietnam to Reagan*, 120–43; Kenneth MacKinnon, *Misogyny in the Movies: The De Palma Question* (Newark: University of Delaware Press, 1990).

40 Dumas, *De Palma*, 12.

41 Badley, 'De Palma's Red Period', 102; *De Palma* (Noah Baumbach and Jake Paltrow, 2015).

42 Keesey, *Split Screen*, 146.

43 *De Palma*; Greven, *Psycho-Sexual: Male Desire,* 214–15.

44 Ibid.

45 Keesey, *Split Screen*, 146.

46 *De Palma.*

47 Wood, *Hollywood from Vietnam to Reagan*, 143.

48 Keesey, *Split Screen*, 156.

49 *De Palma.* Rabe keeps cropping up in this project: not only did he write Altman's *Streamers,* faithfully based on his own play, he wrote *Casualties of War* (1989) for De Palma. He also features briefly in Chapter 5 because of a failed collaboration with Friedkin.

50 Oliver Stone, *Chasing the Light* (London: Monoray, 2020), 182.

51 Ibid., 179; Keesey, *Split Screen*, 164.

52 *De Palma.*

53 Keesey, *Split Screen*, 180.

54 Lynn Hirschberg, 'Brian De Palma's Death Wish', *Esquire*, January 1984, 83 [capitals in original].

55 Badley, 'De Palma's Red Period', 112.

56 Prince, *New Pot of Gold*, 353.

57 Quoted in Keesey, *Split Screen*, 180.

58 Ibid., 183.

59 Ibid., 193.

60 Ibid., 204.

61 Quoted in Biskind, *Easy Riders*, 408.

62 Quoted in Leo Robson, 'Hollywood's Favourite Flop', *New Statesman*, 31 July 2015–13 August 2015, 19.

63 Stratten's tragic story formed the basis for Bob Fosse's 1983 film, *Star 80,* in which Bogdanovich (who objected) is lightly fictionalized as Aram Nicholas (Roger Rees).

64 Biskind, *Easy Riders*, 416.

65 Andrew Yule, *Picture Shows: The Life and Films of Peter Bogdanovich* (New York: Limelight Editions, 1992), 167–8.

180   *Notes*

66   Ibid., 170–6.

67   Biskind, *Easy Riders*, 415.

68   Yule, *Picture Shows*, 184–207.

69   Quoted in ibid., 219.

70   Quoted in ibid., 225.

71   Ibid., 231–50.

72   Quoted in Alfio Leotta, *The Cinema of John Milius* (Lanham: Lexington Books, 2019), x.

73   *Milius* (Joey Figueroa and Zak Knutson, 2013).

74   Leotta, *Milius*, xii.

75   Kolker, *A Cinema of Loneliness*, 3rd edition, 177. This observation about Milius is absent from the 4th edition so perhaps Kolker has modified his views.

76   *Milius*.

77   Jeffords, *Hard Bodies*.

78   *Conan*; *Scarface*; *Year of the Dragon*; *8 Million Ways to Die* (Ashby, 1986).

79   Leotta, *Milius*, 80.

80   Stone, *Chasing the Light*, 142.

81   Leotta, *Milius*, 88.

82   Patrick Goldstein, '*Red Dawn* Is Milius' Kind of Movie', *Los Angeles Times*, 16 August 1984, 11.

83   Ibid.

84   Leotta, *Milius*, 102.

85   Ibid., 103.

86   Kolker, *A Cinema of Loneliness*, 17–105; Wood and Lippe, *Arthur Penn*.

87   Examples include Christopher Beach, *The Films of Hal Ashby* (Detroit: Wayne State University Press, 2009); Nick Dawson, *Being Hal Ashby: The Life of a Hollywood Rebel* (Kentucky: University Press of Kentucky, 2011); Hunter, *Authoring Hal Ashby*; Brenda Austin-Smith, 'Hal Ashby, Gentle Giant', in *The Other Hollywood Renaissance*, 26–43; plus documentary *Hal* (Amy Scott, 2018).

88   Kolker, *A Cinema of Loneliness*, 20.

89   Lippe and Wood, 'An Interview with Arthur Penn', 215.

90   Geoff Andrew, 'Lost and Found: *Four Friends*', *Sight and Sound* 28, no. 2 (February 2018): 88.

91   Lippe and Wood, 'An Interview with Arthur Penn', 218.

92   Kolker, *A Cinema of Loneliness*, 21.

93   Lippe and Wood, 'An Interview with Arthur Penn', 226.

94   Ibid., 229.

95   Beach, *Films of Hal Ashby*, 9.

96   Hunter, *Authoring Hal Ashby*, 155.

Notes   181

97   Drake, 'Reputational Capital', 144.

98   Ibid., 146.

99   Hunter, *Authoring Hal Ashby*, 125–36.

100   Beach, *Films of Hal Ashby*, 144.

101   Quoted in ibid., 146.

102   Drake, 'Reputational Capital', 149.

103   Ibid.

104   Beach, *Films of Hal Ashby*, 149.

105   Hunter, *Authoring Hal Ashby*, 179.

106   Jay Boyer, *Bob Rafelson* (New York: Twayne Publishers, 1996). Rafelson does merit a chapter in the recent collection, *The Other Hollywood Renaissance:* Vincent Longo, 'Bob Rafelson's Ambivalent Authorship', 278–95.

107   Douglas Hildebrand, 'Bob Rafelson', in *Contemporary North American Film Directors: A Wallflower Critical Guide*, ed. Yoram Allon, Del Cullen and Hannah Patterson (London: Wallflower, 2002), 435.

108   Jonathan Kirschner, *Hollywood's Last Golden Age: Politics, Society, and the Seventies Film in America* (Ithaca: Cornell University Press, 2012), 16.

109   Andrew Schroeder, 'The Movement Inside: BBS Films and the Cultural Left in the New Hollywood', in *The World Sixties Made: Politics and Culture in Recent America*, ed. Van Gosse and Richard Moser (Philadelphia: Temple University Press, 2003), 115.

110   *Ossessione* (Luchino Visconti, 1943); *The Postman Always Rings Twice* (Tay Garnett, 1946).

111   Boyer, *Rafelson*, xvii.

112   Ibid., 78–80.

113   Ibid., 94.

114   Maggie Heung, '*Black Widow* (Review)', *Film Quarterly* 41, no. 1 (Autumn 1987): 57.

115   Boyer, *Rafelson*, 93.

116   *Man Trouble* (1992); *Blood and Wine* (1996).

117   Schroeder, 'The Movement Inside', 118.

118   Bart Mills, 'A Misfit Goes Mainstream', *Guardian*, 19 April 1990, 24.

119   Robert Morales, 'Head of Hopper' (1983) in *Dennis Hopper: Interviews,* ed. Nick Dawson (Jackson: University of Mississippi, 2012), 117.

120   Bill Kelley, 'True Colors' (1988) in ibid., 135.

121   Barbara Scharres, 'From Out of the Blue: The Return of Dennis Hopper', *Journal of the University Film and Video Association* 35, no. 2 (Spring 1983): 29.

122   The song comes from one of Young's most acclaimed album, *Rust Never Sleeps,* released in the same year. 'Thrasher', also featured in the film, is from the same album.

182   *Notes*

123   Scharres, 'From Out of the Blue', 29.

124   Nick Pinkerton, 'The Other Side of 80s America', *Sight and Sound* 28, no. 6 (June 2018): 24.

125   Kelley, 'True Colors', 136–7.

126   Ibid., 139.

127   Ibid., 135.

128   Drake, 'Reputational Capital', 146.

Chapter 3

1   Robert P. Kolker, 'The Affection of Death', in *The Later Films and Legacy of Robert Altman,* ed. Lisa Dombrowski and Justin Wyatt (Edinburgh: Edinburgh University Press, 2021), 191.

2   Patrick McGilligan, *Robert Altman: Jumping off the Cliff* (New York: St Martin's Press, 1989), 516; Stephen Farber, 'Five Horsemen of the Apocalypse', *Film Comment,* 21, no. 4 (July/August 1985): 33.

3   Pauline Kael, 'The Current Cinema: Lasso and Peashooter', *New Yorker,* 27 January 1986, 84.

4   Lisa Dombrowski and Justin Wyatt, 'Interview with Allan F. Nicholls', in *The Later Films,* 200.

5   Zuckoff, *The Oral Biography,* 381.

6   Altman's response to being labelled 'The Comeback Kid' on the release of *The Player,* as told to Eleanor Ringel of the *Atlanta Journal* (1993). Quoted in Dimitrios Pavlounis, 'Staging the "Rebel's Return"', in *A Companion to Robert Altman,* ed. Adrian Danks (Chichester: John Wiley & Sons, 2015), 935.

7   Anthony Quinn, 'On Both Sides of the Ledger', *Independent on Sunday,* 20 February 1994, 18.

8   Quoted in Robert Murphy, 'Art, Commerce, Corruption …', *AIP & Co,* no. 55 (June 1984): 29.

9   Quoted in Justin Wyatt, 'Countering Robert Altman's Sexual Outlaws: Visibility, Representation, and Questionable Sexual Progress', in *The Later Films,* 177.

10   Tzioumakis, '"Here Comes the Hot-Stepper": Hollywood Renaissance, Indie Film and Robert Altman's Comeback in the 1990s', in *The Later Films,* 125.

11   André Bazin, *What Is Cinema Volume 1?* (Berkeley: University of California Press, 1967, 2nd edition 2004, trans. Hugh Gray), 85.

12   Gayle Sherwood Magee, *Robert Altman's Soundtracks* (New York: Oxford University Press, 2014), 144.

13   Bazin, *What Is Cinema?,* 90.

Notes   183

14   Ibid., 92.

15   Susan Sontag, 'Film and Theatre', *Tulane Drama Review* 11, no. 1 (Autumn 1966): 28.

16   Martin Esslin, *The Field of Drama: How the Signs of Drama Create Meaning on Stage and Screen* (London: Methuen Drama, 1988), 40.

17   Sontag, 'Film and Theatre', 30.

18   Mark Minett provides a forensic and enlightening chapter-length examination of Altman's use of the zoom. See *Robert Altman and the Elaboration of Hollywood Storytelling* (New York: Oxford University Press, 2021), 77–169.

19   Andrew Sarris, 'The Selling of Sam Shepard', *Village Voice,* 10 December 1985, 59.

20   Nigel Andrews, '*Streamers*', *Financial Times*, 23 March 1984, 17.

21   Sontag, 'Film and Theatre', 28.

22   David Thompson (ed.), *Altman on Altman* (London: Faber and Faber, 2006), 133.

23   Charles Champlin, 'Altman's Getting Back to Basics in *Streamers*', *Los Angeles Times*, 24 March 1983, M1.

24   Lisa Dombrowski and Justin Wyatt, 'Introduction: Autumnal Altman – Rethinking His Last Quarter Century', in *The Later Years*, 2; McGilligan, *Jumping off the Cliff*, 476.

25   Daniel O'Brien, *Robert Altman: Hollywood Survivor* (London: B.T. Batsford, 1995), 86; Thompson, *Altman on Altman*, 124.

26   McGilligan, *Jumping off the Cliff*, 510–12.

27   Tim J. Anderson, 'Offbeat and Out of Sync: *Popeye* and the Failure of an Auteur-Driven Franchise', in *The Later Films*, 102–5.

28   David Levy in ibid., 365; McGilligan, *Jumping off the Cliff*, 520; Arjan Harmetz, 'Robert Altman Sells Studio for $2.3 Million', *New York Times*, 11 July 1981, 15.

29   Harmetz, 'Altman Sells', 15; Kathryn Altman in Zuckoff, *The Oral Biography*, 367.

30   Harmetz, 'Altman Sells', 15.

31   McGilligan, *Jumping off the Cliff*, 518.

32   Farber, 'Four Horsemen', 34.

33   Mark Rydell in Zuckoff, *The Oral Biography*, 365.

34   Justin Wyatt, 'Economic Constraints/Economic Opportunities: Robert Altman as Auteur', *Velvet Light Trap* 17 (Autumn 1996): 55.

35   Wyatt, *High Concept*, 190.

36   'Final Figures: *Two by South*', n.d., Box 162, Robert Altman Archive, Special Collections Library, University of Michigan (RAA hereafter). All monetary figures quoted exclude cents.

37   Frank Rich, 'Stage: Robert Altman Directs Cher', *New York Times*, 19 February 1982, C3.

38   Zuckoff, *The Oral Biography,* 374.

39 Richard Combs, 'Lives of Performers: A Discussion with Robert Altman on Film and Theatre, Past and Present, Toing and Froing ...', *Monthly Film Bulletin* 50 (September 1983): 233.

40 Letter from Denise Breton (European publicist) to Altman, 28 August 1982 (RAA:104).

41 MG Cable Productions, 'Outside Participant Report', 31 March 1985 (RAA:104).

42 Kolker, *A Cinema of Loneliness*, 414.

43 Combs, 'Lives of Performers', 233.

44 Thompson, *Altman on Altman*, 129–30.

45 Ed Graczyk, *Come Back to the 5 & Dime, Jimmy Dean, Jimmy Dean* (London: Samuel French Inc., 1982).

46 McGilligan, *Jumping off the Cliff*, 524.

47 Ibid., 527.

48 Magee, *Altman's Soundtracks*, 146.

49 The other two are *Sticks and Bones* and *The Basic Training of Pavlo Hummel* (both 1971).

50 Agreement between Landscape Films (Altman) and Lampwick Inc., 8 March 1983 (RAA:142); Paul Rosenfield, 'Robert Altman: Ever Ready for the Gauntlet or Gantlet', *Los Angeles Times*, 29 November 1983, G4.

51 Roy Loynd, 'Mileti Ankles SLM to Solo, Buys *Streamers* for $3-Mil', *Variety*, 6 July 1983, 6, 34.

52 'Robert Altman Schedule – *Streamers*', n.d. (RAA:144).

53 Tzioumakis, 'Here Comes the Hot-Stepper', 123; Mary Reinholz, 'UA Classics' Kitt Carrying the Torch, Going for Sophisticates', *The Hollywood Reporter* 278, no. 35 (20 September 1983): 1, 59.

54 Quoted in David Robinson, '*Streamers*', *The Times*, 23 March 1984, 21.

55 Philip C. Kolin, 'Rabe's *Streamers*', *Explicator* 45, no. 1 (Autumn 1986): 63.

56 Carol Rosen, *Plays of Impasse: Contemporary Drama Set in Confining Institutions* (Princeton: Princeton University Press, 1983), 251 (emphasis in original).

57 Quoted in Clarke Taylor, 'Premiere of *Streamers*: Playwright Rabe Cheered at Filmfest', *Los Angeles Times*, 12 October 1983, G2.

58 Sabine Altwein, *The Quest for American Manhood: Issue of Race and Gender in David Rabe's Vietnam Trilogy* (Saarbrücken: VDM Verlag Dr Müller, 2008), 23.

59 Other examinations of the play include Christopher Bigsby, *Contemporary American Playwrights* (Cambridge: Cambridge University Press, 2000), 275–78 and Gerald M. Berkowitz, *American Drama of the Twentieth Century* (London: Longman, 1992), 142–4. Among leading Altman scholars, the film is not mentioned at all by Kolker or by Robert Self in *Robert Altman's Subliminal Reality* (Minneapolis: University of Minnesota Press, 2002).

60 Keyssar, *Altman's America*, 317.

61 Bigsby, *Contemporary American Playwrights*, 275.

62 David Rabe, '*Streamers*: An Interview', n.d. and unattributed, BFI Reuben Library cuttings file on *Streamers*, 23.

63 Ibid., 22.

64 David Rabe, *Streamers*, 'Screenplay' and 'As Shot Screenplay', n.d. (RAA:144).

65 Brent Lewis, 'Altman on *Streamers*', *Nine to Five*, 2 April 1984, 4.

66 Zuckoff, *The Oral Biography*, 383.

67 Minett, *Elaboration of Hollywood Storytelling*, 222.

68 Rabe, *The Vietnam Plays: Volume Two* (New York: Grove Press, 1993), 33–5.

69 Ibid., 5.

70 Champlin, 'Altman's Getting Back to Basics', M6.

71 Mignot was cinematographer on nine Altman projects beginning with *Jimmy Dean* and including nearly everything Altman worked on in the eighties.

72 Bazin, *What Is Cinema?*, 89.

73 Keyssar, *Altman's America*, 316.

74 'Final Accounting Statement', *Streamers*, n.d. (RAA:142).

75 McGilligan, *Jumping off the Cliff*, 528–31.

76 Thompson, *Altman on Altman*, 134.

77 Robert Altman, DVD Commentary, *Secret Honor* (Criterion, 2004).

78 Freed provided the story for *Executive Action* (David Miller, 1973) that offers an alternative theory about [John] Kennedy's assassination some eighteen years before Oliver Stone's similarly themed *JFK* (1991). On Stone, see Richard Combs, 'In a Lonely Place', *Monthly Film Bulletin* 52, no. 612 (January 1985): 5.

79 Patricia Aufderheide, '*Secret Honor: Interviews with Donald Freed and Robert Altman*', *Cineaste* 14, no. 2 (1985): 14.

80 '*Secret Honour* [*sic*]', *New Musical Express*, 9 February 1985, 19.

81 Agreement between Secret Castle Productions and Cinecom International, 11 February 1984 (RAA:137).

82 Lisa Dombrowski and Justin Wyatt, 'Interview with Ira Deutchman', in *The Later Films*, 211–12.

83 University of Michigan Department of Communication Student Questionnaires, January 1984 (RAA: 137).

84 Magee, *Altman's Soundtracks*, 145.

85 Combs, 'In a Lonely Place', 5; Altman, DVD Commentary.

86 Hirschberg, 'Brian De Palma's Death Wish', 82.

87 For example: Rick Armstrong, 'Altman/Nixon/Reagan: Honorable Secrets, Historical Analogies and the Nexus of Anger', in *A Companion to Robert Altman*, 617–63.

88 Donald Freed and Arnold M. Stone, 'Secret Honor, The Last Testament of Richard M. Nixon: A Political Myth', in *New Plays USA 2*, ed. M. Elizabeth Osborn and Gillian Richards (New York: Theatre Communications Group, 1984), 1–32.

89 Altman, DVD Commentary.

90 Combs, 'In a Lonely Place', 5.

91 Freed and Stone, *Secret Honor*, 5.

92 Thompson, *Altman on Altman*, 135.

93 Thomas Monsell, *Nixon on Stage and Screen* (Jefferson: McFarland & Company, 1998), 139.

94 Richard R. Ness, 'A Perfect Couple: The Altman-Rudolph Connection', in *The Later Films*, 72.

95 Freed and Stone, *Secret Honor*, 31.

96 Kael, 'The Current Cinema: Arf', *New Yorker*, 15 July 1985, 73.

97 Keyssar, *Altman's America*, 329.

98 The Bohemian Grove retreat has been the subject of several books. See G. William Domhoff, *The Bohemian Grove and Other Retreats: A Study in Ruling-Class Cohesiveness* (New York: Harper Torchbooks, 1974) for an objective account of the club's history and rituals.

99 At least thirty different financial agreements between Secret Castle and individual theatres or theatre chains (RAA:139).

100 Screen Actors Guild Report for Philip Baker Hall for quarter ending 31 March 1989 (RAA:138).

101 For a scathing response to the film's vision of Nixon, see Stephen Harvey, 'Sympathy for That Devil?', *Village Voice*, 11 June 1985, 60.

102 First draft 24 June 1984; 2nd 9 December 1984; 5th 24 September 1994; Amendments by Stephen Altman, 15 March 1996. Numerous letters and legal agreements, 1978–1996: for example, letter to Altman from Euston Films regarding director and screenplay fees, 14 October 1986 (all RAA:542).

103 Numerous letters, telexes and documents, 1984–1995. For example, see Budget Summary ($2.7 million), 6 November 1984; telex from Thomas Schittler (producer), budget now $6.7m, 23 June 1987 (all RAA:536).

104 *Across the River and Into the Trees*, screenplay by Altman, 9 May 1985 (RAA:534); *The Feud*, 1st draft screenplay by Altman, December 1983 (RAA:542).

105 Letter from Robert Stein (Altman's agent) to Elliott Kastner (producer), 3 February 1986 (RAA:545). *Heat* was made in 1986, directed by Dick Richards, a critical and commercial failure.

106 'Budget Recap: *Nashville/Nashville*', Weintraub Entertainment Productions, 14 September 1987. Drafts dated November 1986, March 1987, April 1987, 26 February 1987, 15 March 1987 (all RAA:555).

Notes

107 Letter from David Kirkpatrick, Weintraub Entertainment to Altman, 5 November 1987 (RAA:555); Letter from Kirkpatrick to Scott Bushnell, 29 October 1987 (RAA:555).

108 Its original title is *Third and Oak: The Laundromat*.

109 Secret Castle Productions, 'Statement of Income', 31 December 1985 (RAA:138).

110 Zuckoff, *The Oral Biography*, 391.

111 Letter from Shepard to Altman, 14 January 1983 (RAA:108).

112 Zuckoff, *The Oral Biography*, 390–1.

113 'Director's Loan-Out Agreement', 'Actor's Loan-Out Agreement', 'Literary Acquisition Agreement', all dated 16 March 1985 (RAA:108).

114 Self, *Altman's Subliminal Reality*.

115 Robert Self, 'The Art Cinema and Robert Altman', *Velvet Light Trap* 19 (1982), 30.

116 Kolker, *A Cinema of Loneliness,* 414.

117 *Fool for Love*, 'Production Notes', n.d., 4 (RAA:109).

118 Stanley Kauffmann, 'Fooling around with Love', *New Republic*, 23 December 1985, 24.

119 Neil Norman, '*Fool for Love*', *Face*, July 1986, 93.

120 Sam Shepard, *Fool for Love and Other Plays* (New York: Bantam, 1984), 21. All other quotations from the play are also in the film unless otherwise stated.

121 *Paris, Texas* (Wim Wenders, 1984), with an original screenplay by Shepard, starred Stanton in a role with some similarities to the Old Man. He too is a man who goes on very long walks.

122 Shepard, *Fool for Love*, 21.

123 Ibid., 19.

124 Thompson, *Altman on Altman*, 139.

125 Zuckoff, *The Oral Biography*, 391.

126 Kimball King, 'Sam Shepard and the Cinema', in *The Cambridge Companion to Sam Shepard*, ed. Matthew Roudané (Cambridge: Cambridge University Press, 2006), 211.

127 Dombrowski and Wyatt, 'Interview with Allan F. Nicholls', 201.

128 *Fool for Love*, Screenplays: Four Drafts (1st n.d.; 2nd 15 April 1985; 3rd 19 April; 4th 25 April); Shooting Script 25 April; 'As Shot Script' n.d. (RAA:108).

129 Thompson, *Altman on Altman*, 140.

130 Shepard, *Fool for Love*, 20.

131 Frank Caso, *Robert Altman: In the American Grain* (London: Reaktion Books, 2015), 195.

132 Thompson, *Altman on Altman*, 140.

133 Shepard, *Fool for Love*, 48.

134 Ibid., 53.

135 Ibid., 54.

188 Notes

136 Ibid., 51.

137 Keyssar, *Altman's America*, 317.

138 Ross Wetzsteon, 'Introduction', in *Fool for Love and Other Plays*, 4.

139 Thompson, *Altman on Altman*, 140.

140 Keyssar, *Altman's America*, 323.

141 Sarris, 'The Selling of Sam Shepard', 59.

142 Cannon Films Inc., '*Fool for Love* Summary', 7 April 1987 (RAA:108).

143 For example, see McGilligan, *Jumping off the Cliff*, 548; O'Brien, *Hollywood Survivor*, 106.

144 Craig Gholson, 'Christopher Durang', *Bomb – Artists in Conversation* 20 (Summer 1987) (http://bombmagazine.org/article/950/christopher-durang).

145 Letter from Durang to Altman, 17 May 1986, 1 (RAA:99).

146 Durang, 'Beyond Therapy', in *Christopher Durang Explains It All for You: Six Plays* (New York: Grove Press, 1983), 215–97.

147 'Production Budget – *Beyond Therapy*', New World Pictures, 23 April 1986 (RAA:99).

148 Thompson, *Altman on Altman*, 141. According to Altman, Conti used his native Scottish accent, whereas, in fact, he employs a broad but dubious Irish brogue; Altman also praises Travolta's cockney accent as 'great' which is certainly generous.

149 Letter from Harold Pinter to Altman, 30 September 1987 (RAA:93).

150 Ibid.

151 Wouk adapted just the courtroom section of his 1951 novel, *The Caine Mutiny*, for the stage as *The Caine Mutiny Court-Martial* in 1953. In 1954, the film of the novel, *The Caine Mutiny* (Edward Dmytryk), was released.

152 Chuck Tyron, 'For Real: *Tanner'88, Tanner on Tanner*, and the Political Spectacle in the Post-Network Era', in *The Later Films*, 30–1.

153 It is probably not coincidental that all three series were/are on HBO. Indicating that the series has retained some form of cultural legacy, Senator Jack Tanner (played again by Michael Murphy) popped up recently as a 'talking head' in Scorsese's quasi-documentary, *Rolling Thunder Revue: A Bob Dylan Story* (Netflix, 2019).

154 Tzioumakis, 'Here Comes the Hot-Stepper', 118–19.

Chapter 4

1 Quoted in Robert Lindsey, 'Francis Coppola: Promises to Keep, the Flamboyant Filmmaker Swears His Best Work Lies Ahead', *New York Times*, 24 July 1988, SM24.

Notes

2 David Breskin, 'Francis Coppola', in *Inner Views: Filmmakers in Conversation* (New York: Da Capo Press, 1997), 32.

3 Francis Coppola, 'Journals 1989–1993', in *Projections 3: Film-makers on Film-making*, ed. John Boorman and Walter Donahue (London: Faber and Faber, 1994), 26.

4 Quoted in Dale Pollock, *Skywalking: The Life and Films of George Lucas* (London: Elm Tree Books, 1983), 78.

5 King, *New Hollywood Cinema*, 90.

6 Lynda Myles, 'The Zoetrope Saga', *Sight and Sound* 51, no. 2 (Spring 1982): 92.

7 Breskin, 'Francis Coppola', 4.

8 *The Outsiders* $25 million; *Peggy Sue*, $41 million; *The Cotton Club*, $25 million.

9 Corrigan, *A Cinema without Walls*, 105.

10 Jeffrey Chown, *Hollywood Auteur: Francis Coppola* (London: Praeger, 1988), 2.

11 Michael Ryan and Douglas Kellner, *Camera Politica: The Politics and Ideology of Contemporary Hollywood Film* (Bloomington: Indiana University Press, 1988), 268.

12 Freedman, *Versions of Hollywood Crime Cinema*, 36.

13 Ibid., 56.

14 *The Electronic Cinema* (Documentary, *One from the Heart* DVD, American Zoetrope, 2003).

15 Cowie, *Coppola*, 142.

16 Lewis, *Whom God Wishes*, 1.

17 Michael Powell, *Million Dollar Movie* (London: William Heinemann, 1992), 573. Powell credited Coppola and Scorsese's support as the beginning of his belated reputational rehabilitation.

18 Lewis, *Whom God Wishes*, 3.

19 Ibid., 21.

20 David Thomson, *The Whole Equation: A History of Hollywood* (London: Abacus, 2004), 396.

21 Lillian Ross, 'Onwards and Upwards with the Arts: Some Figures on a Fantasy', *New Yorker*, 8 November 1982.

22 Lewis, *Whom God Wishes*, 10. My emphasis.

23 Michael Chion, *David Lynch*, 2nd edition (London: BFI Publishing, 2006), 60.

24 Goodwin and Wise, *On the Edge*, 289–91; Schumacher, *Francis Ford Coppola*, 277–81. The only other Zoetrope originals were *The Outsiders* and *Rumble Fish*.

25 Quoted in *The Dream Studio* (Documentary, *One from the Heart* DVD).

26 Lewis, *Whom God Wishes*, 37.

27 He has returned to *Megalopolis* ('instead of it being a novel on the written page, it would be written in cinema') time and again, reviving the idea again recently and claiming he will spend his own money to make it at a cost of $100 million. See Mike Fleming Jr, 'Francis Coppola, "A Gambling Maverick Moviemaker Who Won Big Betting on Star Cast for Epic", *Megalopolis*', *Deadline*, 31 August 2021;

190   *Notes*

Oliver Macnaughton, '*Megalopolis*: Can Francis Ford Coppola's $100m Gamble Pay Off?', *The Guardian*, 3 September 2021. An adaptation of Goethe's *Elective Affinities* is the other 'big' project that Coppola has mentioned over the years. See for example, David Thomson and Lucy Gray, 'Idols of the King', *Film Comment* 19, no. 5 (September–October 1983): 74 and Coppola, *Live Cinema and Its Techniques* (New York: Liveright Publishing, 2017), 72.

28   Coppola, *Live Cinema*, 70.

29   *The Dream Studio*; Coppola, *Live Cinema,* 77. However, it did get some international distribution.

30   Kevin Polowy, 'Francis Ford Coppola Says He Was "depressed" and "had Lost everything" before Kids Encouraged Him to Make *The Outsiders*', *Yahoo Entertainment*, 11 November 2021 (https://www.aol.com/entertainment/francis-ford-coppola-says-depressed-160038377).

31   For some broadly positive viewpoints, see Sheila Benson, '*One from the Heart*', *Los Angeles Times*, 22 January 1982, G1, G6; Carrie Rickey, 'Let Yourself Go! Three Musicals Sing One from the Libido', *Film Comment* 18, no. 2 (March/April 1982): 43–7.

32   Chown, *Hollywood Auteur*, 158.

33   See particularly Cowie, *Coppola*, 146–65. One fairly brief exception is Graham Fuller's sympathetic and astute reconsideration of the film: 'A Second Look: *One from the Heart*', *Cinéaste* 17, no. 4 (January 1990): 58–9.

34   Both have been comprehensively covered elsewhere: on Zoetrope and the film's production/post-production, see particularly Lewis, *Whom God Wishes*, 41–73; Ross, 'Onwards and Upwards'. On the use of new technology, see Raymond Fielding, 'Recent Electronic Innovations in Professional Motion Picture Production', *Journal of Film and Video* 36, no. 2 (Spring 1984): 43–9, 72; Brooks Riley, 'Film into Video', *Film Comment* 18, no. 3 (May–June 1982): 45–8; Coppola, *Live Cinema*; *The Electronic Cinema*.

35   Quoted in Cowie, *Coppola*, 152.

36   Tom Waits and Crystal Gayle, 'Picking up after You'. All songs in the film are composed by Waits.

37   Rick Altman, *The American Film Musical* (Bloomington: Indiana University Press, 1987), 32.

38   Ibid., 29.

39   Rickey, 'Let Yourself Go', 44.

40   Francis Coppola, DVD Commentary, *One from the Heart* (American Zoetrope, 2003).

41   Barney Hoskyns, *Lowside of the Road: A Life of Tom Waits* (London: Faber & Faber, 2009), 244.

Notes 191

42 *One from the Heart*'s soundtrack album comes at an interesting point in Waits's recording career, forming a bridge between two distinct phases of his career. His next album would see him changing direction entirely, moving away from his bar room balladeer persona with the highly original and much-admired *Swordfishtrombones* (1983).

43 Coppola quoted in *Tom Waits and the Music of One from the Heart* (Documentary, *One from the Heart* DVD).

44 Waits and Gayle, 'Old Boyfriends' and 'You Can't Unring a Bell.'

45 Wyatt, *High Concept*, 22, 30.

46 Stanley Cavell, *Pursuits of Happiness: The Hollywood Comedy of Remarriage* (Cambridge, MA: Harvard University Press, 1981).

47 Ibid., 8.

48 Ibid., 49.

49 Coppola quoted in Ross, 'Onward and Upward', 64.

50 Coppola, DVD Commentary, *One from the Heart*.

51 Quoted in Cowie, *Coppola*, 153.

52 Goodwin and Wise, *On the Edge*, 296. Although his influence is obvious in the film, Kelly fell out badly with Coppola during production and insisted his name be excluded from the credits and later press releases. See ibid., 317.

53 Coppola, DVD Commentary, *One from the Heart*.

54 Cowie, *Coppola*, 146.

55 Coppola, *Live Cinema*, 75. The book describes in detail the two workshops conducted in 2015 and 2016.

56 Ibid., 69, 76.

57 Coppola's task would have been more difficult than Hitchcock's similar experiment on *Rope* (1948) because Hitchcock confined himself to a single set and limited character numbers.

58 Riley, 'Film into Video', 46; Fielding, 'Recent Electronic Innovations', 45.

59 Cowie, *Coppola*, 152.

60 Lindsey, 'Coppola', SM25.

61 Goodwin and Wise, *On the Edge* (322) and Schumacher, *Francis Ford Coppola* (317) both say thirty but Chown, *Hollywood Auteur*, puts it at 108 (163).

62 *S. E. Hinton on Location in Tulsa* (Documentary on DVD of *The Outsiders: The Complete Novel* (Studio Canal, 2011)).

63 Arjan Harmetz, 'Making *The Outsiders*: A Librarian's Dream', *New York Times*, 23 March 1983, C19.

64 Goodwin and Wise, *On the Edge*, 323.

65 '*The Outsiders*' files, Film Finances Limited Archives, London (FFA hereafter).

66 Draft of *Variety* advertisement, June 1982 (FFA).

192   *Notes*

67   Lewis, *Whom God Wishes*, 97–8.

68   Telex from Film Finances Limited to Robert Spiotta, Pony Boy Inc. c/o Zoetrope Studios, 2 March 1982 (FFA).

69   Letter from Kurt Woolner (Film Finances' representative) to Film Finances Limited, 26 April 1982 (FFA).

70   *Staying Gold: A Look Back at The Outsiders* (Documentary on DVD of *The Outsiders*, 2011).

71   Coppola, DVD Commentary, *The Outsiders* (Studio Canal, 2011).

72   Thomson and Gray, 'Idols of the Kings', 61.

73   Coppola's continuing tendency to second-guess himself has also resulted in various versions of *The Godfather* trilogy including the recent re-edited *Part III* as *The Godfather Coda: The Death of Michael Corleone* (2020); a third visit to *Apocalypse Now, Final Cut* (2019) following *Redux* in 2001; a new version of *One from the Heart* for DVD in 2003 which features a few superficial, and arguably unnecessary, alterations; a Blu-ray release of the third 1980s film that Coppola has re-edited, *The Cotton Club Encore* (2019), which runs thirteen minutes longer than the original.

74   Jonathan Bernstein, *Pretty in Pink: The Golden Age of Teenage Movies* (New York: St Martin's Griffin, 1997), 114.

75   Lewis, *Whom God Wishes*, 98; Wyatt, *High Concept*, 192.

76   Those who took part in a massive and unconventional audition process, but did not make the cut, included Mickey Rourke (who would star in *Rumble Fish)*, Dennis Quaid, Kate Capshaw and Val Kilmer. See *The Casting of The Outsiders* (Documentary on DVD of *The Outsiders*, 2011).

77   Five articles appeared in five successive issues of *Tiger Beat* magazine (Goodwin and Wise, *On the Edge*, 352). A special edition of *16 Magazine* in December 1982 was devoted to *The Outsiders'* young cast. See 'The Outsiders Production Files', Margaret Herrick Library, Academy of Motion Picture Arts and Sciences, Los Angeles (AMPAS hereafter).

78   Quoted in Molly Lewis, 'The Rumble of Nostalgia: Francis Ford Coppola's Vision of Boyhood', in *Cinemas of Boyhood: Masculinity, Sexuality, Nationality*, ed. Timothy Shary (New York: Berghahn, 2021), 90.

79   The Tulsa setting is not actually mentioned in the film.

80   Swayze was thirty at the time (and looks it). The others were all about ten years younger with Howell the youngest at sixteen.

81   S. E Hinton, *The Outsiders* (London: William Collins, 1967), 128.

82   Quoted in 'Production Information: *The Outsiders*', 25 March 1983 (AMPAS), 3.

83   Quoted in Goodwin and Wise, *On the Edge*, 322.

84   'Production Information: *The Outsiders*', 11.

Notes 193

85 Quoted in *The Outsiders: The True Story*, booklet accompanying DVD release of *The Outsiders* (2011).

86 Lewis, *Whom God Wishes*, 100.

87 'Production Budget', *Rumble Fish*, n.d. (FFA).

88 Memo from Robert Spiotta (Zoetrope) to Barry Hirsch (lawyer), 7 June 1982 (FFA).

89 Lewis, *Whom God Wishes*, 108; Chown, *Hollywood Auteur*, 167.

90 S. E. Hinton, *Rumble Fish* (New York: Delacorte Press, 1975).

91 Cowie, *Coppola*, 169.

92 Thomson and Gray, 'Idols of the King', 61.

93 Lewis, 'The Rumble of Nostalgia', 95.

94 Goodwin and Wise, *On the Edge*, 384.

95 Ibid., 390.

96 Schumacher, *Francis Ford Coppola*, 339.

97 The film's production history has been extensively covered. See particularly, Michael Daly, 'The Making of *The Cotton Club*: A True Tale of Hollywood', *New York,* 7 May 1984, 40–62; Goodwin and Wise, *On the Edge*, 359–413 and Lewis, *Whom God Wishes,* 111–42. Robert Evans offers his own extremely partial account in his memoir, *The Kid Stays in the Picture* (London: Aurum Press, 1994), 327–51.

98 Goodwin and Wise, *On the Edge*, 379.

99 Cowie, *Coppola*, 179. Puzo ended up with only a 'Story' credit.

100 The recent re-edit, *The Cotton Club Encore,* is noticeably different. Some of the film's obvious problems have been addressed but, arguably, this has the effect of creating others.

101 Schumacher, *Francis Ford Coppola*, 380.

102 Chown, *Hollywood Auteur*, 201.

103 Lewis, *Whom God Wishes*, 149.

104 Quoted in Ibid.

105 Schumacher, *Francis Ford Coppola*, 380.

106 Lee Lourdeaux, *Italian and Irish Filmmakers in America: Capra, Coppola and Scorsese* (Philadelphia: Temple University Press, 1990), 178.

107 Coppola's episode was not shown until March 1987.

108 Goodwin and Wise, *On the Edge*, 416; Cowie, *Coppola*, 189.

109 Quoted in Goodwin and Wise, *On the Edge*, 407.

110 Palmer, *Films of the Eighties,* 52.

111 Cowie, *Coppola*, 199.

112 Gene Phillips, 'Francis Coppola', *Films in Review* 40, no. 3 (March 1989): 159.

113 Gabriella Oldham, 'Barry Malkin, the Supreme Collaboration', in *First Cut: Conversations with Film Editors* (Berkeley: University of California Press, 1992), 331.

114 Goodwin and Wise, *On the Edge*, 432.

115 Steve Oney, '*Tucker*: The Director Finally Makes the Picture of His Dreams', *Premiere*, August 1988, 69.

116 Lindsey, 'Coppola', SM26.

117 Quoted in Pollock, *Skywalking*, 79.

118 Delorme, *Francis Ford Coppola*, 68; Jill Kearney, 'The Road Warrior', *American Film* 13, no. 8 (May–September 1988): 23.

119 Lewis, *Whom God Wishes*, 151.

120 Oney, '*Tucker*', 70.

121 For an insight into Eleanor's personality and relationship with her husband, see her *Notes: On the Making of Apocalypse Now* (London: Faber and Faber, 1979).

122 Kearney, 'The Road Warrior', 26.

123 For example, see Lewis, *Whom God Wishes*, 152.

124 Cowie, *Coppola*, 215.

125 Although, in reality, Tucker was indeed acquitted, he did not make his own closing address. See Oney, '*Tucker*', 69.

126 Arvid Linde, *Preston Tucker and Others: Tales of Brilliant Automotive Inventors and Innovations* (Dorchester: Veloce Publishing, 2011), 29–47.

127 Kearney, 'The Road Warrior', 27.

128 Cowie, *Coppola*, 213.

129 Ibid., 221.

130 Coppola, *Live Cinema*, 84 (emphasis in original).

131 For example, see Lindsey, 'Coppola'; Kearney, 'The Road Warrior'; Brent Lewis, 'Coppola's Coup', *Films and Filming*, no. 410 (November/December 1988): 6–8; Michael Sragow, 'Hot-rodding Down the Street of Dreams', *L.A. Herald-Examiner*, 10 August 1988, B1, B4.

132 Lindsey, 'Coppola', SM27.

133 Kearney, 'The Road Warrior', 26-7.

134 Oldham, 'Barry Malkin', 338.

135 Lindsey, 'Coppola', SM27.

136 Cowie, *Coppola*, 223.

137 Schumacher, *Francis Ford Coppola*, 415.

138 In Napa Valley, Los Angeles, San Francisco, New York and Belize. See Lindsey, 'Coppola', SM25.

139 For an interesting analysis of the three, see Calum Marsh, 'Small Change: The Late Films of Francis Ford Coppola', *Cinéaste* 40, no. 3 (Summer 2015): 32.

140 Prince, *New Pot of Gold*, 229.

Notes 195

Chapter 5

1 Larry Gross, 'Whatever Happened to William Friedkin?', *Sight and Sound* 5, no. 12 (December 1995): 14.

2 *The Boys in the Band* (1970), *The French Connection, The Exorcist, Sorcerer* and *The Brink's Job* (1978).

3 Friedkin speaking in June 1982, quoted in Clagett, *Films of Aberration*, 278.

4 Walon Green (writer of *Sorcerer* and *The Brink's Job*) talking about executives at the Hollywood studios. Quoted in Biskind, *Easy Riders*, 413.

5 Quoted in Biskind, *Easy Riders*, 413–14.

6 Although *To Live and Die* is credited to Friedkin and Gerald Petievich, Friedkin was the sole writer (discussed shortly). He was also co-writer on *The Guardian* (1990).

7 Wyatt, *High Concept*, 191.

8 Nat Segaloff, *Hurricane Billy: The Stormy Life and Films of William Friedkin* (New York: William Morrow, 1990), 276.

9 Ibid., 190.

10 Clagett, *Films of Aberration*, 274. Blatty eventually directed it himself as *The Exorcist III* in 1990.

11 Segaloff, *Hurricane Billy*, 190, 213. *Blood and Money* was not made.

12 Ibid., 190.

13 Alex Simon, '*Cruising* with Billy', *Venice*, September 2007, 69.

14 Clagett, *Films of Aberration*, 238–9. They were caught, convicted for extortion, but no murder was proved. They *were* men in uniform, but were boat crew not policemen.

15 Arthur Bell, 'Another Murder at the Anvil', *Village Voice*, 22 January 1979. William Friedkin Papers (WFP hereafter), Margaret Herrick Library, Academy of Motion Pictures and Sciences: item f.168.

16 Simon, '*Cruising* with Billy', 69.

17 Friedkin, *Friedkin Connection*, 361.

18 Clagett, *Films of Aberration*, 240.

19 Lawrence Grobel, *Al Pacino: The Authorized Biography* (London: Pocket Books, 2006), 92.

20 Clagett, *Films of Aberration*, 259.

21 Mark Kermode, 'Cruise Control', *Sight and Sound* 8, no. 11 (November 1998): 22.

22 Segaloff, *Hurricane Billy*, 199.

23 Linda Ruth Williams, 'No Sex Please, We're American', *Sight and Sound* 14, no. 1 (January 2004): 19.

24 Examples, among many, include Les Ledbetter, '1000 in "Village" Renew Protest against Movie on Homosexuals', *New York Times*, 26 July 1979, B2; Fred Ferretti, 'Filming of *Cruising* Goes More Calmly', *New York Times*, 7 August 1979, C7;

196 *Notes*

Dale Pollock, 'Friedkin Film *Cruising* into a Storm of Protest', *Los Angeles Times*, 4 February 1980, G1, G8.

25 Eugenio Ercolani and Marcus Stiglegger, *Cruising* (Liverpool: Auteur, 2020), 85. '[Friedkin] took the film before the MPAA board nearly 50 times at a cost of $50,000, and deleted forty minutes of footage from the original cut before he got the desired R rating.'

26 Prince, *New Pot of Gold*, 346.

27 Ibid., 345–7. For more on the rating dispute, see also Arjan Harmetz, 'How *Cruising* Received Its "R" Rating', *New York Times*, 16 February 1980, 12; Segaloff, *Hurricane Billy*, 204–5; Pollock, '*Cruising*: The Battle Continues', *Los Angeles Times*, 27 June 1980, Part VI, 9; '*Cruising* Gets a New "R" Label', *Variety*, 10 June 1980. WFP: f.167.

28 Edgar Gross (Friedkin's business manager), File Memo, 12 May 1980. WFP: f.167; Pollock, 'R- Rated *Cruising*: The MPAA Seal of Disapproval', *Los Angeles Times Calendar*, 4 May 1980, 1, 6–7.

29 'Statement of William Friedkin and Jerry Weintraub Relative to *Cruising* and Its "R" Rating', 17 June 1980. WFP: f.167.

30 Gross, File memo, 7 March 1980. WFP: f.167.

31 Prince, *New Pot of Gold*, 347.

32 Vito Russo, *The Celluloid Closet: Homosexuality in the Movies* (New York: Harper & Row, 1981, revised ed. 1987), 259.

33 Jason Bailey, 'Making Sense of *Cruising*', *Village Voice*, 21 March 2018, 1–5.

34 Letter from Keith Williams to Friedkin, 14 August 1979. WFP: f.113.

35 Letter from Friedkin to Mayor Koch, 9 October 1979. WFP: f.113.

36 Vincent Canby, 'Screen: Pacino Stars in Friedkin's *Cruising*', *New York Times*, 15 February 1980, C6.

37 George Grella, '*Cruising*: Artful, Shocking', *Rochester-City Newspaper*, n.d. WFP: f.113.

38 Letter from Grella to Friedkin, 11 April 1980. WFP: f.113. Emphasis in original.

39 Letter from Friedkin to Grella, 17 June 1980. WFP: f.113.

40 Ercolani and Stiglegger, *Cruising*, 87.

41 There has also been a recent 2019 Blu-ray release.

42 Gary Needham, '"*Cruising* Is a Picture We Sincerely Wish We Did Not Have to Show": United Artists, Ratings, and the Controversy of William Friedkin's *Cruising* (1980)', in *United Artists*, ed. Peter Kramer, Gary Needham, Yannis Tzioumakis and Tino Balio (Abingdon: Routledge, 2020), 192–210; R. Barton Palmer, 'Redeeming *Cruising*: Tendentiously Offensive, Coherently Incoherent, Strangely Pleasurable', in *B Is for Bad Cinema: Aesthetics, Politics, and Cultural Value*, ed. Claire Perkins and Constantine Verevis (Albany: SUNY Press, 2014), 85–104; see also Derek Nystrom,

Hard Hats, Rednecks, and Macho Men (New York: Oxford University Press, 2009); D. A. Miller, 'Cruising', *Film Quarterly* 61, no. 2 (January 2007): 70–3.

43 Paul Burston, 'So Good It Hurts', *Sight and Sound* 8, no. 11 (November 1998): 24.

44 Wood, 'The Incoherent Text: Narrative in the 70s' reprinted in *Hollywood from Vietnam to Reagan*, 41–62.

45 Ibid., 42.

46 Bill Krohn, 'Friedkin Out', *Rouge*, no. 3 (2004), 1–12 (www.rouge.com.au/3/friedkin.html); Adrian Martin, 'Cruising: The Sound of Violence', *Undercurrent*, no. 4 (October 2008). See also R. Barton Palmer, 'Redeeming *Cruising*'; Dominic Lennard, 'William Friedkin: Frayed Connections', in *The Other Hollywood Renaissance*, 148–60.

47 Martin, 'The Sound of Violence'.

48 Krohn, 'Friedkin Out', 5.

49 Quoted in Janet Maslin, 'Friedkin Defends His *Cruising*', *New York Times*, 18 September 1979, C12.

50 *Cruising* scripts 26 April 1979; 1 June; 25 June; 29 June. WFP: f.85; f.90; f.92; f.97.

51 Scripts, both 14 February 1980. WFP: f.103; f.104.

52 Script, 14 February 1980. WFP: f.104.

53 Martin, 'The Sound of Violence'.

54 Script 2nd draft, 26 April 1979. WFP: f.85.

55 Ibid.

56 Script revised 4th draft, 29 June 1979. WFP: f.92.

57 Krohn, 'Friedkin Out', 12.

58 Wood, *Hollywood from Vietnam to Reagan*, 61.

59 Steve Choe, *The Films of William Friedkin* (Edinburgh: Edinburgh University Press, 2021), 102.

60 Alex Simon, 'William Friedkin: Auteur of the Dark (1997)', in *William Friedkin Interviews*, ed. Christopher Lane (Jackson: University Press of Mississippi, 2020), 69.

61 Steven Gaydos, 'William Friedkin and *To Live and Die in L.A.*', in *Movie Talk from the Front Lines: Filmmakers Discuss Their Work with the Los Angeles Critics Association*, ed. Jerry Roberts and Steven Gaydos (Jefferson: McFarland and Co., 1994), 252. See also documentary *The Directors: William Friedkin* (Robert J. Emery, 1995).

62 Alexander Wilson, 'Friedkin's *Cruising*, Ghetto Politics and Gay Sexuality', *Social Text*, no. 4 (Autumn 1981): 98; Dale Pollock, 'Cruising in War Zone; Finished on Sked, Bow Set', *Variety* (12 September 1979): 6.

63 Ercolani and Stiglegger, *Cruising*, 87.

64 Friedkin, *Friedkin Connection*, 376.

65 Quoted in John Corry, 'Broadway: Chodorov-Panama Mystery to Star Claudette Colbert', *New York Times*, 12 June 1981, C2.

198   *Notes*

66 *New York Times,* '*Duet* Closing Saturday', 29 December 1981, C7.

67 Carrie Rickey, 'Has Success Spoiled Paul Brickman?' *Wall Street Journal*, 4 January 1984, 20.

68 Clagett, *Films of Aberration*, 277.

69 Bud Yorkin, File memo, 18 August 1982: 'The Navy turned it down. No F-14. The Army Air has turned us down … AT THIS TIME WE HAVE NO AIR FIELD, NO PLANES, NOR ANY COOPERATION FROM ANY OF THE ARMED SERVICES (capitals in original)', WFP: f.213.

70 Memo from Yorkin to Bob Shapiro (Warners), 25 August 1982. WFP: f.291.

71 Clagett, *Films of Aberration*, 277.

72 Segaloff, *Hurricane Billy*, 220.

73 Ibid., 245.

74 Ibid., 243.

75 Ibid., 246–7.

76 Roderick Mann, 'The Director behind the Crime', *Los Angeles Times*, 27 October 1985 (AMPAS Production File).

77 Gaydos, 'William Friedkin', 235.

78 Clagett, *Films of Aberration*, 291.

79 Will Tusher, 'Friedkin to Direct and Write *L.A.*', *Variety*, 25 July 1984 (AMPAS).

80 'Tentative Proposed Budget', *To Live and Die*, 12 October 1984; 'Projected Shooting Budget', 14 November 1984. WFP: f.939.

81 '*To Live and Die in L.A.* Cost Summary', 22 November 1985. WFP: f.951.

82 Ibid.; Letter from Irving Levin to Friedkin, 1 March 1984. WFP: f.959.

83 Quoted in Mann, 'The Director behind the Crime'.

84 Phillip Lopate, *Totally, Tenderly, Tragically: Essays and Criticism from a Lifelong Love Affair with the Movies* (New York: Anchor Books, 1998), 135.

85 'Cast Deal Memos', 1984. WFP: f.944.

86 'Cost Summary', 22 November 1985. WFP: f.951.

87 Ibid.

88 Segaloff, *Hurricane Billy*, 224.

89 Choe, *The Films*, 60.

90 Friedkin, *Friedkin Connection*, 384.

91 Sharon Willis, 'Disputed Territories: Masculinity and Social Space', in *Male Trouble,* ed. Constance Penley and Sharon Willis (Minneapolis: University of Minnesota Press, 1993), 273.

92 Friedkin, *Friedkin Connection*, 249.

93 There was some disagreement about the authorship of the screenplay. Friedkin said, 'I put Gerald Petievich's name on it because he did create characters and situations. I used a lot of his dialogue … even though I wrote the entire script.'

Petievich, on the other hand, claimed that they 'worked on it together'. Validating Friedkin's claims, all the drafts are marked 'screenplay by William Friedkin (based on a novel by Gerald Petievich)'. The change to the joint credit appears only on the shooting script. See *To Live and Die in L.A.,* handwritten scripts n.d. WFP: f.890 and f.892; 1st draft, 25 April 1984. WFP: f.893; Script, 8 November 1984. WFP: f.974.

94 Gerald Petievich, *To Live and Die in L.A.* (New York: Pocket Books, 1984).

95 Scripts n.d. WFP: f.890, f.892; 1st draft. 25 April 1984; Friedkin's handwritten notes on script n.d. WFP: f.935.

96 Letter from William Peter Blatty to Friedkin, 1. WFP: f.950.

97 Script, 1 October 1984. WFP: f. 916.

98 Letter from Blatty to Friedkin, 2.

99 Ibid., 3.

100 Script, 8 November 1984.

101 Clagett, *Films of Aberration*, 289.

102 Ibid., 290.

103 Handwritten script n.d.; script, 25 April 1984.

104 Script, 1 October 1984.

105 Krohn, 'Friedkin Out', 6.

106 Gaydos, 'William Friedkin', 248.

107 Robert Arnett, 'Eighties Noir: The Dissenting Voice in Reagan's America', *Journal of Popular Film and Television* 34, no. 3 (2006): 125; Ian Mantgani, 'Ending … To Live and Die in LA', *Sight and Sound* 26, no. 11 (November 2016): 112.

108 Clagett, *Films of Aberration*, 288.

109 Michael Wilmington, '*Live and Die* Chases *French Connection*', *Los Angeles Times*, 1 November 1985, G4.

110 Choe, *The Films*, 62.

111 Segaloff, *Hurricane Billy*, 236.

112 Richard Lippe and Florence Jacobwitz, 'Masculinity in the Movies: *To Live and Die in L.A*', *CineAction!*, no. 6 (Summer/Autumn 1986): 38–40.

113 Vincent Canby, 'How *Live and Die* Hooks Its Viewers', *New York Times*, 17 November 1985, H17.

114 Quoted in Gaydos, 'William Friedkin', 232.

115 Segaloff, *Hurricane Billy*, 248.

116 Ibid., 248-9.

117 William Wood, *Rampage* (London: Star Books, 1985).

118 Friedkin, *Friedkin Connection*, 398.

119 Ibid.

120 On costs, letter from Ken Ryan, Rampage Productions, to European American Bank, 3 January 1987. WFP: f.566. On budget, letter from Thomas Hansen (lawyer) to Steve Ransohoff (Film Finances Inc.), 16 October 1986. WFP: f. 580.

121 Letter from Friedkin to Film Finances Inc., 2 October 1986. WFP: f.580.

122 'Director Agreement', 15 August 1986; 'Writer Agreement', 14 July 1986. WFP: f.580.

123 Segaloff, *Hurricane Billy*, 267.

124 'Cast Deal Memos', 1986. WFP: f.567.

125 'Music Agreement Ennio Morricone', 22 July 1987. WFP: f.581; Friedkin, *Friedkin Connection*, 400.

126 Ibid.

127 Clagett, *Films of Aberration*, 311.

128 'Bank Files Action over *Rampage* Funds', *Variety*, 6 June 1988; Segaloff, *Hurricane Billy*, 268.

129 Friedkin, *Friedkin Connection*, 401 (emphasis in original).

130 Quoted in Clagett, *Films of Aberration*, 309.

131 The Hinckley case is pertinent. A controversial verdict found him not guilty by reason of insanity and he was released in 2016 after thirty-five years. See Elizabeth Chuck, 'John Hinckley Freed from Mental Hospital 35 Years after Reagan Assassination Attempt', *NBC News*, 10 October 2016 (www.nbcnews.com/news/us-news/john-hinckley-freed-mental-hospital-35-years-after-reagan-assassination-n646076).

132 Fred Barbash, 'Life or Death: It's in Your Mind – or His', *Washington Post*, 27 February 1981, A7.

133 *Rampage*, 1st draft n.d. WFP: f.525; Script, 8 August 1986. WFP: f.548.

134 Letter from John Daugherty (Office of the District Attorney, Sacramento) to Kathy Lambert (Rampage Productions), 4 February 1986, accompanying materials about 'People vs. Richard Trenton Chase'. WFP: f.653.

135 *NewsRounds*, January 1986, 16. WFP: f. 623.

136 Letters in 'Hate Mail 1986' files. WFP: f.612 and f.613. Example from Helen Smith, 14 May 1986: 'Surely you can make money some way without hurting so many people.'

137 Friedkin, 'A Statement from William Friedkin', *NewsRounds*, June/July 1986, 5.

138 Iris Yang, *The Sacramento Bee*, 7 February 1979. WFP: f.653.

139 Friedkin, *Friedkin Connection*, 401.

140 Letter from Office of the D.A. Sacramento, John Daugherty to Kathy Lambert, 4 February 1986; file marked 'Research (Richard Chase) 1978–1986' including newspaper articles, books. All WFP: f.653.

141 Letter from Colleen Grace to Friedkin, 15 January 1986. WFP: f.656.

142   Clagett, *Films of Aberration*, 310.
143   The real-life model, Chase, was dubbed the 'Dracula Killer' in the press.
144   1st draft n.d., 5. WFP: f.525.
145   Segaloff, *Hurricane Billy*, 265.
146   Revised Continuity Script, 11 July 1991. WFP: f.557.
147   Choe, *The Films*, 135–6.

Conclusion

1   Wyatt, *High Concept*, 191.
2   Farber, 'Five Horsemen after the Apocalypse', 32. The five featured are Altman, Bogdanovich, Scorsese, John Sayles and Alan Rudolph.
3   Biskind, *Easy Riders*, 16.
4   For full details of these music videos, see Filmography.

Bibliography

Archival sources

BFI Reuben Library, London
Cuttings files for films by key directors (articles cited individually in bibliography and notes)
Film Finances Limited Archives, London (abbreviated to FFA)
Production Files for *The Outsiders* (1983) and *Rumble Fish* (1983)
Margaret Herrick Library, Academy of Motion Pictures & Sciences, Los Angeles (abbreviated to AMPAS)
William Friedkin Papers (abbreviated to WFP)
Production files for films by key directors (articles cited individually in bibliography and notes)
University of Michigan Library (Special Collections), Ann Arbor
Robert Altman Archive (abbreviated to RAA)

Books and edited collections

Altman, Rick. *The American Film Musical*. Bloomington: Indiana University Press, 1987.

Altwein, Sabine. *The Quest for American Manhood: Issue of Race and Gender in David Rabe's Vietnam Trilogy*. Saarbrücken: VDM Verlag Dr Müller, 2008.

Andrew, Geoff. *Stranger than Paradise: Maverick Filmmakers in Recent American Cinema*. London: Prion Books, 1998.

Bach, Steven. *Final Cut: Dreams and Disaster in the Making of Heaven's Gate*. London: Pimlico, 1996.

Bazin, André. *What Is Cinema Volume 1?* 2nd edn. Trans. Hugh Gray. 1967. Berkeley: University of California Press, 2004.

Beach, Christopher. *The Films of Hal Ashby*. Detroit: Wayne State University Press, 2009.

Bergan, Ronald. *Francis Coppola*. London: Orion, 1998.

Berkowitz, Gerald M. *American Drama of the Twentieth Century*. London: Longman, 1992.

Berliner, Todd. *Hollywood Incoherent: Narration in Seventies Cinema*. Austin: University of Texas Press, 2010.

Bibliography

Bernstein, Jonathan. *Pretty in Pink: The Golden Age of Teenage Movies*. New York: St Martin's Griffin, 1997.

Bigsby, Christopher. *Contemporary American Playwrights*. Cambridge: Cambridge University Press, 2000.

Biskind, Peter. *Easy Riders, Raging Bulls*. London: Bloomsbury, 1998.

Biskind, Peter. *Down and Dirty Pictures: Miramax, Sundance and the Rise of Independent Film*. London: Bloomsbury, 2004.

Boyer, Jay. *Bob Rafelson*. New York: Twayne Publishers, 1996.

Breskin, David. *Inner Views: Filmmakers in Conversation*. New York: Da Capo Press, 1997.

Caso, Frank. *Robert Altman: In the American Grain*. London: Reaktion Books, 2015.

Cavell, Stanley. *Pursuits of Happiness: The Hollywood Comedy of Remarriage*. Cambridge, MA: Harvard University Press, 1981.

Chapman, James, Mark Glancy and Sue Harper (eds). *The New Film History: Sources, Methods, Approaches*. London: Palgrave Macmillan, 2007.

Chion, Michael. *David Lynch*. 2nd edn. London: BFI Publishing, 2006.

Choe, Steve. *The Films of William Friedkin*. Edinburgh: Edinburgh University Press, 2021.

Chown, Jeffrey. *Hollywood Auteur: Francis Coppola*. London: Praeger, 1988.

Clagett, Thomas. *William Friedkin: Films of Aberration, Obsession and Reality*. 2nd edn. Los Angeles: Silman-James Press, 2003.

Cook, David A. *Lost Illusions: American Cinema in the Shadow of Watergate and Vietnam, 1970–1979*. Berkeley: University of California Press, 2002.

Coppola, Eleanor. *Notes: On the Making of Apocalypse Now*. London: Faber and Faber, 1979.

Coppola, Francis Ford. *Live Cinema and Its Techniques*. New York: Liveright Publishing, 2017.

Corrigan, Timothy. *A Cinema without Walls: Movies and Culture after Vietnam*. London: Routledge, 1991.

Cowie, Peter. *Coppola*. London: Andre Deutsch, 1989.

Dawson, Nick. *Being Hal Ashby: The Life of a Hollywood Rebel*. Kentucky: University Press of Kentucky, 2011.

Delorme, Stéphane. *Francis Ford Coppola: Masters of Cinema*. Paris: Cahiers du cinéma Sarl, 2010.

Diawara, Mantia. *Black American Cinema*. New York: Routledge, 1993.

Domhoff, G. William. *The Bohemian Grove and Other Retreats: A Study in Ruling-Class Cohesiveness*. New York: Harper Torchbooks, 1974.

Dumas, Chris. *Brian De Palma and the Political Invisible*. Bristol: Intellect Books, 2012.

Durang, Christopher. *Christopher Durang Explains It All for You: Six Plays*. New York: Grove Press, 1983.

Bibliography

Elsaesser, Thomas, Alexander Horwath, Noel King (eds). *The Last Great American Picture Show: New Hollywood Cinema in the 1970s*. Amsterdam: Amsterdam University Press, 2004.

Ercolani, Eugenio and Marcus Stiglegger. *Cruising*. Liverpool: Auteur, 2020.

Esslin, Martin. *The Field of Drama: How the Signs of Drama Create Meaning on Stage and Screen*. London: Methuen Drama, 1988.

Evans, Robert. *The Kid Stays in the Picture*. London: Aurum Press, 1994.

Finler, Joel W. *The Hollywood Story*. New York: Crown Publishers, 1988.

Freedman, Carl. *Versions of Hollywood Crime Cinema: Studies in Ford, Wilder, Coppola, Scorsese, and Others*. Chicago: Intellect, 2013.

Friedkin, William. *The Friedkin Connection*. New York: Harper Perennial, 2013.

Godfrey, Nicholas. *The Limits of Auteurism: Case Studies in the Critically Constructed New Hollywood*. New Brunswick: Rutgers University Press, 2018.

Gomery, Douglas. *The Hollywood Studio System: A History*. London: BFI Publishing, 2005.

Goodwin, Michael and Naomi Wise. *On the Edge: The Life and Times of Francis Coppola*. New York: William Morrow and Co., 1989.

Graczyk, Ed. *Come Back to the 5 & Dime, Jimmy Dean, Jimmy Dean*. London: Samuel French Inc., 1982.

Greven, David. *Psycho-Sexual: Male Desire in Hitchcock, De Palma, Scorsese and Friedkin*. Austin: University of Texas Press, 2013.

Grist, Leighton. *The Films of Martin Scorsese, 1978–99: Authorship and Context II*. Basingstoke: Palgrave Macmillan, 2013.

Grobel, Lawrence. *Al Pacino: The Authorized Biography*. London: Pocket Books, 2006.

Hillier, Jim. *The New Hollywood*. New York: Continuum, 1992.

Hinton, S. E. *The Outsiders*. London: William Collins, 1967.

Hinton, S. E. *Rumble Fish*. New York: Delacorte Press, 1975.

Hoskyns, Barney. *Lowside of the Road: A Life of Tom Waits*. London: Faber & Faber, 2009.

Hunter, Aaron. *Authoring Hal Ashby: The Myth of the Hollywood Auteur*. New York: Bloomsbury Academic, 2016.

Jacobs, Diane. *Hollywood Renaissance*. London: The Tantivy Press, 1977.

Jeffords, Susan. *Hard Bodies: Hollywood Masculinity in the Reagan Era*. New Brunswick: Rutgers University Press, 1994.

Keesey, Douglas. *Brian De Palma's Split-Screen: A Life in Film*. Jackson: University of Mississippi, 2015.

Keyssar, Helene. *Robert Altman's America*. New York: Oxford University Press, 1991.

King, Geoff. *New Hollywood Cinema: An Introduction*. London: I.B. Tauris, 2002.

King, Geoff. *American Independent Cinema*. London: I.B. Tauris, 2005.

King, Geoff. *Indiewood USA: Where Hollywood Meets Independent Cinema*. London: I.B. Tauris, 2009.

Kirschner, Jonathan. *Hollywood's Last Golden Age: Politics, Society, and the Seventies Film in America*. Ithaca: Cornell University Press, 2012.

Kirschner, Jonathan and Jon Lewis (eds). *When the Movies Mattered: The New Hollywood Revisited*. Ithaca: Cornell University Press, 2019.

Kolker, Robert. *A Cinema of Loneliness: Penn, Stone, Kubrick, Scorsese, Spielberg, Altman*. 3rd edn. Oxford: Oxford University Press, 2000.

Kolker, Robert. *A Cinema of Loneliness*. 4th edn. Oxford: Oxford University Press, 2011.

Krämer, Peter. *The New Hollywood: From Bonnie and Clyde to Star Wars*. London: Wallflower Press, 2005.

Krämer, Peter and Yannis Tzioumakis (eds). *The Hollywood Renaissance: Revisiting America's Most Celebrated Era*. New York: Bloomsbury Academic, 2018.

Langford, Barry. *Post-Classical Hollywood: Film Industry, Style and Ideology since 1945*. Edinburgh: Edinburgh University Press, 2010.

Leotta, Alfio. *The Cinema of John Milius*. Lanham: Lexington Books, 2019.

Levy, Emanuel. *Cinema of Outsiders: The Rise of American Independent Film*. New York: New York University Press, 1999.

Lewis, Jon. *Whom God Wishes to Destroy: Francis Coppola and the New Hollywood*. London: Duke University Press, 1997.

Linde, Arvid. *Preston Tucker and Others: Tales of Brilliant Automotive Inventors and Innovations*. Dorchester: Veloce Publishing, 2011.

Lindlof, Thomas R. *Hollywood under Siege: Martin Scorsese, the Religious Right, and the Culture Wars*. Lexington: University Press of Kentucky, 2008.

Lopate, Phillip. *Totally, Tenderly, Tragically: Essays and Criticism from a Lifelong Love Affair with the Movies*. New York: Anchor Books, 1998.

Lourdeaux, Lee. *Italian and Irish Filmmakers in America: Capra, Coppola and Scorsese*. Philadelphia: Temple University Press, 1990.

MacKinnon, Kenneth. *Misogyny in the Movies: The De Palma Question*. Newark: University of Delaware Press, 1990.

Magee, Gayle Sherwood. *Robert Altman's Soundtracks*. New York: Oxford University Press, 2014.

Maltby, Richard. *Hollywood Cinema*. 2nd edn. 1995. Oxford: Blackwell Publishing, 2003.

Man, Glenn. *Radical Visions: American Film Renaissance, 1967–1976*. Westport: Greenwood Press, 1994.

McGilligan, Patrick. *Robert Altman: Jumping off the Cliff*. New York: St Martin's Press, 1989.

Merritt, Greg. *Celluloid Mavericks: A History of American Independent Film*. New York: Thunder's Mouth Press, 2000.

Middleton, Darren J. N. *Scandalizing Jesus? Kazantzakis's The Last Temptation of Christ Fifty Years On*. New York: Continuum, 2005.

Minett, Mark. *Robert Altman and the Elaboration of Hollywood Storytelling*. New York: Oxford University Press, 2021.

Monaco, James. *American Film Now*. New York: New American Library, 1984.

Monsell, Thomas. *Nixon on Stage and Screen*. Jefferson: McFarland and Co., 1998.

Nadel, Alan. *Flatlining on the Fields of Dreams: Cultural Narratives in the Films of President Reagan's America*. New Brunswick: Rutgers University Press, 1997.

Nystrom, Derek. *Hard Hats, Rednecks, and Macho Men*. New York: Oxford University Press, 2009.

O'Brien, Daniel. *Robert Altman: Hollywood Survivor*. London: B.T. Batsford, 1995.

Oldham, Gabriella. *First Cut: Conversations with Film Editors*. Berkeley: University of California Press, 1992.

Palmer, William. *The Films of the Eighties: A Social History*. Carbondale: Southern Illinois University Press, 1995.

Peretz, Eyal. *Becoming Visionary: Brian De Palma's Cinematic Education of the Senses*. Stanford: Stanford University Press, 2007.

Perkins, V. F. *Film as Film: Understanding and Judging Movies*. 2nd edn. London: Da Capo Press, 1993.

Petievich, Gerald. *To Live and Die in L.A.* New York: Pocket Books, 1984.

Pierson, John. *Spike, Mike, Slackers & Dykes*. New York: Hyperion, 1995.

Pollock, Dale. *Skywalking: The Life and Films of George Lucas*. London: Elm Tree Books, 1983.

Powell, Michael. *Million Dollar Movie*. London: William Heinemann, 1992.

Prince, Stephen. *A New Pot of Gold: Hollywood under the Electronic Rainbow, 1980–1989*. Berkeley and London: University of California Press, 2000.

Pye, Michael and Linda Myles. *The Movie Brats: How the Film School Generation Took over Hollywood*. London: Faber and Faber, 1979.

Rabe, David. *The Vietnam Plays: Volume Two*. New York: Grove Press, 1993.

Riley, Robin. *Film, Faith and Cultural Conflict: The Case of Martin Scorsese's 'The Last Temptation of Christ'*. London: Praeger, 2003.

Rosen, Carol. *Plays of Impasse: Contemporary Drama Set in Confining Institutions*. Princeton: Princeton University Press, 1983.

Russo, Vito. *The Celluloid Closet: Homosexuality in the Movies*, rev. edn. 1981. New York: Harper & Row, 1987.

Ryan, Michael and Douglas Kellner. *Camera Politica: The Politics and Ideology of Contemporary Hollywood Film*. Bloomington: Indiana University Press, 1988.

Schumacher, Michael. *Francis Ford Coppola: A Filmmaker's Life*. London: Bloomsbury, 1999.

Segaloff, Nat. *Hurricane Billy: The Stormy Life and Films of William Friedkin*. New York: William Morrow, 1990.

Self, Robert. *Robert Altman's Subliminal Reality*. Minneapolis: University of Minnesota Press, 2002.

Shepard, Sam. *Fool for Love and Other Plays*. New York: Bantam, 1984.

Shone, Tom. *Blockbuster: How Hollywood Learned to Stop Worrying and Love the Summer*. London: Simon and Schuster, 2004.

Smukler, Maya Montañez. *Liberating Hollywood: Women Directors and the Feminist Reform of 1970s American Cinema*. New Brunswick: Rutgers University Press, 2019.

Stone, Oliver. *Chasing the Light*. London: Monoray, 2020.

Thomson, David. *The Whole Equation: A History of Hollywood*. London: Abacus, 2004.

Thompson, David (ed.). *Altman on Altman*. London: Faber and Faber, 2005.

Thompson, David and Ian Christie (eds). *Scorsese on Scorsese*. London: Faber and Faber, 1989.

Thompson, Kristin. *Storytelling in the New Hollywood: Understanding Classical Narrative Techniques*. Cambridge, MA: Harvard University Press, 1999.

Tzioumakis, Yannis. *American Independent Cinema: An Introduction*. Edinburgh: Edinburgh University Press, 2006.

Von Gunden, Kenneth. *Postmodern Auteurs: Coppola, Lucas, De Palma, Spielberg and Scorsese*. Jefferson: McFarland and Co., 1991.

Wood, Robin. *Hollywood from Vietnam to Reagan*. 2nd edn. 1986. New York: Columbia University Press, 2003.

Wood, William. *Rampage*. London: Star Books, 1985.

Wyatt, Justin. *High Concept Movies and Marketing in Hollywood*. Austin: University of Texas Press, 1994.

Yule, Andrew. *Picture Shows: The Life and Films of Peter Bogdanovich*. New York: Limelight Editions, 1992.

Zuckoff, Mitchell. *Robert Altman: The Oral Biography*. New York: Alfred A. Knopf, 2009.

Articles and chapters

Anderson, Tim J. 'Offbeat and Out of Sync: *Popeye* and the Failure of an Auteur-Driven Franchise'. In *The Later Films and Legacy of Robert Altman*, edited by Lisa Dombrowski and Justin Wyatt, 102–05. Edinburgh: Edinburgh University Press, 2021.

Andrew, Geoff. 'Lost and Found: *Four Friends*'. *Sight and Sound* 28, no. 2 (February 2018): 88.

Andrews, Nigel. '*Streamers*'. *Financial Times*, 23 March 1984, 17.

Armstrong, Rick. 'Altman/Nixon/Reagan: Honorable Secrets, Historical Analogies and the Nexus of Anger'. In *A Companion to Robert Altman*, edited by Adrian Danks, 617–63. Chichester: John Wiley & Sons, 2015.

Arnett, Robert. 'Eighties Noir: The Dissenting Voice in Reagan's America'. *Journal of Popular Film and Television* 34, no. 3 (2006): 123–9.

Aufderheide, Patricia. '*Secret Honor*: Interviews with Donald Freed and Robert Altman'. *Cinéaste* 14, no. 2 (1985): 13–14.

Austin-Smith, Brenda. 'Hal Ashby, Gentle Giant'. In *The Other Hollywood Renaissance*, edited by Dominic Lennard, R. Barton Palmer and Murray Pomerance, 26–43. Edinburgh: Edinburgh University Press, 2020.

Badley, Linda. 'Brian de Palma's Embattled Red Period: Hitchcock, Gender, Genre, and Postmodernism'. In *The Other Hollywood Renaissance*, edited by Dominic Lennard, R. Barton Palmer and Murray Pomerance, 100–16. Edinburgh: Edinburgh University Press, 2020.

Bailey, Jason. 'Making Sense of *Cruising*'. *Village Voice*, 21 March 2018, 1–5.

Barbash, Fred. 'Life or Death: It's in Your Mind – or His'. *Washington Post*, 27 February 1981, A7.

Bell, Arthur. 'Another Murder at the Anvil'. *Village Voice*, 22 January 1979. (WFP: f168).

Benson, Sheila. '*One from the Heart*'. *Los Angeles Times*, 22 January 1982, G1, G6.

Braudy, Leo. 'The Sacraments of Genre: Coppola, DePalma, Scorsese'. *Film Quarterly* 39, no. 3 (April 1986): 17–28.

Britton, Andrew. 'Blissing Out: The Politics of Reaganite Entertainment (1986)'. In *Britton on Film: The Complete Film Criticism of Andrew Britton*, edited by Barry Keith Grant, 97–154. Detroit: Wayne State University, 2009.

Burston, Paul. 'So Good It Hurts'. *Sight and Sound* 8, no. 11 (November 1998): 24.

Canby, Vincent. 'Screen: Pacino Stars in Friedkin's *Cruising*'. *New York Times*, 15 February 1980, C6.

Canby, Vincent. 'How *Live and Die* Hooks Its Viewers'. *New York Times*, 17 November 1985, H17.

Champlin, Charles. 'Altman's Getting Back to Basics in *Streamers*'. *Los Angeles Times*, 24 March 1983, M1, M6.

Chuck, Elizabeth. 'John Hinckley Freed from Mental Hospital 35 Years after Reagan Assassination Attempt'. *NBC News*, 10 September 2016 (www.nbcnews.com/news/us-news/john-hinckley-freed-mental-hospital-35-years-after-reagan-assassination-n646076).

Combs, Richard. 'Lives of Performers: A Discussion with Robert Altman on Film and Theatre, Past and Present, Toing and Froing …'. *Monthly Film Bulletin* 50, no. 596 (September 1983): 233.

Combs, Richard. 'In a Lonely Place'. *Monthly Film Bulletin* 52, no. 612 (January 1985): 4–6.

Cook, Pam. 'Authorship Revised and Revived'. In *The Cinema Book*. 3rd edn., edited by Pam Cook, 479–86. London: BFI Publishing, 2007.

Coppola, Francis Ford. 'Journals 1989–1993'. In *Projections 3: Film-makers on Film-making*, edited by John Boorman and Walter Donahue, 3–46. London: Faber and Faber, 1994.

Corry, John. 'Broadway: Chodorov-Panama Mystery to Star Claudette Colbert'. *New York Times*, 12 June 1981, C2.

Daly, Michael. 'The Making of *The Cotton Club*: A True Tale of Hollywood'. *New York*, 7 May 1984, 40–62.

Dombrowski, Lisa, and Justin Wyatt. 'Interview with Allan F. Nicholls'. In *The Later Films and Legacy of Robert Altman*, edited by Lisa Dombrowski and Justin Wyatt, 197–201. Edinburgh: Edinburgh University Press, 2021.

Dombrowski, Lisa, and Justin Wyatt. 'Interview with Ira Deutchman'. In *The Later Films and Legacy of Robert Altman*, edited by Lisa Dombrowski and Justin Wyatt, 211–12. Edinburgh: Edinburgh University Press, 2021.

Dombrowski, Lisa and Justin Wyatt. 'Introduction: Autumnal Altman – Rethinking His Last Quarter Century'. In *The Later Films and Legacy of Robert Altman*, edited by Lisa Dombrowski and Justin Wyatt, 1–10. Edinburgh: Edinburgh University Press, 2021.

Drake, Philip. 'Reputational Capital, Creative Conflict and Hollywood Independence'. In *American Independent Cinema: Indie, Indiewood and Beyond King*, edited by Geoff King, Claire Molloy and Yannis Tzioumakis, 140–92. London: Routledge, 2012.

Farber, Stephen. 'Five Horsemen after the Apocalypse'. *Film Comment* 21, no. 4 (July/August 1985): 32–5.

Ferretti, Fred. 'Filming of *Cruising* Goes More Calmly'. *New York Times*, 7 August 1979, C7.

Fielding, Raymond. 'Recent Electronic Innovations in Professional Motion Picture Production'. *Journal of Film and Video* 36, no. 2 (Spring 1984): 43–9, 72.

Fleming Jr, Mike. 'Francis Coppola A Gambling Maverick Moviemaker Who Won Big Betting on Star Cast for Epic *Megalopolis*'. *Deadline*, 31 August 2021.

Freed, Donald and Arnold M. Stone. 'Secret Honor, The Last Testament of Richard M. Nixon: A Political Myth'. In *New Plays USA 2*, edited by M. Elizabeth Osborn and Gillian Richards, 1–32. New York: Theatre Communications Group, 1984.

Friedkin, William. 'A Statement from William Friedkin'. *NewsRounds*, June/July 1986, 5.

Fuller, Graham. 'A Second Look: *One from the Heart*'. *Cinéaste* 17, no. 4 (January 1990): 58–9.

Gaydos, Steven. 'William Friedkin and *To Live and Die in L.A.*'. In *Movie Talk from the Front Lines: Filmmakers Discuss Their Work with the Los Angeles Critics Association*, edited by Jerry Roberts and Steven Gaydos, 231–52. Jefferson: McFarland and Co., 1994.

Gholson, Craig. 'Christopher Durang'. *Bomb – Artists in Conversation* 20 (Summer 1987). (http://bombmagazine.org/article/950/christopher-durang).

Goldstein, Patrick. '*Red Dawn* Is Milius' Kind of Movie'. *Los Angeles Times*, 16 August 1984, 11.

Grella, George. '*Cruising*: Artful, Shocking'. *Rochester-City Newspaper*. n.d. WFP: f.113.

Gross, Larry. 'Whatever Happened to William Friedkin?'. *Sight and Sound* 5, no. 12 (December 1995): 14–15.

Harmetz, Arjan. 'How *Cruising* Received Its "R" Rating'. *New York Times*, 16 February 1980, 12.

Harmetz, Arjan. 'Robert Altman Sells Studio for $2.3 Million'. *New York Times*, 11 July 1981, 15.

Harmetz, Arjan. 'Making *The Outsiders*: A Librarian's Dream'. *New York Times*, 23 March 1983, C19.

Harvey, Stephen. 'Sympathy for That Devil?'. *Village Voice*, 11 June 1985, 60.

Heung, Maggie. '*Black Widow* (Review)'. *Film Quarterly* 41, no. 1 (Autumn 1987): 54–8.

Hildebrand, Douglas. 'Bob Rafelson'. In *Contemporary North American Film Directors: A Wallflower Critical Guide*, edited by Yoram Allon, Del Cullen and Hannah Patterson, 435–6. London: Wallflower, 2002.

Hirschberg, Lynn. 'Brian De Palma's Death Wish'. *Esquire*, January 1984, 79–83.

Kael, Pauline. 'The Current Cinema: Arf'. *New Yorker*, 15 July 1985, 70, 73.

Kael, Pauline. 'The Current Cinema: Lasso and Peashooter'. *New Yorker*, 27 January 1986, 84, 87.

Kaufmann, Stanley. 'Fooling around with Love'. *New Republic*, 23 December 1985, 24–5.

Kearney, Jill. 'The Road Warrior'. *American Film* 13, no. 8 (May–September 1988): 21–7, 52.

Kelley, Bill. 'True Colors (1988)'. In *Dennis Hopper: Interviews*, edited by Nick Dawson, 135–40. Jackson: University of Mississippi, 2012.

Kermode, Mark. 'Cruise Control'. *Sight and Sound* 8, no. 11 (November 1998): 22–4.

King, Kimball. 'Sam Shepard and the Cinema'. In *The Cambridge Companion to Sam Shepard*, edited by Matthew Roudané, 210–26. Cambridge: Cambridge University Press, 2006.

Kolin, Philip C. 'Rabe's *Streamers*'. *Explicator* 45, no. 1 (Autumn 1986): 63–4.

Kolker, Robert. 'The Affection of Death'. In *The Later Films and Legacy of Robert Altman*, edited by Lisa Dombrowski and Justin Wyatt, 190–4. Edinburgh: Edinburgh University Press, 2021.

Krohn, Bill. 'Friedkin Out'. *Rouge*, no. 3 (2004): 1–12 (www.rouge.com.au/3/friedkin.html).

Ledbetter, Les. '1000 in "Village" Renew Protest against Movie on Homosexuals'. *New York Times*, 26 July 1979, B2.

Lehman, Peter. 'The American Cinema and the Critic Who Guided Me through It'. In *Citizen Sarris, American Film Critic: Essays in Honor of Andrew Sarris*, edited by Emanuel Levy, 71–6. Lanham: The Scarecrow Press, Inc., 2001.

Lennard, Dominic. 'William Friedkin: Frayed Connections'. In *The Other Hollywood Renaissance*, edited by Dominic Lennard, R. Barton Palmer and Murray Pomerance, 148–60. Edinburgh: Edinburgh University Press, 2020.

Lewis, Brent. 'Altman on *Streamers*'. *Nine to Five*, 2 April 1984, 4.

Lewis, Brent. 'Coppola's Coup'. *Films and Filming*, no. 410 (November/December 1988): 6–8.

Lewis, Molly. 'The Rumble of Nostalgia: Francis Ford Coppola's Vision of Boyhood'. In *Cinemas of Boyhood: Masculinity, Sexuality, Nationality*, edited by Timothy Shary, 87–102. New York: Berghahn, 2021.

Lindsey, Robert. 'Francis Coppola: Promises to Keep, the Flamboyant Filmmaker Swears His Best Work Lies Ahead'. *New York Times*, 24 July 1988, SM22–29.

Lippe, Richard and Florence Jacobwitz. 'Masculinity in the Movies: *To Live and Die in L.A*'. *CineAction!*, no. 6 (Summer/Autumn 1986): 35–44.

Lippe, Richard and Robin Wood. 'An Interview with Arthur Penn'. In *Arthur Penn*, edited by Robin Wood with Richard Lippe and Barry Keith Grant, rev edn., 202–11. Detroit: Wayne State University Press, 2014.

Longo, Vincent. 'Bob Rafelson's Ambivalent Authorship'. In *The Other Hollywood Renaissance*, edited by Dominic Lennard, R. Barton Palmer and Murray Pomerance, 278–95. Edinburgh: Edinburgh University Press, 2020.

Loynd, Roy. 'Mileti Ankles SLM to Solo, Buys *Streamers* for $3-Mil'. *Variety*, 6 July 1983, 6, 34.

Macnaughton, Oliver. '*Megalopolis*: Can Francis Ford Coppola's $100m Gamble Pay Off?' *Guardian*, 3 September 2021.

Maltby, Richard. '"Nobody Knows Everything": Post-classical Historiographies and Consolidated Entertainment'. In *Contemporary Hollywood Cinema*, edited by Steve Neale and Murray Smith, 21–44. London: Routledge, 1998.

Mann, Roderick. 'The Director behind the Crime'. *Los Angeles Times*, 27 October 1985 (AMPAS).

Mantgani, Ian. 'Ending … *To Live and Die in LA*'. *Sight and Sound* 26, no. 11 (November 2016): 112.

Marsh, Calum. 'Small Change: The Late Films of Francis Ford Coppola'. *Cinéaste* 40, no. 3 (Summer 2015): 32.

Martin, Adrian. '*Cruising*: The Sound of Violence'. *Undercurrent*, no. 4 (October 2008).

Maslin, Janet. 'Friedkin Defends His *Cruising*'. *New York Times*, 18 September 1979, C12.

Miller, D. A. '*Cruising*'. *Film Quarterly* 61, no. 2 (January 2007): 70–3.

Miller, Mark Crispin. 'Introduction: The Big Picture'. In *Seeing Through Movies*, edited by Mark Crispin Miller, 3–13. New York: Pantheon Books, 1990.

Mills, Bart. 'A Misfit Goes Mainstream'. *Guardian*, 19 April 1990, 24.

Morales, Robert. 'Head of Hopper (1983)'. In *Dennis Hopper: Interviews*, edited by Nick Dawson, 116–20. Jackson: University of Mississippi, 2012.

Murphy, Robert. 'Art, Commerce, Corruption …'. *AIP & Co*, no. 55 (June 1984): 24–9.

Myles, Lynda. 'The Zoetrope Saga'. *Sight and Sound* 51, no. 2 (Spring 1982): 91–3.

Needham, Gary. '"*Cruising* Is a Picture We Sincerely Wish We Did Not Have to Show": United Artists, Ratings, and the Controversy of William Friedkin's *Cruising* (1980)'. In *United Artists*, edited by Peter Krämer, Gary Needham, Yannis Tzioumakis and Tino Balio, 192–210. Abingdon: Routledge, 2020.

New Musical Express. 'Secret Honour [sic]'. 9 February 1985, 19.

New York Times. '*Duet* Closing Saturday'. 29 December 1981, C7.

Newland, Christina. '*Joker*'. *Sight and Sound* 29, no. 11 (November 2019): 70–1.

Ness, Richard R. 'A Perfect Couple: The Altman-Rudolph Connection'. In *The Later Films and Legacy of Robert Altman*, edited by Lisa Dombrowski and Justin Wyatt, 65–80. Edinburgh: Edinburgh University Press, 2021.

Norman, Neil. '*Fool for Love*'. *Face*, July 1986, 93.

Oney, Steve. '*Tucker*: The Director Finally Makes the Picture of His Dreams'. *Premiere*, August 1988, 69–74.

Palmer, R. Barton. 'Redeeming *Cruising*: Tendentiously Offensive, Coherently Incoherent, Strangely Pleasurable'. In *B Is for Bad Cinema: Aesthetics, Politics, and Cultural Value*, edited by Claire Perkins and Constantine Verevis, 85–104. Albany: SUNY Press, 2014.

Pavlounis, Dimitrios. 'Staging the "Rebel's Return"'. In *A Companion to Robert Altman*, edited by Adrian Danks, 932–86. Chichester: John Wiley & Sons, 2015.

Phillips, Gene. 'Francis Coppola'. *Films in Review* 40, no. 3 (March 1989): 155–60.

Pinkerton, Nick. 'The Other Side of 80s America'. *Sight and Sound* 28, no. 6 (June 2018): 20–7.

Pollock, Dale. '*Cruising* in War Zone; Finished on Sked, Bow Set'. *Variety*, 12 September 1979, 6.

Pollock, Dale. 'Friedkin Film *Cruising* into a Storm of Protest'. *Los Angeles Times*, 4 February 1980, G1.

Pollock, Dale. 'R- Rated *Cruising*: The MPAA Seal of Disapproval'. *Los Angeles Times Calendar*, 4 May 1980, 1, 6–7.

Pollock, Dale. '*Cruising*: The Battle Continues'. *Los Angeles Times*, 27 June 1980, Part VI, 9.

Polowy, Kevin. 'Francis Ford Coppola Says He Was "depressed" and "had lost everything" before Kids Encouraged Him to Make *The Outsiders*'. *Yahoo Entertainment*, 11 November 2021. (https://www.aol.com/entertainment/francis-ford-coppola-says-depressed–160038377).

Prince, Stephen. 'Hollywood in the Age of Reagan'. In *Contemporary American Cinema*, edited by Linda Ruth Williams and Michael Hammond, 229–45. Maidenhead: McGraw-Hill, 2006.

Prince, Stephen. 'Introduction: Movies and the 1980s'. In *American Cinema of the 1980s: Themes and Variations*, edited by Stephen Prince, 1–21. Oxford: Berg, 2007.

Quinn, Anthony. 'On Both Sides of the Ledger'. *Independent on Sunday*, 20 February 1994, 18–20.

Rabe, David. '*Streamers*: An Interview'. *BFI Reuben Library* cuttings file on *Streamers*, n.d. and unattributed, 20–3.

Ramaeker, Paul. 'Notes on the Split-Field Diopter'. *Film History* 19 (2007): 191.

Reinholz, Mary. 'UA Classics' Kitt Carrying the Torch, Going for Sophisticates', *The Hollywood Reporter* 278, no. 35 (20 September 1983): 1, 59.

Rich, Frank. 'Stage: Robert Altman Directs Cher'. *New York Times*, 19 February 1982, C3.

Rickey, Carrie. 'Let Yourself Go! Three Musicals Sing One from the Libido'. *Film Comment* 18, no. 2 (March/April 1982): 43–7.

Rickey, Carrie. 'Has Success Spoiled Paul Brickman?'. *Wall Street Journal*, 4 January 1984, 20.

Riley, Brooks. 'Film into Video'. *Film Comment* 18, no. 3 (May–June 1982): 45–8.

Robinson, David. '*Streamers*'. *The Times*, 23 March 1984, 21.

Robson, Leo. 'Hollywood's Favourite Flop'. *New Statesman*, 31 July 2015–13 August 2015, 19.

Rosenfield, Paul. 'Robert Altman: Ever Ready for the Gauntlet or Gantlet'. *Los Angeles Times*, 29 November 1983, G1, G4.

Ross, Lillian. 'Onwards and Upwards with the Arts: Some Figures on a Fantasy'. *New Yorker*, 8 November 1982, 48–50.

Roudané, Matthew. 'Introduction'. In *The Cambridge Companion to Sam Shepard*, edited by Matthew Roudané, 1–6. Cambridge: Cambridge University Press, 2006.

Sarris, Andrew. 'The Selling of Sam Shepard'. *Village Voice*, 10 December 1985, 59.

Sarris, Andrew. 'Notes on the Auteur Theory in 1962'. In *Auteurs and Authorship: A Film Reader*, edited by Barry Keith Grant, 35–45. Oxford: Blackwell Publishing, 2008.

Scharres, Barbara. 'From out of the Blue: The Return of Dennis Hopper'. *Journal of the University Film and Video Association* 35, no. 2 (Spring 1983): 25–33.

Schatz, Thomas. 'The New Hollywood'. In *Film Theory Goes to the Movies*, edited by Jim Collins, Hilary Radnor and Ava Preacher Collins, 8–36. Abingdon: Routledge, 1993.

Schroeder, Andrew. 'The Movement Inside: BBS Films and the Cultural Left in the New Hollywood'. In *The World the Sixties Made: Politics and Culture in Recent America*, edited by Van Gosse and Richard Moser, 114–36. Philadelphia: Temple University Press, 2003.

Self, Robert. 'The Art Cinema and Robert Altman'. *Velvet Light Trap*, no. 19 (1982): 30–4.

Simon, Alex. '*Cruising* with Billy'. *Venice*, September 2007, 69–71.

Simon, Alex. 'William Friedkin: Auteur of the Dark (1997)'. In *William Friedkin Interviews*, edited by Christopher Lane, 68–79. Jackson: University Press of Mississippi, 2020.

Sinwell, Sarah S. 'Fantasies and Fangirls: Gender and Sexuality in Robert Altman's *Come Back to the 5 & Dime, Jimmy Dean, Jimmy Dean*'. In *The Later Films and Legacy of Robert Altman*, edited by Lisa Dombrowski and Justin Wyatt, 159–71. Edinburgh: Edinburgh University Press, 2021.

Sontag, Susan. 'Film and Theatre'. *Tulane Drama Review* 11, no. 1 (Autumn 1966): 24–37.

Sragow, Michael. 'Hot-rodding Down the Street of Dreams'. *L.A. Herald-Examiner*, 10 August 1988, B–1, B–4.

Taylor, Clarke. 'Premiere of *Streamers*: Playwright Rabe Cheered at Filmfest'. *Los Angeles Times*, 12 October 1983, G2.

Thomson, David. 'Who Killed the Movies?'. *Esquire* 126, no. 6 (December 1996): 56.

Thomson, David and Lucy Gray. 'Idols of the King'. *Film Comment* 19, no. 5 (September–October 1983): 61–75.

Tsay, I-Lien. "'Let Me Love You": Ambiguous Masculinity in Michael Cimino's Melodramas'. In *The Other Hollywood Renaissance*, edited by Dominic Lennard, R. Barton Palmer and Murray Pomerance, 88–101. Edinburgh: Edinburgh University Press, 2020.

Tusher, Will. 'Friedkin to Direct and Write *L.A.*'. *Variety*, 25 July 1984 (AMPAS).

Tyron, Chuck. 'For Real: *Tanner '88, Tanner on Tanner*, and the Political Spectacle in the Post-Network Era'. In *The Later Films and Legacy of Robert Altman*, edited by Lisa Dombrowski and Justin Wyatt, 30–46. Edinburgh: Edinburgh University Press, 2021.

Tzioumakis, Yannis. "'Independent", "Indie" and "Indiewood": Towards a Periodisation of Contemporary (Post-1980) American Independent Cinema'. In *American Independent Cinema: Indie, Indiewood and Beyond*, edited by Geoff King, Claire Molloy and Yannis Tzioumakis, 28–40. London: Routledge, 2012.

Tzioumakis, Yannis. "'Here Comes the Hot-Stepper": Hollywood Renaissance, Indie Film and Robert Altman's Comeback in the 1990s'. In *The Later Films and Legacy of Robert Altman*, edited by Lisa Dombrowski and Justin Wyatt, 117–36. Edinburgh: Edinburgh University Press, 2021.

Variety. 'Bank Files Action over *Rampage* Funds', 6 June 1988 (AMPAS).

Variety. '*Cruising* Gets a New R Label', 10 June 1980. WFP: f.167.

Wetzsteon, Ross. 'Introduction'. In *Sam Shepard: Fool for Love and Other Plays*, 1–16. New York: Bantam, 1984.

Williams, Linda Ruth. 'No Sex Please, We're American'. *Sight and Sound* 14, no. 1 (January 2004): 18–20.

Willis, Sharon. 'Disputed Territories: Masculinity and Social Space'. In *Male Trouble*, edited by Constance Penley and Sharon Willis, 263–81. Minneapolis: University of Minnesota Press, 1993.

Wilmington, Michael. '*Live and Die* Chases *French Connection*'. *Los Angeles Times*, 1 November 1985, G4.

Wilson, Alexander. 'Friedkin's *Cruising*, Ghetto Politics and Gay Sexuality'. *Social Text*, no. 4 (Autumn 1981): 98–109.

Wyatt, Justin. 'Economic Constraints/Economic Opportunities: Robert Altman as Auteur'. *Velvet Light Trap*, no. 17 (Autumn 1996): 51–8.

Wyatt, Justin. 'The Formation of the "Major Independent": Miramax, New Line and the New Hollywood'. In *Contemporary Hollywood Cinema*, edited by Steve Neale and Murray Smith, 74–90. London: Routledge, 1998.

Wyatt, Justin. 'Countering Robert Altman's Sexual Outlaws: Visibility, Representation, and Questionable Sexual Progress'. In *The Later Films and Legacy of Robert Altman*, edited by Lisa Dombrowski and Justin Wyatt, 172–89. Edinburgh: Edinburgh University Press, 2021.

Yang, Iris. 'Untitled'. *The Sacramento Bee*, 7 February 1979 (WFP: f.653).

Filmography

The following are complete filmographies for all filmic work between 1980 and 1989 directed by the eleven featured Renaissance auteurs.

All are feature films made for theatrical release unless otherwise stated as follows: television films (tv), television episodes (tve), television series (tvs), music videos (v) and documentaries (d).

Robert Altman

HealtH (sc. Frank Barhydt, Robert Altman and Paul Dooley, 1980)
Popeye (sc. Jules Feiffer, 1980)
Come Back to the 5 and Dime, Jimmy Dean, Jimmy Dean (sc. Ed Graczyk, 1982)
Precious Blood (sc. Frank South, 1982) – tv *(Two by South)*
Rattlesnake in a Cooler (sc. Frank South, 1982) – tv *(Two by South)*
Streamers (sc. David Rabe, 1983)
Secret Honor (sc. Donald Freed and Arnold Stone, 1984)
Fool for Love (sc. Sam Shepard, 1985)
The Laundromat (sc. Marsha Norman, 1985) – tv
Beyond Therapy (sc. Christopher Durang and Robert Altman, 1987)
The Dumb Waiter (sc. Harold Pinter, 1987) – tv (*Basements*)
O.C. and Stiggs (sc. Ted Mann and Donald Cantrell, 1987)
'Les Boréades' (sc. Robert Altman, 1987) – segment in *Aria*
The Room (sc. Harold Pinter, 1987) – tv (*Basements*)
The Caine Mutiny Court-Martial (sc. Herman Wouk, 1988) – tv
Tanner '88 (sc. Gary Trudeau, 1988) – tvs

Hal Ashby

Second-Hand Hearts (sc. Charles Eastman, 1981)
'Going to A Go-Go' – live version (1982) – The Rolling Stones – v
Let's Spend the Night Together (1982) – The Rolling Stones – d
Lookin' to Get Out (sc. Al Schwartz and Jon Voight, 1982)
'Solo *Trans*' (1984) – Neil Young – v
The Slugger's Wife (sc. Neil Simon, 1985)
8 Million Ways to Die (sc. Oliver Stone and R. Lance Hill, 1986)

216 *Filmography*

'Pilot' (sc. David Milch and Jeffrey Lewis, 1987) – *Beverley Hills Buntz* – tve
Jake's Journey (sc. Graham Chapman, Andy Schatzberg and David Sherlock, 1988) – tv

Peter Bogdanovich

They All Laughed (sc. Peter Bogdanovich and Blaine Novak, 1981)
Mask (sc. Ann Hamilton Phelan, 1985)
Illegally Yours (sc. M.A. Stewart and Max Dickens, 1988)

Francis Coppola

One From the Heart (sc. Armyan Bernstein and Francis Coppola, 1981)
The Outsiders (sc. Kathleen Rowell, 1983)
Rumble Fish (sc. S.E. Hinton and Francis Coppola, 1983)
The Cotton Club (sc. William Kennedy and Francis Coppola, 1984)
Captain EO (sc. George Lucas, Rusty Lemorande and Francis Coppola, 1986) – short
   (Disneyland)
Peggy Sue Got Married (sc. Jerry Scheitling and Arlene Sarner, 1986)
Gardens of Stone (sc. Ronald Bass, 1987)
'Rip Van Winkle' (sc. Mark Curtiss and Rod Ash, 1987) – *Faerie Tale Theater* – tve
'Life Without Zoe' (sc. Francis and Sofia Coppola, 1988) – segment in *New York Stories*
Tucker: The Man and His Dream (sc. Arnold Schulman and David Seidler, 1988)

Brian De Palma

Dressed to Kill (sc. Brian De Palma, 1980)
Blow Out (sc. Brian De Palma, 1981)
Scarface (sc. Oliver Stone, 1983)
Body Double (sc. Robert J. Avrech and Brian De Palma, 1984)
'Dancing in the Dark' (1984) – Bruce Springsteen – v
'Relax' version 3 (1984) –Frankie Goes to Hollywood – v
Wise Guys (sc. George Gallo, 1986)
The Untouchables (sc. David Mamet, 1987)
Casualties of War (sc. David Rabe, 1989)

William Friedkin

Cruising (sc. William Friedkin, 1980)
Deal of the Century (sc. Paul Brickman, 1983)
'Self-Control' (1984) – Laura Brannigan – v

Filmography

217

'Nightcrawlers' (sc. Philip DeGuere, 1985) – *The Twilight Zone* – tve
To Live and Die in L.A. (sc. William Friedkin and Gerald Petievich, 1985)
'To Live and Die in LA' (1985) – Wang Chung – v
'Putting It Together: The Making of the *Broadway Album*' (1986) – Barbra Streisand – v
C.A.T. Squad (sc. Gerald Petievich, 1986) –tv
Rampage (sc. William Friedkin, 1987)
C.A.T. Squad: Python Wolf (sc. Robert Ward, 1988) – tv

Dennis Hopper

Out of the Blue (sc. Leonard Yakir and Brenda Nielson, 1980)
Colors (sc. Michael Schiffer, 1988)

John Milius

Conan the Barbarian (sc. John Milius and Oliver Stone, 1982)
Red Dawn (sc. John Milius and Kevin Reynolds, 1984)
'Opening Day' (sc. John Milius, 1985) – *The Twilight Zone* – tve
Farewell to the King (sc. John Milius, 1989)

Arthur Penn

Four Friends (sc. Steve Tesich, 1981)
Target (sc. Howard Berk and Don Peterson, 1985)
Dead of Winter (sc. Mark Schmuger and Mark Malone, 1987)
Penn and Teller Get Killed (sc. Penn Jillette and Teller, 1989)

Bob Rafelson

Modesty (sc. Bob Rafelson, 1981) – short
The Postman Always Rings Twice (sc. David Mamet, 1981)
'All Night Long' (1983) – Lionel Richie – v
Black Widow (sc. Ronald Bass, 1987)

Martin Scorsese

Raging Bull (sc. Mardik Martin and Paul Schrader, 1980)
The King of Comedy (sc. Paul D. Zimmerman, 1982)
After Hours (sc. Joseph Minion, 1985)

218   *Filmography*

The Color of Money (sc. Richard Price, 1986)
'Mirror, Mirror' (sc. Joseph Minion, 1986) – *Amazing Stories* (tve)
'Bad' (sc. Richard Price, 1987) – Michael Jackson – v
The Last Temptation of Christ (sc. Paul Schrader, 1988)
'Life Lessons' (sc. Richard Price, 1989) – segment in *New York Stories*

****

Documentaries cited

The Directors: William Friedkin (Robert J. Emery, 1995)
The Dream Studio (*One from the Heart* DVD, 2002)
The Electronic Cinema (*One from the Heart* DVD, 2002)
S.E. Hinton on Location in Tulsa (*The Outsiders: The Complete Novel* DVD, 2011)
Staying Gold: A Look Back at The Outsiders (*The Outsiders: The Complete Novel* DVD, 2011)
The Casting of The Outsiders (*The Outsiders: The Complete Novel* DVD, 2011)
Milius (Joey Figueroa and Zak Knutson, 2013)
Electric Boogaloo: The Wild, Untold Story of Cannon Films (Mark Hartley, 2014)
De Palma (Noah Baumbach and Jake Paltrow, 2015)
Hal (Amy Scott, 2018)

Index

Academy Awards (1979) 97–8
Across the River and Into the Trees (novel) 83. *See also* Ernest Hemingway
After Hours (1985) 27, 35, 39
agents, the power of 20, 28
Allen, Karen 138, 142
Allen, Woody 40, 127
Altman, Robert 1–2, 8–16, 21, 28, 30, 35, 51, 59, 61–94, 96, 129–31, 161–2, 164, 167
   'Altmanesque', the 13, 79, 85, 90
   critical reception 65, 69, 75, 82, 92
   fidelity to plays 63–5, 69, 73, 78, 81, 85, 87, 89–90, 92–3
   major studios, relationship with 61–2, 65–6, 76
   mobile camera, use of 65, 72, 74–5, 80, 88, 93
   negative perceptions of 1980s 62, 66–7, 69
   unmade films 83–4
Altman, Stephen 78, 83
American Friend, The (1978) 56
American Graffiti (1973) 121
Animal House (1978) 76
Anne-Down, Lesley 155
anti-heroes 54, 131, 148–9, 161–2
Antonioni, Michelangelo 11, 41, 99, 141
Apocalypse Now (1979) 8–9, 47–8, 56, 95, 97, 100, 119, 120, 126–7, 129, 167
Apted, Michael 55
Aria (1988) 93. *See also* 'Les Boréades'
Ashby, Hal 9, 11, 22, 44, 49, 51–3, 58, 133, 168
auteurism and auteur theory 1–3, 5–6, 9–13, 15
   commercial auteurism 5–6, 24, 97, 128, 142
   post-auteurism 13
Avventura, L' (1960) 144

Back to the Future (1985) 25, 27
Basements (1987) 93. *See also The Dumb Waiter* and *The Room*
Basic Instinct (1992) 162
Basinger, Kim 85–92
Bazin, André 63–4, 80
BBS Productions *See under* Raybert Productions
Beatty, Warren 10, 37, 126
Being There (1979) 9, 51–2
Bell, Arthur 132–3, 135
Berger, Thomas 83. *See also The Feud* (novel)
Beverly Hills Cop (1984) 37
Beyond Therapy (1987) 61, 71, 84, 92–3
Beyond Therapy (play) 87, 92
Biarritz 83
Biehn, Michael 154
Big Wednesday (1978) 47
Biskind, Peter 1, 6, 23, 167
Black, Karen 68, 84
Black Narcissus (1947) 106
Black Stallion Returns, The (1983) 99
Black Widow (1987) 54–5
Blade Runner (1982) 5
Blatty, William Peter 131, 147, 149
Blauner, Steve 10, 54
blockbusters and the blockbuster era 1, 4–7, 23–5, 27–8, 166
Blood and Money (novel) 132. *See also* Thomas Thompson
Blow Out (1981) 31, 41–2, 50, 57
Blow-Up (1967) 41
Bludhorn, Charlie 26
Blue Chips (1994) 162
Blue Velvet (1986) 30, 154
Body Double (1984) 33, 40–3
Bogdanovich, Peter 1, 10–11, 30, 33, 44–6, 49, 54
Bohemian Grove Retreat, the 82
Bonnie and Clyde (1967) 4, 49

220   *Index*

'Boréades, Les' (1988) 93. *See also Aria*
Boys in the Band, The (1970) 144
Bram Stoker's Dracula (1992) 95
Brannigan, Laura 143
Brat Pack, the 111, 115
Breaking Away (1979) 49
Brickman, Paul 142–3
Bridges, Jeff 121, 123
Brief Encounter (1945) 50
Brink's Job, The (1978) 131, 143, 153
Britton, Andrew 4–5, 23, 29
Brubaker (1980) 54
Bug (2006) 162
Burum, Stephen 115

C.A.T. Squad (1985) 153
C.A.T. Squad: Python Wolf (1988) 153
cable television 22, 24, 29, 62, 67
cahiers du cinéma 13
Caine Mutiny Court Martial, The (1988) 93
Caligula (1980) 33
Cannon Group 30, 84, 89, 92
Cape Fear (1991) 40
Capra, Frank 123
Carolco Pictures 29–30
Carrie (1976) 40
Carroll, Tod and Ted Mann 75
Cassavetes, John 11, 30
Casualties of War (1989) 43, 119
Catchfire (1990) 58
Cavell, Stanley 104. *See also* comedy of
    remarriage
CBS 26, 50
censorship and controversy 33–4, 41–2,
    134–5
Chartoff, Robert 36
Chase, Chevy 16, 143
Chase, Richard 158–9
Chemical Bank 109, 116
Chinatown (1974) 55
Chvatal, Cindy 144
Cimino, Michael 5, 8, 11, 30, 95, 99, 129
Cinecom International 77. *See also* Ira
    Deutchman
Cineplex-Odeon 38
Citizen Kane (1941) 124
Classifications and Ratings
    Administration (CARA) 135

Clouzot, Henri 129, 141
Coca-Cola Company 26
Cocteau, Jean 64, 116
Color of Money, The (1986) 35, 37–9, 165
Columbia Pictures 21, 26–7, 42–3, 53, 98
*Come Back to the 5 and Dime, Jimmy
    Dean, Jimmy Dean* (1982) 16, 67–9,
    71–2, 75, 77, 87, 102
comedy of remarriage 104. *See also*
    Stanley Cavell
Coming Home (1978) 52
Conan the Barbarian (1982) 30, 44, 47–8
Conformist, The (1970) 126
Conti, Tom 93
Conversation, The (1974) 41–2
Coppola, Eleanor 122–3
Coppola, Francis 1–2, 5–6, 8–11, 14–16,
    26, 33, 35, 41, 46, 59, 95–128,
    129–31, 154, 162, 163–4, 167–8
    contradictions and ego, his 95–9,
      121–2
    director for hire 96, 117–18, 120
    electronic cinema 107–8, 115, 122
    family, depictions of 118, 122–3
    Hollywood genres, engagement with
      101–5, 114, 123
    technology, use of 106–8, 111–12, 119,
      125
    visual stylist, as a 96, 100, 104–8,
      112–16, 118, 124–6
Coppola, Gio 120, 122
Corman, Roger 38
Cotton Club, The (1984) 96, 117–18, 127
Creative Artists Agency (CAA) 20, 38, 46.
    See also Michael Ovitz
Cruise, Tom 111
Cruising (1980) 16–17, 24, 33, 41, 130–42,
    145, 148–9, 162, 164
Cruising (novel) 132. *See also* Gerald
    Walker
Curb Your Enthusiasm (2000–) 94

Dafoe, Willem 145, 154
Davis, Martin 26
De Laurentiis, Dino (DEG) 30, 46, 48, 130,
    153–5, 161
De Niro, Robert 36, 43, 50
De Palma (2015) 41

Index

De Palma, Brian 10–11, 28, 31, 33–5, 40–4, 78, 168
Dead of Winter (1987) 51
Deal of the Century (1983) 16, 142–3, 161, 164
Deer Hunter, The (1978) 8
DeGuere, Philip 143
Deutchman, Ira 77. *See also* Cinecom International
Dick Tracy (1990) 37, 126
Dillinger (1973) 47
Dillon, Matt 110–12, 115–16
Disney 21, 37–8, 40, 61
Distant Vision (2016) 107
'Doctor Death' (James Grigson) 156
Dr Strangelove (1964) 143
Dressed to Kill (1980) 33, 40–3
Dreyer, Carl 65
Duet for One (play) 142
Dumb Waiter, The (1987) 93. *See also* Basements.
Durang, Christopher 87, 92

Easter Egg Hunt, An (novel) 83. *See also* Gillian Freeman
Easy Rider (1969) 44, 53–4, 56
8 Million Ways to Die (1986) 53
Embassy Pictures 30
Enfants du Paradis, les (1946) 101
Escape Artist, The (1982) 99, 127
Estevez, Emilio 111
Eszterhas, Joe 162
Euston Films 83
Exorcist, The (1973) 7, 11, 129, 131, 147, 149, 155
Exorcist, The III (1990) 131. *See also* Legion (novel)
E.T. The Extra-Terrestrial (1982) 7, 27, 111
Evans, Robert 117

'Faerie Tale Theater' 119. *See also Rip Van Winkle*
Falling in Love (1984) 50
Farewell to the King (1989) 48
Fellini, Federico 82, 141
Feud, The (novel) 83. *See also* Thomas Berger
Fiddler on the Roof (1971) 7
Film Finances Limited 14, 109, 115–16, 154

Filmways 31, 41, 49
First Blood (1982) 47
Five Easy Pieces (1970) 53–4
Flight of the Intruder (1991) 48
Fool for Love (1985) 12, 16, 30, 64, 84–92, 168
Fool for Love (play) 84–92
Forman, Milos 11
Forrest, Frederick 101
Four Friends (1982) 31, 49
Fox. *See under* 20th Century Fox
Fox Searchlight Pictures 29
Frankenheimer, John 107
Freed, Donald and Arnold M. Stone 76–7, 82. *See also Secret Honor* (play)
Freeman, Gillian 83. *See also An Easter Egg Hunt* (novel)
French Connection, The (1971) 3, 129, 132, 145–7, 149, 155
Friedkin, William 1–3, 8–11, 15–17, 24, 30, 33, 35, 41, 54, 59, 99, 129–62, 164, 167–8
 ambiguity 130–1, 139–41, 148, 162
 documentaries, influence of 144, 153, 158–9
 genre conformity 130–1, 138, 152, 161–2
 incoherence 136–40, 149
 major studios, relationship with 130, 143
 protests and censorship 133–5, 158
 screenwriting and adaptation 130, 137–41, 147–9, 154, 160, 162

Game of Thrones (2011–2019) 47
Gardens of Stone (1987) 26, 119
Garr, Teri 101
Gayle, Crystal 102–3
Geffen Company 37
General Cinema Corp (GCC) 134
Gere, Richard 117
Gertrud (1964) 65
Gibson, Henry 84
Globus, Yoram and Menahan Golan. *See under* Cannon Group
Godard, Jean-Luc 30, 106, 141
Godfather, The (1972) 7, 11, 95, 97, 117, 126–7

222   *Index*

Godfather Part III, The (1980) 9, 128
Golden Raspberry Awards 136
Goodfellas (1990) 7, 40
Gone with the Wind (novel and 1939 film)
    113–15
Gorillas in the Mist (1988) 55
Graczyk, Ed 67, 87
Graduate, The (1967) 4
Green, Walon 130
Grosbard, Ulu 50
Guardian, The (1990) 162
Gulf and Western. *See under* Paramount

Hackman, Gene 42
Hall, Philip Baker 76–82
Hammett (1982) 99, 116
Harders, Robert 78, 84
Harold and Maude (1970) 52
Hawks, Howard 15, 42
HealtH (1980) 61, 65, 68
Heat (1986) 83
Heaven's Gate (1980) 5, 8–9, 24, 36, 100,
    129, 132, 141, 167
Heffner, Richard 135
Hemingway, Ernest 83. *See also Across the
    River and Into the Trees*
Herzog, Werner 99
high concept filmmaking 6, 15, 20, 66–7,
    94, 103, 111, 130, 165–6
Hinckley, John 156
Hines, Gregory 143
Hinton S. E. (Susan) 108–9, 112–13, 115
Hitchcock, Alfred 15, 41–3, 74
Hollywood General Studios. *See under*
    Zoetrope Studios
Hollywood major studios 8–9, 15–17,
    19–28, 36–7, 61, 65, 98, 123,
    129–30, 165, 167
Hollywood Renaissance auteurs, defining
    10–12, 34
Hollywood Renaissance filmmaking 7,
    10–16, 19–22, 28, 33–4, 94, 96, 107,
    129, 163–6, 168
Hollywood Renaissance, periodization of
    7–10
Home Box Office (HBO) 26, 119
Home Movies (1979) 78
home video 22, 24–5, 29, 31–2, 62

Hopper, Dennis 10–11, 53–4, 56–8, 116
Hot Spot, The (1990) 58
Howard the Duck (1986) 127
Howell, C. Thomas 111–12
Hunt, Linda 93
Hunted, The (2003) 153, 162
Hustler, The (1961) 37, 166

Illegally Yours (1988) 30, 46
Images (1972) 68
In the Heat of the Night (1967) 51
independent cinema 7–9, 15–17, 19–23,
    27–32, 130, 142, 161, 165–6
Indiewood cinema 9, 28–9
Ishioka, Eiko 119
Ishtar (1987) 10

Jade (1995) 162
Jarmusch, Jim 7, 94, 166
Jaws (1975) 1, 4, 6, 24
Jewison, Norman 7, 51
Joker (2019) 36
Julia, Raul 101
Jurgensen, Randy 132–3, 153

Kael, Pauline 61, 81
Kelly, Gene 105
Kennedy, William 118
King Lear (1987) 30
King of Comedy, The (1983) 5, 35–7
King of Marvin Gardens, The (1972) 54
Kinney Corporation, The. *See under*
    Warner Brothers
Kinski, Nastassja 101
Koch, Mayor Ed 135
Kolker, Robert 3, 47, 49–51, 61, 68, 85
Kubrick, Stanley 11–12, 34, 143
Kurosawa, Akira 141

Landau, Martin 123, 125
Lane, Diane 111, 116
Landlord, The (1970) 51
Larry Sanders Show, The (1992–8) 94
Las Vegas, artificial representation of 101–5
Last Movie, The (1971) 56
Last Picture Show, The (1971) 45–6, 54
Last Temptation of Christ, The (1988) 20,
    24, 33, 36, 38–9, 46, 145

Index

223

Laundromat, The (1985) 84
Lee, Spike 7, 31, 166
Legion (novel) 131. See also *The Exorcist III* (1990)
Lennox, Annie 93
Levin, Irving H. 144–5, 148
Lewis, Jerry 36
'Life Lessons' (1989) 40, 127. See also *New York Stories*
'Life without Zoe' (1989) 127. See also *New York Stories*
Lightning Over Water (1980) 78
Lookin' To Get Out (1982) 22, 52–3
Lorimar Productions 22, 52–3, 55, 133
Los Angeles Actors Theater 76
Love Story (1970) 7
Love Streams (1984) 30
Lowe, Rob 46, 111–12
Lucas, George 1, 4, 10, 46, 95, 119, 121, 126–7
Lumet, Sidney 11, 24, 34, 65

M*A*S*H (1970) 11, 62, 65, 70
Macchio, Ralph 111, 115
Magnificent Ambersons, The (1942) 124
Makavejev, Dusan 99
Malkin, Barry 120, 127
Mamet, David 55
Mandate (magazine) 135
Manhunter (1986) 145
Margaret Herrick Library, Los Angeles 14, 131
Marquetti, Angelo 144
Mask (1985) 44–6
Matsushita Electric 27
May, Elaine 10
Mazursky, Paul 11, 34
McArthur, Alex 154
McCabe and Mrs Miller (1971) 65
Metro Goldwyn Mayer (MGM) 21, 48, 55, 66, 76, 105, 144, 148
Mignot, Pierre 74, 78, 80, 88
Mileti, Nick 69
Milius (2013) 47
Milius, John 10–11, 30, 46–8, 82
mini-major studios 21, 27–8
Miramax Films 29, 155, 161
mirrors, symbolic use of 64, 68–9, 80, 91, 102

Misakian, Jo Ellen 108
Mishima: A Life in Four Chapters (1985) 119
Mission Impossible (1996) 44
Missouri Breaks, The (1976) 49
Modine, Matthew 71, 73
Monkees, The (1966–1968) 54
Moore, Michael 31
Morricone, Ennio 154–5, 160
Mountains of the Moon (1990) 55
Mr Smith Goes to Washington (1939) 123
MTV 106, 167
Murdoch, Rupert 27, 144
Murphy, Michael 93
Music Corporation of America (MCA). *See under* Universal

Napoleon (1927) 116
Nashville (1975) 8, 62, 65, 83, 93, 132
Nashville XIII/Nashville, Nashville 83–4
National Lampoon magazine 75
New Film History 13, 165
New Line Films 29
New World Pictures 93
New York, New York (1977) 36
New York Stories (1989) 40, 26–7. See also 'Life Lessons', 'Life without Zoe', 'Oedipus Wrecks'
Newman, Paul 37
Newman, Peter 68, 75–6
NewsRounds (newspaper) 158
Nicholls, Allan F. 61, 87
Nichols, Mike 4, 11, 24, 34, 69
Nicholson, Jack 54–5, 143
Night Moves (1975) 49
Night They Raided Minsky's, The (1968) 143
'Nightcrawlers' (1985) 143. See also *The Twilight Zone*
Nixon, Richard M. 76–82
Norman, Marsha 84
Nykvist, Sven 55

OC and Stiggs (1987) 61, 71, 75–6, 92–3
'Oedipus Wrecks' (1989) 127. See also *New York Stories*
On the Town (1949) 105
One from the Heart (1981) 16, 95–108, 114, 119, 122–7, 168

Orion Films 27, 31, 48
Out of the Blue (1980) 20, 56-8
Outsiders, The (1983) 14, 16, 96, 108-17, 124, 154
Outsiders, The (novel) 108-10, 112
Ovitz, Michael 20. *See also* Creative Artists Agency (CAA)

Pacino, Al 24, 42, 133-5, 138, 142, 145
Pankow, John 145
Paper Moon (1973) 45
Paramount 21, 24-6, 37, 43, 61, 83, 98, 117, 127
Paramount Decree, the 1948 38
Pathé 30
Peckinpah, Sam 11
Peggy Sue Got Married (1986) 26, 96, 118-19, 128
Penn and Teller Get Killed (1989) 49, 51
Penn, Arthur 4, 10-11, 30-1, 44, 49-51
Penn, Sean 58
People vs Paul Crump, The (1962) 153
Perfect Couple, A (1979) 65
Peterson, William 145, 154
Petievich, Gerald 131, 147, 152-3
Pinter, Harold 93
Platoon (1986) 43, 119, 145
Player, The (1992) 62
Pleasance, Donald 93
Pollack, Sydney 11, 25, 34, 53
Popeye (1980) 9, 28, 61, 66
Porky's (1981) 76
Postman Always Rings Twice, The (1981) 54
Powell, Michael 98, 106
Precious Blood (1981) 67. *See also Two by South*
Producers Sales Organisation (PSO) 45, 53
Puzo, Mario 117, 126.

Quintet (1979) 65

Rabe, David 42, 69-73, 132
Rafelson, Bob 10-11, 33, 53, 56-8, 168
Raging Bull (1980) 1, 10, 36
Rainmaker, The (1997) 128

Rake's Progress, A (opera) 69
Rampage (1987) 16-17, 20, 30, 130, 153-61
Rampage (novel) 153, 156, 158, 160. *See also* William Wood
Rattlesnake in the Cooler (1981) 67. *See also Two by South*
Ray, Nicholas 78
Raybert Productions 10-11, 53-5
Reaganite entertainment and ideology 1, 4-7, 15, 29, 37, 142, 167
Rebel without a Cause (1955) 115
Red Dawn (1984) 44, 48
Rip Van Winkle (1987) 119. *See also* 'Faerie Tale Theater'
Risky Business (1983) 111, 142
Rocky III (1982) 27
Room, The (1988) 93. *See also Basements*
Ross, Steve 25, 28
Rourke, Mickey 116
Rules of Engagement (2000) 153, 162
Rumble Fish (1983) 14, 16, 110, 114-17, 124, 154
Rumble Fish (novel) 115-16
Runaway Train (1985) 30

Sarris, Andrew 13, 64
Sayles, John 94, 166
Scarface (1983) 40-4
Schneider, Bert 10, 54
Schrader, Paul 11, 36
Schulman, Sam 144
Scorsese, Martin 5, 8-11, 20, 24, 28, 33-40, 44, 46, 62, 145, 165, 168
Second Hand Hearts (1981) 22, 52
Secret Honor (1984) 16, 62, 70-3, 76-83, 93-4
Secret Honor, The Last Testament of Richard M. Nixon: A Political Myth (play) 76-82. *See also* Donald Freed and Arnold M. Stone
'Self-Control' (video) 143
Serling, Rod 143
Serpico (1974) 133
sex, lies and videotape (1989) 9, 29
Shampoo (1975) 52
Shepard, Sam 13, 84-92
SLM Productions 144-5

Slugger's Wife, The (1985) 53
Smith, Bud 148, 150
'Somewhere' (video) 144
Sontag, Susan 64, 80
Sony Pictures 26
Sony Picture Classics 29
Sorcerer (1977) 8–9, 100, 129, 131, 142, 146, 149, 167
South, Frank 67
Spielberg, Steven 1, 4, 7, 10–11, 28, 34, 47, 132
Stanton, Harry Dean 86, 88, 91
Stark, Ray 118
Star Wars (1977) 1, 4–7, 19, 24, 27, 99, 127, 129
Stay Hungry (1976) 54
Stewart, James 123
Stone, Oliver 42, 47–8, 137
Storaro, Vittorio 104, 107, 123, 126
Stratten, Dorothy 45
Streamers (1983) 16, 62, 64–5, 69–75, 119, 132
Streamers (play) 70–75
Streisand, Barbra 144
Sundance Festival 29, 82
Swayze, Patrick 111–12
Syberberg, Hans-Jürgen 99

Tanner '88 (1988) 61, 93
Target (1984) 50
Tavoularis, Dean 126
Taxi Driver (1976) 8, 36, 39
Terminator, The (1984) 154
Terminator 2 (1991) 29
Tesich, Steve 49
Tetro (2009) 128
Tevis, Walter 37
Tex (1982) 111
Texasville (1990) 46
That Cold Day in the Park (1969) 83
They All Laughed (1981) 21, 45
Thief of Baghdad, The (1940) 98, 106
Thompson, Thomas 132. *See also Blood and Money*
3 Women (1977) 68
THX1138 (1971) 121
Time-Life Films 26, 45
To Live and Die in L.A. (1985) 17, 130–1, 144–52, 157, 162, 164, 168

To Live and Die in L.A. (novel) 131, 144, 147, 149
Tootsie (1983) 25, 53
Touchstone Pictures. *See under* Disney
Travolta, John 31, 41, 93
Tri-Star Pictures 26–7, 118–19
Tucker: The Man and his Dream (1988) 16, 114, 118, 121–7
Turner Broadcasting 29
Turner, Kathleen 118
Twelve Angry Men (1957) 65
20th Century Fox 21, 27, 36, 45, 54, 61, 65, 144
24 Hours in Los Angeles (book) 150
Twilight Zone, The 143. *See also* 'Nightcrawlers'
Twixt (2011) 128
Two by South (1981) 67. *See also Precious Blood and Rattlesnake in the Cooler*

United Artists 8, 24, 36, 48, 136
United Artists Classics 69
United States Secret Service 144–5, 148
Universal 21, 25, 26, 28, 45–6, 116
University of Michigan 14, 69, 77
Untouchables, The (1987) 35, 40, 43

Venice Film Festival, and Golden Lion award 69
Vietnam war 70, 77, 119–120, 143
Vincent and Theo (1990) 94

Waits, Tom 102–3, 106
Walker, Gerald 132. *See also Cruising* (novel)
Wang Chung 146
Ward, Robert 153
Warner Brothers 21, 24, 26–8, 109, 133, 142–3
Wasserman, Lew 25–6, 28, 98
Weaver, Sigourney 143
Wedding, A (1978) 65
Weintraub, Jerry 83–4, 132–5
Welles, Orson 116, 124
Wenders, Wim 56
What's Up Doc? (1972) 45–6
Winkler, Irvin 36, 45
Wise Guys (1986) 42

Witness (1985) 37
Wood, Robin 4–5, 23, 29, 40, 42, 49, 51, 136–7, 140–1
Wood, William 153, 158. *See also Rampage* (novel)
Wouk, Hermann 93
Wyatt, Justin 5–6, 67, 103, 111, 130, 165

Year of the Dragon (1985) 30
Youth without Youth (2007) 128
Young, Neil 57
'yuppie nightmare' film cycle 37

Zemeckis, Robert 25
Zoetrope Studios 99, 105, 107, 109
Zukor, Adolph 25